THE HANDKERCHIEF TREE

The Handkerchief Tree

The Journal of Frederick Grice, 1946-83

Edited by

Gillian and Colin Clarke

Anthony Eyre
MOUNT ORLEANS PRESS

Frontispiece, plate 1:
Fred Grice at home in Worcester, 1982.

Published in Great Britain in 2021
by Anthony Eyre, Mount Orleans Press
23 High Street, Cricklade SN6 6AP
www.anthonyeyre.com

ISBN 978-1-912945-28-3

A CIP record for this book is available
from the British Library

Printed in England by the
Short Run Press

To Aidan and Veronica:
children of Gillian and Colin Clarke,
the editors, and grandchildren of
Frederick Grice, the author

Contents

List of Plates

List of Figures

Acknowledgements

We are grateful to our son and daughter, Aidan Clarke and Veronica Clarke-Scholes—grandchildren of Frederick Grice—for their advice and support in the preparation and publication of this book, which we dedicate to them.

Rosemary Hull, Colin's cousin, kindly located the handkerchief tree in the Priory Gardens in Malvern and advised us when to photograph it at its best.

Ailsa Allen, Cartographic and Graphics Officer in the School of Geography and the Environment, Oxford University, drew the maps—Figures 1 and 2. Ailsa has also prepared the nine photographs for publication as the plates of this book. We are indebted to her for her skills.

Gillian and Colin Clarke

Maps

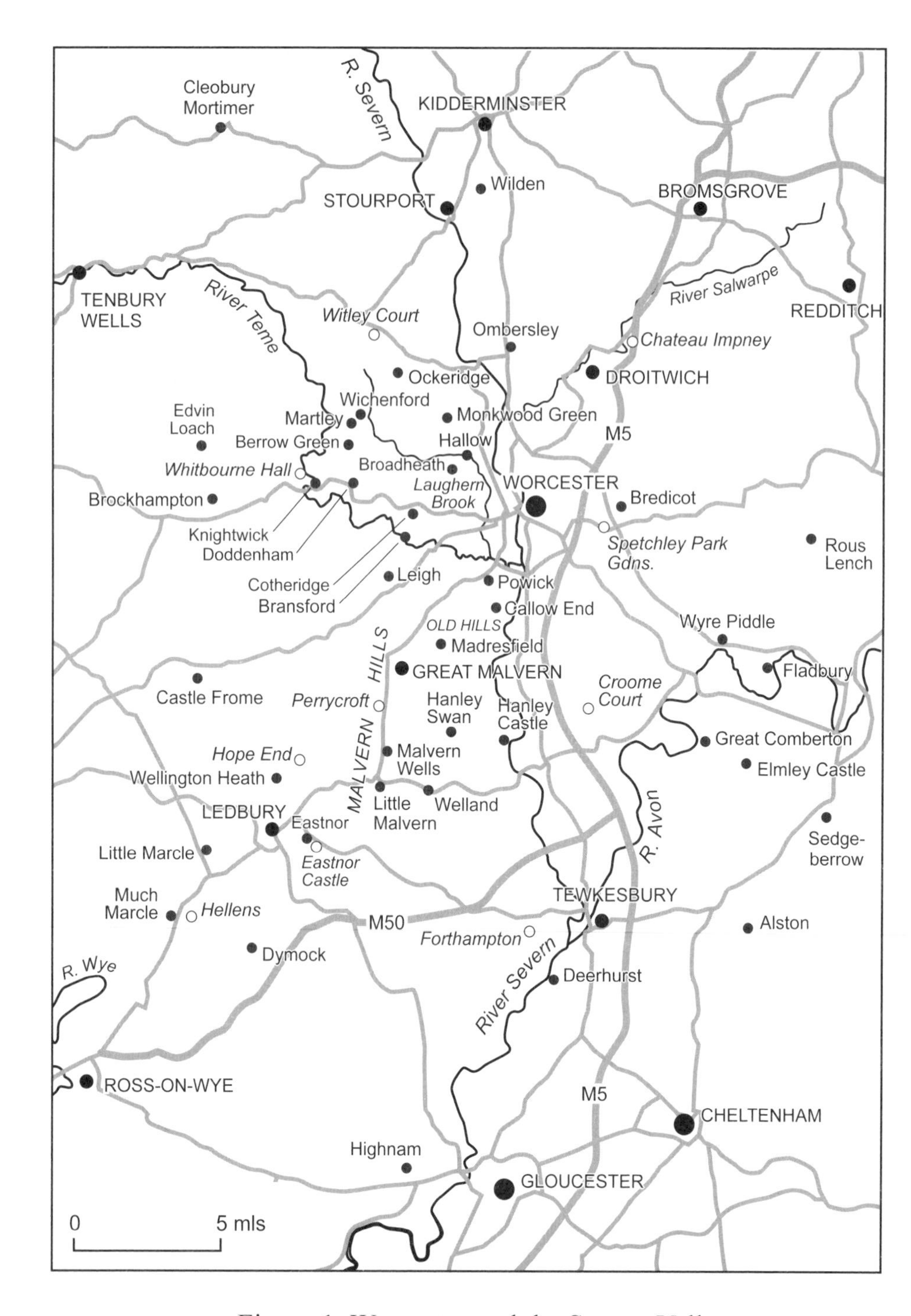

Figure 1. Worcester and the Severn Valley

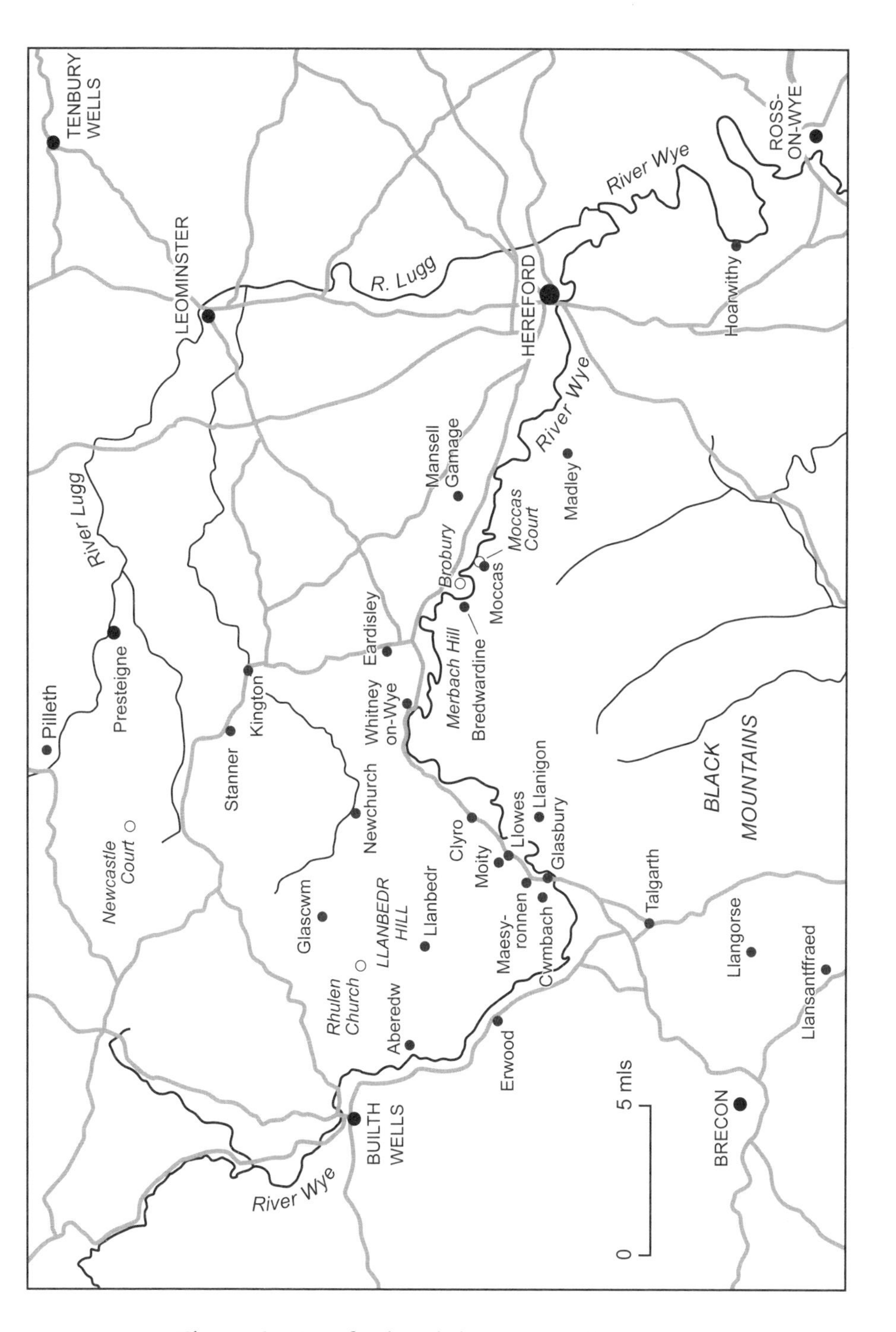

Figure 2. Hereford and the Wye Valley

Introduction

Colin and Gillian Clarke

Early life and career in education

In his retirement in the early 1970s Frederick Grice recalled:

> I was born in the North-East of England, in the far north, within hearing distance of the bells of Durham Cathedral. My father, who was a miner, worked in a small colliery a few miles out of Durham. I always think that I had the best of three worlds: the world of the pit village with its strikes, lockouts, evictions and accidents, and the warm company of a close-knit neighbourly community; the world of the beautiful medieval city of Durham, where I went to school, a city of fine architecture and novel traditions of piety and erudition; and the world of the austerely beautiful and unspoilt countryside that encircled the colliery village, merging into the lonely dales to the west and the borderland moors of Northumberland to the north (Commire 1974, 96).

Although Fred spent the greater part of his adult life in Worcester, the inspiration for much of his writing came from his childhood years in Durham. He was born in 1910 in Brandon where his father worked as a coal miner. At the age of eleven he won a scholarship to the Durham Johnston School, where he developed a deep love of English Literature that stayed with him for the rest of his life. After graduating with first-class honours from King's College, London in 1931, he returned home to the north and spent a happy year at Hatfield College, Durham University, where he obtained a teaching qualification and coxed one of the college boats. By 1941 Fred, now married to Gwen and with a daughter, Gillian, was teaching English at the A.J. Dawson Grammar School in Wingate, when he was called up into the Royal Air Force and posted to a small mobile radar unit in North Africa. When he was demobbed in 1946 he had spent the last two-to-three years as a Flight Lieutenant in the Education Corps based at Eastleigh near Nairobi.

Fred Grice's post-war journals (1946-83) began almost as soon as he was demobbed from the RAF and took up his civilian post as Lecturer in English at the newly-established Worcester Emergency Teacher Training College.

Fred's telegram home to Gwen in Durham following his successful interview read 'chaotic but promising'.[1] This training college (later to be made permanent and now the University of Worcester) had been set up by the government to train the backlog of primary and secondary school teachers, previously eligible for National Service during the Second World War. The situation was novel: the students were predominantly ex-service men and women, and the lecturers and their families were required to live on campus—often in overcrowded and communal circumstances. Nonetheless, the college had many attractions: it was new, created in peacetime, co-educational, and run along democratic lines; the staff and the mature students blended and formed an attractive education-orientated community (Cheesewright 2008).

This book is about the life and interests of Fred Grice—a writer of children's books, a devotee of English literature, especially as a poet and regular theatregoer, and an enthusiastic walker and observer of landscapes, people and place. At the time the journal begins in 1946 Fred was making a double adjustment to his new surroundings in Worcester away from his experiences in North and East Africa where he had served in the RAF and, further back in time, the Durham coalfield of his childhood and early years as a grammar school master. It was his experience as an Education Officer in the RAF in Kenya that enabled him to make the transition from secondary teaching in County Durham to lecturing in adult education in Worcester. Separated from Gwen from 1942 to 1945, the recently reunited couple now had two daughters, Gillian aged six and Erica five months.

Later Fred became Head of the English Department at the training college and devoted himself to the two activities he loved most—teaching and writing. He was also involved as a lecturer in extramural courses for the University of Birmingham held in Worcester and at Welland, near Malvern. As Cheesewright observed, Fred was one of the many staff at Worcester who blossomed: 'Fred Grice became a poet, author of children's stories, and a local broadcaster and critic.'[2] The first signs of yearning for the life he had left behind in the north of England are evident in Fred's post-war diaries. Here he began to record the world of his childhood, recreating with accuracy everyday conversation, but above all, paying homage to the unsung bravery of men like his father, who spent the greater part of their life underground in discomfort and danger.

Author

Fred's first book, *Folk Tales of the North Country* (1944)—prepared for publication by his wife while he was in Africa—was a collection of legends and folk tales, many of them told by his father and other acquaintances, but all embodying something of the spirit of the land that was the mainspring of his inspiration.[3] This was followed by *Folk Tales of the West Midlands* (1953) and *Folk Tales of Lancashire* (1954). His first novel for children came with the publication of *Aidan and the Strollers* (1960), a story based on the life of strolling players in the early nineteenth century. Later that year *The Bonny Pit Laddie* (1960) was also published. The most popular of all his books, it is the one closest to his heart in that it is set in his native colliery village, incorporating much of the personal history of his own family, especially his mother and father, and drawing heavily on the vicissitudes of the mining community of Durham. *The Bonny Pit Laddie* was shortlisted for the Carnegie Medal for children's fiction.

Fred wrote prolifically during the sixties and early seventies, taking inspiration from his own adventures during World War II in North Africa—*The Moving Finger* (1962), from Worcester—*A Severnside Story* (1964), from the north country—*The Oak and the Ash* (1968) and *The Courage of Andy Robson* (1969), and from the lives of the navvies who built the British railways in the mid-nineteenth century—*Young Tom Sawbones* (1972). The fourteen books he published in the 1960s and 1970s took up a large part of his diary during many of these years since all the first drafts were handwritten before being typed by Fred and re-typed professionally for publication. Of his children's books he said, 'I do not write with children in the forefront of my mind. Rather I write about children and the adult world as seen through the eyes of children... I think I am helped by the fact that in general I distrust overwrought writing, and prefer a simpler less involved style' (Commire 1974, 97).

After his retirement in 1972 Fred continued to write, give lectures—especially to children and educationalists with an interest in his books—and to write poetry. His collected works for children received The Other Award in 1977, but he increasingly turned his attention to writing and editing for adults. He edited the *Transactions of the Worcestershire Archaeological Society* for most of the 1970s and became President of the Archaeological Society in the early 1980s while also researching the nineteenth-century diarist, the Revd Francis Kilvert. With the support of the Kilvert Society, of which he was Deputy President (from 1974), he spent the last ten years of his life writing articles and completing the research for his final book, *Francis Kilvert and his World* (1982). Fred died suddenly in early 1983, shortly after the publication of this significant contribution to Kilvert studies, but with every intention of turning his own diary into a book (perhaps for publication) not unlike Kilvert's famous diary of country life.

'To keep a diary is to attempt a difficult literary form,' noted William Plomer, Kilvert's editor (1973, 5). 'Its effectiveness is likely to derive from a special blend of honesty and appetite for life which gives the power to record everyday happenings while magically freeing them from banality and triviality.' Mark Bostridge, in similar vein, has commented that 'I try not to let a good story pass without catching it on the wing' (Mark Bostridge, *TLS*, 24 Jan. 2020, p 17). The editors think that seizing the moment in words free from banality and triviality is precisely what Fred achieves in his journal. Fred focuses at first on Worcester, the Severn Valley and Worcestershire in the 1940s, 1950s, and 1960s (Figure 1), with excursions into other parts of the West Midlands, Oxfordshire, London, Durham and the north; but in retirement in the 1970s and early 1980s, as he explores Kilvert country, he becomes increasing engaged with Herefordshire, Radnorshire and the Wye Valley (Figure 2), in addition to his earlier post-war fascination with the catchments of the Rivers Severn, Teme and Salwarpe.

Fred's diaries and their relationship to his journal

From 1937 Fred kept a regular diary in which he recorded the varied activities of his literary and personal life, and noted changes in the natural environment witnessed on the walks he took on the moors around Durham. In short, when he was drafted to North Africa in 1942 he was a budding professional writer with a keen eye for environmental detail and ear for language. Moreover his first book, *Folk Tales of the North Country,* was published towards the end of the war in 1944. The war years 1942-3 were portrayed in his early diaries and are based on two handwritten notebooks (0 and 1) plus a memoir.[5] His editors —Gillian and Colin Clarke (his son-in-law)—have already juxtaposed and, where necessary, blended these three sources into *War's Nomads: A Mobile Radar Unit in Pursuit of Rommel During the Western Desert Campaign, 1942-3* (Grice 2015). *War's Nomads* was nominated for Book of the Year by *History Today.*

The editors are treating the published version of *War's Nomads* as the first volume of his autobiography, with the second volume to be this book,

The Handkerchief Tree—The Journal of Frederick Grice, 1946-83. We have not included in *The Handkerchief Tree* Volumes 2 or 3 of his original diary which deal with East and North Africa and are extraneous to our concerns. The source of *The Handkerchief Tree* lies in 32 post-war diaries beginning with volume 4 and running until 1983, and contains the handwritten entries from which Fred made his own selection for the journal.[6] On 23 April 1977 he wrote in his diary, 'I am typing out the best parts of my notebooks onto loose sheets'; and on 26 May he added, 'the prose accounts are to be interspersed with poems—the best I have done. I must make sure that Gillian knows about it.'

These journal selections, which Fred started to work on in May 1977 and continued until his death in 1983, were made from his original diary entries, and sometimes rewritten to polish them for style and coherence. Fred gave his journal selections the same date as the similar entries in the original diaries, and it is feasible to move backwards and forwards between the two accounts. Occasionally, in addition to rewriting and smoothing his original entry from the diary, Fred intrudes a piece of new text that represents a backward look from his vantage point as author. Some of the journal entries were misplaced by him during his editing, but we were able to sort out problems of chronology by going back to his original diary accounts and reordering the journal where necessary. Tellingly, Fred noted in his diary on 28 May 1977: 'I suppose I am drawn to a Kilvert-like oeuvre because I feel as he did about life. However unsensational, however obscure—I feel that it must not be wholly forgotten. It has brought me so many pleasures that I cannot but tell them. So I will go in for something longer and even more revealing.'

The editors have divided the text into 10 chapters—plus an Introduction and Prologue—separated into two parts: Part I, Chapters 1 to 4, is entitled 'College Lecturer and Children's Author'; and Part II, Chapters 5 to 10, are called 'In the Footsteps of Francis Kilvert.' Part I covers the last 26 active years of Fred's life, mostly as Head of Department and part-time author, and the first two chapters deal with the immediate post-war periods 1946-57 and 1958-63. When read sequentially, they give a sense of the quickening recovery of Worcester and the Worcester area immediately after World War II, and especially after the mid-1950s; moreover, there is more for Fred to report in the second chapter, including the text of his four books published between 1960 and 1963. Chapter 3 continues with Worcester's economic recovery, but what is striking is the comparative shortness of this chapter. Fred published seven books between 1964 and 1972, and almost all were recorded in first draft in the diaries for this 9-year period—including the handwritten narratives referred to in Chapter 4.

Part II marks the beginning of Fred's retirement and the increased opportunity he has to devote himself entirely to children's writing, research, and publishing about Kilvert. Although this section covers only ten years—the last decade of his life—there is a great deal for him to report and adequate time in which to record it; some years have a chapter to themselves. Both his 1976 and 1978 OUP books were published out of freehand versions later typed up by Fred; they account once more for the reduced space for recording alternative matters, especially in 1977-8. The final chapter—Chapter 10—is one of the longest in Part II, largely because it contains most of his 'late poems', is extended in time to cover the death of Fred's mother, and the memorial service of one of his close associates, Matley Moore, a distinctive Worcester character.

Worcester's decay

When Fred began his journal in 1946 Worcester looked decidedly post-war—and drab, though the city had never experienced more than a casual bombing raid during World War II. Wartime rationing still applied but was gradually reduced in the late 1940s and early 1950s and sweet rationing disappeared before the mid-1950s. Buying a new car was rationed until the late 1950s by which time wartime waiting lists finally disappeared. Worcester in the 1940s was a dour place and pleasures were homespun, amateurish and inexpensive. Before television became commonplace nationally in the late 1950s, cinemas were the main source of weekly entertainment following the closure in 1955 of the Theatre Royal in Worcester. However, football and cricket were popular sports at all amateur levels as well as professionally, and Worcestershire County Cricket Club had the distinction of opening the season each summer with a three-day match against the international tourists.

By the 1960s the post-war gloom had begun to lift: the M5 motorway linking Birmingham and Bristol was opened, and soon after that the M50 Ross Spur—changing time-space relationships throughout the county. Pre-war cars were slowly replaced by post-war models. By the early 1970s, a second bridge was built south of Worcester to reduce crowding on the road to Malvern and eliminate the bottleneck in St John's. However, despite these improvements, there was also deterioration in transport: for example Beeching's cuts to rail services in the 1960s saw many rural lines and stations closed. Later the track north of Oxford to Worcester and Hereford was reduced to a single line, on the false assumption that the private car would more than take up the slack—but only at the cost of road congestion.

There was also decay in the urban fabric of central Worcester after the neglect of the 1930s and the war years, and slum clearance in the areas adjacent to the city's medieval walls became the order of the day in the 1950s. In this way it was possible to accommodate the cars, lorries and buses that clogged the inner-city streets until the logjam was reduced by the regional motorways that were completed in the 1960s. Although Worcester had a planning department, set up as part of the UK Town and Country Planning Act of 1947, stewardship of the city by local councillors and planning officials was unimaginative and neglectful to the point of vandalism. A great deal that was medieval and Georgian in inner Worcester was demolished without hesitation, and insufficient care was given to the quality of the replacement buildings. One of the few early successes in inner-city conservation was the preservation of Greyfriars in Friar Street, Worcester, a Grade I merchant's house built in 1480, owned and restored by the Matley Moores, and donated by them to the National Trust in 1966.[4]

It was in the light of these changes for good or ill in Worcester that Fred wrote about Worcester's decay in the 1970s—the last full decade of his life.

> When George III came to Worcester to listen to the music of the Three Choirs [Festival], he was greatly taken with the city, and admired the neat streets, its paved ways, its cleanliness and its beauty. Since then it has had to endure many decades of spoliation and neglect. Now it is like a city in decay. Many interesting houses have been allowed to fall into serious disrepair, and have been demolished and replaced by office blocks which no one wants to occupy. The famous Countess of Huntingdon's Chapel is now almost a total wreck. There are neither private nor public funds to keep it from declining into complete ruin.
>
> The Georgian houses at the end of Bridge Street are empty, waiting for some developer to get permission at last to demolish them and erect more superfluous office blocks. The Georgian Crown Hotel in Broad Street has been derelict for years. The unsafe parapet of All Saints' Church has been taken down and not replaced. No one can find the money for the repairs. The new heating system in the cathedral is proving too expensive to maintain. St Peter's Church in Sidbury has been demolished, and more will follow. The Monday cattle market is in decline, and month by month the business done there dwindles. Meanwhile vandals flourish, and a few years ago all the riverside benches along Hylton Road were systematically smashed.

> Lavatories in stores are closed from time to time because of vandalism. Unspeakable things happen in the Cathedral toilets. A scrap metal merchant litters the South Quay with his rubbish and refuse. Our car parks are the ugliest I have seen anywhere—not car parks but merely weedy derelict waste lots. Ugliness spreads like a disease, and the authorities are too benighted to see how far our city has declined from the tight compact admirable little city that George III praised.
>
> A city in decay, indifferent to its glories, too mercenary and shortsighted to see that what is being destroyed will never be replaced.

Approaching old age

In the 1970s Fred was in his 60s and retired, but hardly elderly. Nonethless, he was unwell in a variety of unspecific ways, and he died from a heart attack in February 1983. Unwell he might have been, but his mind was sharp to the end, and he was always striving to create something new through his writing.

> Isn't it strange to be drawing near to old age, and yet be so powerfully in the presence of the past—not yesterday, not last week, but the far past, as if half a century had passed in a night, in one's sleep, in one sequence of dreams; and that slow eclipse of faculties seems to have happened with the speed of an accident. Now it appears to me that I am only momentarily alive—perhaps when I slip out into the night, and see the vague blossom of another Spring blurring the orchard trees, and catch for a second only the scent of the streaked wallflowers. The long still twilight, the grey blanket of the darkening night, the scent of lilac, the sound of a solitary train! How brief are the moments of our living. How soon life turns into a hallucination! I search constantly for life but it eludes me. I turn away from it to muse, reflect, forget.
>
> Yet I still have visions. After the act of love, in the agony of fulfilment I have often for a moment had strange visions of fabulous beasts, and strange-coloured visions like things seen after drug-taking sessions. Once, recently, I saw with closed eyes a procession of grey and dappled horses, like eroded statues, rear and prance in a sacrificial frieze, with arched and stony necks, and flanks, pitted and noble, straining towards some unknown end, as I sometimes strain, as I am straining now, towards some undivined destination.

Fred's vignettes—Worcester's decay and his old age—give the reader a clear impression of the quality of his writing and the strong sense of place that he evokes. His prose ranges widely over urban and rural environments, seasons and the self, but, as we shall discover when we turn to his journals at the core of the book, it also reports on his social encounters, especially his conversations with students, colleagues, citizens, townspeople and country folk. In his retirement,

Kilvert comes increasingly into focus, as do Herefordshire and Radnorshire, the Worcestershire Archaeological Society and the Kilvert Society.

The poems

Set against the prose in which they are embedded, the seventy-four poems in the journal concentrate on rural landscapes, Fred's own personality and character, elegiac themes, and finally urban topics—largely associated with the city of Worcester. Just over three-quarters of the poems are dated and located close to the appropriate prose passages. The remaining quarter of undated poems, the editors assume, were placed by Fred to illustrate what he considered the most apposite prose passages, and seem to have been composed without reference to the precise dating sequence used elsewhere.

Fred explained:

> I write a great deal of poetry, mainly for my own satisfaction, and my mentors in this field are, in the main, those whose viewpoint and style are relatively uncomplicated—Wordsworth, Hardy, Edward Thomas and Robert Frost. Though I have great sympathy with avant-garde writers and avant-garde artists I learn from them rather than seek to imitate them (Commire 1974, 97).

Worcestershire in the 1970s was characterised by networks of villages and farms, cottages and barns, separated by small undulating fields of brown ploughed land, orchards or meadows of green grass, hedgerows heavily planted with trees—an intimate landscape dominated by the bare Malvern Hills. The subjects of Fred's poems touch on many of these landscape elements—plus those he later encountered in Herefordshire and Radnorshire. Although almost a quarter of the poems deal with this rural world, a slightly higher proportion are devoted to the seasons and to the weather. Taken together, the rural landscape and its buildings plus its climatology account for more than half the poems.

Much more revealing of the state of mind, values and feelings of the poet are the twenty or so poems dealing with the self and the elegiac inner preoccupations of the people he is writing about. Among the elegiac poems several stand out. Thomas Hardy's last possessions turn out to be modest—his jacket, a piece of string and a pocket knife. Emma's room at Max Gate is revealed as an inaccessible garret and Hardy's silence as unbearable. As Fred drives south after his mother's funeral in Durham, his tears on arrival back in Worcester are manifested as raindrops.

If more than half the poems deal with the rural landscape and skyscape, a residual group appropriately deals with Worcester—where he lived, first on the campus of the training college and later in his own home in the outskirts beyond the narrow streets of the crumbling core of the medieval city of the 1940s and 1950s. In contrast, poems dealing with foreign lands are few in number, as are the slender verses dealing with Fred's grandchildren and ageing. Many of the poems are short—between 6 and 12 lines in length, with 'Queen Adelaide's Window' by far the longest with 28 lines. Compact and cleverly constructed, they move swiftly to a conclusion or resolution over the last few lines.

Conclusion

Although he made his name as a children's author and Kilvert's biographer, there were many other sides to Fred in addition to his reputation as a fine lecturer. He was a keen walker and lover of the countryside, attuned to nature, birdsong and the trees. In later years the bracing, empty moorland of his youth was replaced by the gently undulating Worcestershire lanes. He was frequently seen tramping around Wichenford and Broadheath, and he never lost his childlike love of paddling in brooks, catching minnows and flying kites—much to the delight of his grandchildren.

He was a great raconteur with an impish sense of fun, a lover of football (he was a lifelong supporter of Newcastle United), the theatre and the arts. All these aspects of his life and interests are mirrored in his journals—in his autobiographical poems and his verses describing landscapes, skyscapes, townscapes; in his prose accounts of topography; his anecdotes about unusual people or events witnessed, whether humble or elevated; his recording of plays seen and books read; his visits to theatres, galleries and local and national exhibitions. In short, Fred's journal, though inevitably episodic, is an invaluable source of contemporary history.

On his travels through the Severn and Wye valleys between 1946 and 1983 Fred wove an engaging narrative of his visits and experiences, his encounters with others—sometimes amusing, occasionally deeply troubled—whether in lanes or country houses, in classes or on field trips, in the cities of Worcester and Hereford or on the rivers. His ear for a good story and his capacity for capturing the accent and phraseology of ordinary people bring his prose vividly to life and make it accessible, memorable and timeless. Fred's poems are set in a matrix of lyrical, poetic prose that make a substantial and insightful contribution to the quality and texture of his journal.

While this Introduction has recounted Fred's life as a lecturer and author and explained his interest in literature and the arts, the Prologue which follows takes us into the heart of his concerns as a writer on the theme of a sense of place. The Prologue deals with Worcestershire: an English county, and an account of the changing seasons of the year. It also acts as a stepping stone to the journal.

Notes

1 Quoted in Cheesewright, Paul (2008) *The University of Worcester: An Illustrated History.*
2 Cheesewright, 46.
3 Fred's major books are listed by date of publication in Appendix 1.
4 Matley Moore and his sister Elsie were known as the Matley Moores, and Elsie as Elsie Matley Moore.
5 The war years were portrayed in his early diaries covering 1942-1945, and are based on two handwritten notebooks: Volume 0 (Invaluable: not to be lost, and captioned 'On Draft,' 26 April to 7 August 1942) and Volume 1 'Black Book, bought Cape Town,' 25 June to December 1942), plus a typed memoir, 'Erk in the Desert', completed in Eastleigh, Nairobi in 1944.
6 *The Handkerchief Tree* begins with extracts from Volume 4 of the diary, theoretically covering British peace-time entries from 31 December 1937, but which in reality run from 1946 to 11 January 1950.

References

Bostridge, Mark (2020) 'Dear diaries: archiving personal records,' *Times Literary Supplement*, 24 January, 2020, p 17. Mark Bostridge (2019) has recently written a new 'Introduction' to *Kilvert's Diary, 1870-79*, pp vii-xxv. Selections from the diary of Francis Kilvert, chosen, edited and prefaced by William Plomer (based on the three-volume first edition published in 1944). London: Vintage.

Cheesewright, Paul (2008) *The University of Worcester: An Illustrated History.* London: James and James.

Commire, Anne (ed.) (1974) *Something About the Author: Facts and Pictures about Contemporary Authors and Illustrators of Books for Young People.* Detroit, Michigan: Gale Research, Vol.6, pp 96-97.

Grice, Frederick (1982) *Francis Kilvert and his World.* Horsham, Sussex: Caliban Books.

Grice, Frederick, edited by Gillian and Colin Clarke (2015) *War's Nomads: A Mobile Radar Unit in Pursuit of Rommel During the Western Desert Campaign, 1942-3.* Oxford: Casemate Publishers.

Plomer, William (1973) 'Preface', *Kilvert's Diary.* London: Jonathan Cape, Vol 1, p 5.

Prologue

Frederick Grice

There is no better way of familiarising oneself with Worcestershire of the post-war period—the world that Fred embraced as a newcomer—than by allowing him to take us on a visit, recorded in his own words (in a separate typescript of about 1953 but not included in his diary), describing some of his favourite locations in Worcester and Worcestershire. He called the typescript 'An English County', and his familiarity with, and affection for, the area show that shortly after the Second World War he was beginning to regard it as home. This was Fred feeling his way into Worcestershire and its landscapes, natural and man-made; meeting the eccentrics who lived there and made it their own; reflecting on Worcester Cathedral, the Malverns, the Old Hills, Bredon, Eastnor Castle; and depicting the local tradesmen who made cider and repaired Worcester Racecourse, and the gypsies who picked hops in the Teme Valley. Finally there is his complementary account of the changing seasons of the year.

An English county: Worcestershire

It is when I am alone that I discover most—although discover is too magnificent a word for the surprises I have enjoyed in my wanderings over this county—and of all my solitary walks the first that comes to my mind was one I undertook one lovely August evening not long ago. I was warily exploring the grounds of the great estate of Croome Court *(Fig 1)*. I was in some fear of being turned away for I had no leave to be there and had been too shy to ask for it. I think that if truth were told I preferred to explore in this manner, for there was a certain boyish thrill in entering the forbidden ground: and to steal from field to field almost in expectancy of being surprised added piquancy to my exploration.

I ventured first from the great arch that marks the official entrance to Croome, and crossed a derelict field where a demolition gang had been busy all day removing the unsightly remains of a service camp which had been built there. Then, suddenly and without warning, I came upon a building which surprised me with its beauty. It was a charming little rotunda, no more than a simple circular gazebo with five or six windows and no furniture; but its proportions were so chaste and elegant, and its beautifully weathered stone glowed so magnificently against the gloomy and noble grove of cedars and firs in which it stood, that it seemed to me to be one of the most beautiful buildings I had ever seen.[1]

I walked round it with great pleasure, examining the wide and curving walk that led to it, the row of classical statues that adorned the slope below it, and the massive memorial urn that stood silent and alone in the grove nearby; but already I had caught sight of further discoveries. Glimpsing another little building in the distance I walked on. On my left stretched now the sad plain of Defford aerodrome, with its broad and ugly landing strip and violent orange cranes; but to the right the magnificent estate of Croome with its fields and trees looked towards the vague grey Malvern Hills. I crossed a field rough with thistles, their downy heads filled with the light from the west, and came to a second little retreat.

This, to my disappointment, was in ruins. Its columns were damaged, its roof leaking, and the crumbling plasterwork scribbled over with names and indecencies; but as I looked at it, wondering how anyone could bring himself to deface it, a third discovery rose before my eye. It was the form of Dunstall Castle, tall, removed, solitary, standing among the nettles and brambles on the open common. Though Croome itself brooded in the shadows, massive and sombre, the masonry of this strange folly, built for nothing but to serve a fantastic and transient taste, glowed and took life in the pale western light. I did not go to see it. I was content to watch it from a distance, and to leave it so in my mind, the image of an artificial yet strangely moving Gothic ruin.

It was during this summer that I set out to look more closely at other follies in the county. It was an unparagoned summer, and the long continuous Edwardian warmth seemed to have drawn everyone to the sea. I had the strange impression of wide inland acres forsaken and left clear for the lover of solitude. It was in this mood that I came one evening to the quiet village of Rous Lench *(Fig 1)*. I had read of the eccentric Dr Chafy, one-time vicar and squire of the village, and was familiar with his career and nature. Dr Chafy was a Victorian eccentric, tall, handsome, wealthy and earnest. One of his first reforms on coming to Rous Lench was to close the one public house which the village possessed. No doubt the port circulated at the Court, but beer was not to be permitted to the parishioners. He remodelled the inn, enlarging it and fitting it out as a parish room, which was to be one of his main instruments in his plan to educate the villagers. There he encouraged them to listen to his lectures and to grace their uncouth and bucolic ways with a little culture.

Dr Chafy's philanthropy seems to have taken strange forms. His last gift to his parish was two postboxes. It is hardly correct to call them boxes, for they were more like toy houses. One is almost hidden in the trees by the roadside at Radford. The other stands in the middle of Rous Lench, a miniature cottage with tiles, stone walls, the arms of the donor on the gables, and no other opening than a red letter-box, still bearing the initials of Victoria Regina. While I was there I did not see anybody put a letter in the box, but young men were sitting and smoking on the stones steps upon which the folly was erected.

During the course of that warm summer I went out to see the famous Clock Tower at Abberley; Broadway Tower that the Earl of Coventry built to serve as an eyecatcher for Croome, which the Coventry forbade him to begin until he had lit a bonfire on the spot and satisfied her that it was visible from her windows; and Sanderson Miller's 'ruined castle' in the grounds of Hagley Hall. But more often I went out to see nothing of importance, being content to look at the flowers and fields and trees, pleased with looking, and needing, as Wordsworth said, no other interest 'unborrowed from the eye'.

I have always, with Wordsworth, believed in the power of nature to illuminate and refine; and all my life the most healing and uplifting of my pleasures has been to walk in lonely places. No sooner do I begin to put one foot before the other than my mind begins to revive. Then plans and prospects and visions seem to rise in my imagination, as if the motion of walking had disengaged them and given them freedom to circulate. Traffic and the circulation of people distract me; but when I enter quiet lanes and unvisited side-roads, then strange consolations and confirmation come into mind, and the sense of contact and communion with the unfailing uninhibited life of grass and tree, bird and beasts, informs me with its vigour. When I cannot walk in the company of green things, a fearful numbness and deadness creeps over me, and the nullity of my existence fills me with misgiving and despondency.

The sky was perfectly clear, and the colour of lavender, and the pure morning sun made the bare twigs gleam and glisten. The trunks of the trees were green, but the branches and twigs were dove grey, except where a branch of mistletoe, still vivid and emerald, caught the light and flared. The sunshine, the clearness of the air, the warmth—all gave an illusion of spring, and the birds flashed and called in their excitement. The rooks strode in the stubble, already with that aldermanic self-importance the Spring brings to them. The pigeons broke constantly out of the trees, going up with a clatter of wings and seeking refuge in the brown woods. There were redwings and fieldfares in every field.

Wondering at their excitement I looked around. To the critical observer there was nothing new in the scene. Last year's oak leaves stuck stiffly on the twigs and rustled as the wind reached them, but did not fall. The catkins were brown and tight. There was not a bud swelling. The haws stood blackened by the recent frosts. The ash keys, the maple keys, thistle and teazle were dry and dead. Yet there was something, some intimation that roused the birds to immense excitement. The pigeons rose and dived. The little birds kept still but went from twig to twig; the great green woodpeckers loped from tree to tree, breasting the air as if they were swimming through it. As I walked I caught the infection of their excitement, and wondered what had happened to the cosy and demure afternoon land that I had grown used to. But I never found out.

Another afternoon in November, suddenly, on the quiet road between Wichenford turning and King's Green I had a miraculous access of joy that I could not explain and have never forgotten *(Fig 1)*. It was not merely pleasure, but a sharp visitation of ecstasy that suddenly revealed the ordinary and sombre landscape as a scene of indescribable joy. There was nothing before me but the common vista—the last leaves, the ruined nests in the hedges, the distant crowns of bare elms, the black and antlered orchards, the blanched skeletons of parsley stalks, the faintly bloomed sky. Yet suddenly, for five minutes, the whole ordinary scene was invested with a beauty and a significance that I could not explain but simply marvel at.

I have always been fascinated by the strange almost imperceptible crises in the passage of the year, and to see these scarcely visible transformations has always brought me the certainty of an insight which I value more than life itself. Some such awareness came to me one night in late summer, as I sat on the edge of a wide dark field. Low in the south the moon, uneven as a lemon, threw across the world its yellow light. High above, the mid-sky was blue as a beetle, and against its darkness the stars burnt and flickered. They were innumerable like the glinting fragments of some great explosion, arrested in space, jagged and white with heat.

All was tranquillity. The trees stood motionless, and their shadows lay like cloaks thrown on to the yellow grass. Sometimes across the still air came the noise of a car going uphill, or a train going through a cutting; or a bird went overhead heading through the silent air for the south and the sea, uttering an elegiac note now and then as it made its way over hedges and roofs. But the air did not breathe or stir; it was utterly tranquil.

Slowly the moon fell, turned on its side and reddened as it sank. The long black shadows crept stalk by stalk across the fields. Then as the first clock began to strike midnight, and wakened all its fellows one by one, suddenly the elm gave a little shiver. One big dry leaf somewhere up the tree detached itself. It fell dropping from bough to bough, turning and turning till at last it fell to the ground. When it reached the dark turf, the clocks had stopped striking and the moon had gone down; and I knew that at that moment the summer had come to an end. When I went in, I looked at the calendar and found that the leaf had fallen at the turning of the month and it was now September.

Moments of beauty and recognition like these have been the highlights of my life, and I cannot forbear to mention one more which occurred to me in the ordinary and mundane Worcester suburb of St John's. I had had tea with friends who live in an old house on the main street, and after tea I went into the garden. It was a surprisingly lovely garden, with a big weeping willow, its branches sweeping down and touching the ground, and a bed of lily-of-the-valley still in green leaf. Beyond these, however, was a rubbish heap, two or three neglected hives, then a rusty length of railing, with here and there a spike missing.

I went over to the railing to look at the neglected orchard beyond, and suddenly caught sight of Worcester Cathedral, glimpsed between the unkempt orchard branches. The western sun was falling flush upon it, and by some miraculous coincidence the glow was reflected in the great western window right into the garden where I stood. The burning bush! Every pane in the west window glittered and reflected the dying light until it seemed made of gold. In the brilliance of the glow nothing else was visible—no house or riverside shack, no chimney or boathouse, nothing but the cathedral, transfigured and splendid.

No one who lives in Worcestershire and loves the open air can ignore the Malverns *(Fig 1)*. I have walked on them in all weathers and at all times of the day and night; and whenever I put foot on that springy ridge I wonder why I have not gone there more frequently. One brilliant winter morning I saw the sun, far to the south, flame on the waters of the Bristol Channel, and the pale shape of the Mendips rise in the distance. On another occasion in Olympian remoteness I watched storms of field-grey rain sweep by the corners of the hills, overrun the plain with unwelcome and diagonal showers, then spend themselves on the far ridge of the Cotswolds.

In winter or summer, storm or dry weather, it is a thrilling experience to look along the ridge and see the hills stretched out like a brontosaurus across the landscape, and to turn from the placid English plain in the east to the tumbled Celtic ranges that mount, wave on wave, towards Wales until they rise to the long level crest of the Black Mountains. Below, the houses stand like boxes, and the meadow pipit goes from bush to bush, the hawk hangs in the air, and the train takes breath before it dives through the great prehistoric wave of the rock; and always the air is bright and invigorating and pure.

One day I climbed from the car park up the side of British Camp. Climbing was a labour. The flies rose from every patch of bracken, the air was still and sultry, the haze had closed in upon the views. I walked south over the brow of the hill, by the edge of an old twisted tree—that wood of brown branches that swarms so mysteriously over the slope—through a delicious coppice with new nuts spilt on the pathway, and so on through the hot bracken to the obelisk. This is a wonderful vantage point. Eastnor Castle looms through the woods; the wooded valleys roll and fold, and far away on May Hill a line of trees shows like a strange caterpillar that never moves *(Fig 1)*. But my moments of exultation over the solitude of the place and the beauty of the parched landscape alternated with moods of weariness, and the flies seized on me as if they were all dying of thirst and I were the only moist thing for miles.

Strange and ancient trades have always fascinated me. I feel a great pity for those who are condemned to work in factories, and even the skilled designers and decorators in the Porcelain Works in Worcester seem to me to live like prisoners; but those who have elected to work in the open air have always drawn me as the leech gatherers drew Wordsworth. One day I came across a solitary cider maker who had set up his jig on the verge of the road near Madresfield, and he seemed to me as near the personification of Autumn as Hardy's Giles Winterborne.

On another occasion I came on Pitchcroft upon a gang of men who called themselves treaders, and whose humble function it was to walk over the Worcester Racecourse at the end of the meeting and press back the divots that the horses had kicked. On a third day, I came upon a scene such as Hardy describes in *The Return of the Native*. Two men in great hedgers' gloves were cutting the furze on the Old Hills *(Fig 1)*. At first I thought they were ancient fuel gatherers but, alas, they told me that the furze was needed for repairing the racecourse hurdles.

I have never wanted to live with the gypsies who from May to October live as pickers, but the sight of their wagons and lean horses, and the tanned skins and close-combed hair of their women is one I cherish. No doubt they live meanly and sordidly, but when their sleazy cortèges hold up the traffic in the city, they seem to be exercising an ancient and honourable right of which I would not like to see them deprived. Indolent, dirty, irresponsible, they nevertheless declare their reluctance to be conventional, and bring colour and panache into the streets of the city.

The seasons

Spring is always beautiful here; at times, it can be magical. I remember in particular the Spring of 1951. Early months of the year had been vexatious and rainy, but out of the soaked and fruitful earth there came that year such a profusion of growth as I have rarely seen. All the common flowers grew high. Buttercups rose higher than the knees and their cups seemed almost to float in the air. All the white flowers of the verges, Jack-by-the-hedge and all the wild parsley were waist high, and seemed to froth over the roadsides more like clouds than flowers.

All the trees put out a great denseness of foliage, and the juicy black bryony shot out enormous tendrils. Everything was out in abundance—bluebells disdaining to wait till the primroses had died, stitchwort leaning upward and outward as children lean out of their desks to answer their teachers, herb Robert and leggy cowslips, ground ivy, periwinkle, yellow archangel. And the wonderful profusion of everything created a curious illusion. The grasses and flowers were as tall as they were when we were children. They seemed magically to have put back the clock, and we wandered again in a world we thought we had lost.

Some years later these miracles were almost repeated; but then it was not the profusion but the brilliance of the Spring flowers and blossoms that enchanted me. I remember very clearly the end of April, the time of cherry and pear blossom. We had near us at that time some old fruit trees, gnarled, nibbled by goats, split and wormy. They bore nothing but bitter, scarcely-edible fruit, but that year they were all clouded with the most brilliant display of blossom—each like a great cumulus cloud, rising and unfolding richness and whiteness. Behind them stood horse chestnuts, heavy with a wonderful density of leaf, and decorated everywhere with brown candles ready to open as soon as May came in. The beech was tardy. It disdained yet to open, and from a distance looked strangely swart, reddening as if it were blushing for its lethargy. Nearby was an old felled poplar. Its trunk had been sawn up long ago, but the slain tree still put out shoots from its ruined base.

It was the gardens that mainly caught the eye that year—spiraea spilling its whiteness in a great white splash, broom golden as the yolk of eggs; prunus now a browning froth, but lovely even in decay; pink tassels of flowering currant, the jasmine still yellow. The daffodils were tarnished but narcissi shone in great galaxy under the yew hedge, slim, pointed, invulnerable, a glorious assembly of lissom beauty. And all day long the air hung wonderfully still as if the year was saying, 'Look what I've done! Pause and look a little before I begin again.' I could not help looking hour after hour. It was a wonderful climax in a lovely spring.

In the north, the Spring comes slowly: but in Worcestershire the flowers hurry pell-mell, crowding upon one another, bringing surprise upon surprise. If there is anything to lament, it is that Summer comes too quickly. Then too often the air seems to thicken and the days grow languorous. These are the days of the 'tempest', sultry and brooding weather when the thunderous air thickens and broods, and does not break into storms. Eyes turn longingly to the hills, the blue crest of the Malverns and the whaleback of Bredon; to the north with its sharp air, and the far distant sea. The river sinks and leaves sandy spits where the willowherb and tansy grow. The year is dazed and tranced until at last August is gone, and the delicious melancholy days of Autumn have begun.

It was early in September when I was writing this page. I had just returned from the river, and the first cool airs of Autumn were blowing in at my open window. I had been on the river above Bevere. All of the swimmers of Summer had departed; the cabin cruisers had returned to their anchorages. No steamers crowded with innocent and noisy passengers were now to be seen above the lock. And all the true and native life of the river was reclaiming the waters—the waterhens ferrying themselves slowly from bank to bank, taking fright at footfall or the dip of an oar. The water voles nosed along the banks, disappearing with their sudden plop.

Here and there a single swan, indescribably beautiful in the sinking Autumn light quested in a lonely reach. The last of the anglers, the quietest of men, sat immobile on the banks, and the friendly whirr of their reels was like the sound of a river bird. The evening was completely still, so that the river scarce seemed to move, and every reflection was complete and perfect. The willows leaned over the water, as if to admire themselves, and every now and then a slim yellow leaf disengaged itself and fell with a tiny ripple on to the surface of the stream. The Severn, too often muddied or tormented with barges and motorboats, seemed to have refound its ancient composure. And if Sabrina herself had risen among the roots of the alders there would have been no surprise.

Several years ago, we enjoyed an Autumn of unusual mildness that turned in the end to unusual disaster. The Summer had been bad, but the last days of Autumn shone with unusual brilliance. The wet August had left the trees heavy with foliage, and in the clear late sunshine they stood as if in a trance between growth and dissolution. Even the great chestnut trees, always quick to denude themselves, could do no more than surrender from time to time one dry papery leaf that lazily swung from rung to rung till it settled lightly on the ground. The air was a muted blue, the colour of a Michaelmas daisy, and day after day the sun rose and paced serenely across a windless and cloudless sky.

There is a certain group of trees that wait all the year for the Autumn. In Spring and Summer, they receive no more notice than any other chestnuts in the county; but as soon as October comes, every year, with mysterious regularity, the leaves of this little stand of trees, a handful of chestnuts growing by the cross roads at Ombersley, acquire a burning beauty all of their own—ochre and rust, umber and orange, lemon and blood—colours of individual and striking beauty, blending and matching with more than human subtlety. By what secret process of growth does this annual miracle happen? What rareness of soil brings out these rich colours, and gives this clump of trees an individuality? I do not know. All I know is that every year I look forward to seeing the Ombersley chestnuts in their beauty, and they never disappoint me *(Fig 1)*.

Sometimes, but not often, Winter brings a hard frost. Even less frequently the frost sets in when the river is in flood. Then for a while Pitchcroft, the city's playground and racecourse, becomes a vast skating rink; but as the water seeps back into the ground, a space forms under the ice which begins to buckle, and then to crack. On one unforgettable occasion, a hard frost came just when the County Cricket Ground was under three or four inches of water, and the green that had seen the triumphs of the Fosters and other Worcestershire worthies became for three days and nights the loveliest skating ground in the world. Evenings like these do not come so often that they can be forgotten. It may be the mark of a foolish mind, but I can recall that day far more clearly and completely than I can recall the end of the war that claimed so much of our lives.

Once I watched from Broadheath a fine snowstorm *(Fig 1)*. It was mid-December, but not unduly cold. In the west over the low Ankerdines the sun was very bright, a brilliant fox-red; but in the east beyond the city a great range of cloud began to thicken and roll like the dust from some great cataclysm. Like some astonishing and unreal organism, it began to heave and writhe, then to swell and enlarge till it towered in the middle sky. It was blue like a bruise, and yellow like pus—a great fester that meant to burst. Then suddenly it began to spread, fast as contagion. The telegraph wires began to sing and little icicles that had formed on the gates began to tinkle as they fell obliquely in the rising wind. There was a deep hollow noise, high in the air, as if someone had blown into a long-resounding tube; and the frayed ragged edge of the overspreading cloud fell over the sun, which faded to the colour of yolk, to primrose, to the purest lemon, and then went out. In a moment the whole landscape was overrun, and the air was filled with snow.

On another day I was overtaken by such a storm as I was crossing Spetchley Park *(Fig 1)*. It was a cold inhospitable day. The great house, the lake, the boat-house, all loomed sadly and mistily through the wet snow. The deer huddled under the slopes where hay had been spread for them. The does and fawns turned away from us, but the stags lifted their proud heads, their horns looking like peeled twigs in the muted light. One man went trudging across the park with his head down, taking notice of nothing. On the lake swans, duck and coot were feeding, swimming quietly in the still unfrozen water in the middle of the lake. Then suddenly across the thin ice came a fox, his pelt standing out for warmth, his great brush trailing slackly behind him. He came by the ducks, looked hungrily at them, turned, looked again, and then with resignation disappeared into the copse beyond.

Storms like these come, however, rarely. I have often picked primroses on Christmas Day, and most winters my skates have remained unused.

Notes

1 Fred's fascination with Croome and its landscape garden continued, and more than two decades later he published a paper on the park ornaments: Frederick Grice, 'The Park Ornaments of Croome D'Abitôt,' *Transactions of the Worcestershire Archaeological Society*, Third series, Vol 5, 1976, pp 41-9.

Part I

College Lecturer and Children's Author

Chapter 1: 1946-54

1946

Worcester

When we first came to Worcester, just after the end of the Second World War, we were greatly intrigued with one street that seemed determined to keep its links with the past. It was the Shambles, a short street running parallel to the main street, and made up, as its name signified, largely of butchers' shops. Yet there were other shops, shoe shops, greengrocers, clothiers, china and crockery shops and open-air fruit stalls. These shops were far more numerous than one might imagine, because they were, in general, small. The Shambles was the home of the small dealer, the tradesman whose stock could almost go on a handcart, who never aspired to huge profits, men who had encamped cheek by jowl, as if they felt a security in crowding together and living in one another's laps.

There are other streets in Britain far more mediaeval in appearance than our Shambles was, but few more mediaeval in spirit. Here not only did the shopkeepers crowd together in mediaeval neighbourliness; they seemed to retain mediaeval habits. In most cases the tradesman let his goods spill out of his shop into the pathway. There, brushed by the crowds of shoppers, they fell, rolled, broke and were trodden on; but the shopkeeper briskly swilled away the rubbish and the leavings of his customers till the litter was deposited like flotsam halfway across the road, and the gutters ran with streams of muddy water. But the last to object were the shoppers themselves. They were not to be ranked with those who shopped in the High Street, or the Foregate. It was the well-to-do, the uninitiated visitors, the socially ambitious who shopped there.

The patrons of the Shambles were the folk who had lived in Worcester for generations, and who knew where older and more entertaining practices of buying and selling survived. Here came the poor, the old-fashioned, the vagrant. In a corner before a pot shop, an old man sat selling *Old Moore's Almanac*. Near him stood a group of travelling people, grimy and garrulous. Past came an old man, with the kind of deep-carved features seen in mediaeval misericords, wheeling a pram filled with old clothes, unacknowledged by the portly Edwardian shopkeeper surrounded by his china seconds, his Aladdin's cave of a shop lit by gaslights reflected in every plate and cup and jug.

From time to time a car would enter the street and try to nudge its way through the crowd. No one moved for it. Before anyone would make way, the driver had to abandon his silly noise and butt his way gently along, reduced to the pace of the pedestrians, whose ownership of the street he had been rash enough to dispute. The people of the Shambles neither disliked nor feared cars, but they were not prepared to give them any privileges, and the wise motorist soon learnt that it never paid him to try to assert rights which no one was prepared to concede.

I wrote this poem some time after we had settled in Worcester.

Song of the Pedestrians in the Shambles

You'd better keep out of the Shambles,
If you fancy yourself in a car.
You may be an eminent person,
But it's nothing to us what you are.

For we've all come to shop in the Shambles,
And you ought to know just how we feel.
We don't like to be pushed when we're buying
Our liver and tripe and cow-heel.

In the Foregate, in Barbourne and Deansway,
You can go at your own silly rate,
But the speed you may go in the Shambles
We pedestrians mean to dictate.

So keep out, or come on at your peril,
For you'll find us an obstinate band.
We don't mind a pram, but we don't give a damm
For the biggest Rolls-Royce in the land.

In the Shambles we're cocks of the midden,
Just try to push past if you dare.
Don't glower and toot, for we don't care a hoot,
And you'd better find out an alternative route -
The Shambles is OUR affair.

10 March 1956

I find summer in Worcestershire a burdensome time, sultry, airless and enervating. There is here a special kind of weather which they call the 'tempest'. The air grows still and hot, dark thundery clouds gather overhead, everyone longs for a breath of fresh air, or at least for a sudden burst of lightening and thunder; but nothing happens. The sultriness, the airlessness, the oppressive heat remain hour after hour, until they begin very slowly to move away.

But the other day the tension was broken by a spectacular storm. Before it broke the sky darkened and thickened until it looked more solid than the earth. All the houses and walls gleamed ghostly, and the field before me was pale, milky, almost phosphorescent; but beyond the houses the sky rose a thick heavy threatening black. Then through this darkness came quick flickering, like the panic-stricken signallings of someone in distress, the distant and incoherent motions of someone trying to warn of coming disaster. Then the stillness of the air was broken by a restless swishing and rustling. It was the upper branches of the elms that had caught the alarm. They brushed themselves restlessly, and moved like a flock of rooks that rise uneasily, settle and rise again.

As the branches tossed more wildly, the blackness of the sky began to engulf the walls of the houses around me. The flickering in the clouds grew more and more frantic—and then a strange sound was heard, like the sound of rinsing. It was the noise of the rain rushing through the upper air. I heard it reach the tops of the trees then splash on roadway and field, a torrential downpour that beat the blossom off the trees and scattered it like snow on the ground, broke flowers from their stems, filled every hollow space, and ran in furious streams down every gutter, cascading noisily through grids into blacks sinks.

Conversations with Gillian
4 March 1946

'Daddy, have I to put a big f or a little f?'

'A little f. Just as you've done it.'

'But I don't know if I've put it in the right place.'

'It's in the right place. I can see it from here.'

'You should come round and look at it properly.'

'I tell you, I can see it from here. It's right. Get on with it.'

'If it had been Mummy, you'd have come round and had a proper look.'

'Oh shush, Gillian. Put the f in and finish off.'

'But I don't know if it's right. And you have no call to speak to me like that.'

'Oh for God's sake, Gillian, shut up and leave me in peace.'

'I think you might have a bit more sense and look after your own daughter.'

'Holy Moses, I told you it was right. Why don't you finish it?'

'If you were a good Daddy you'd help your own daughter.'

'Shut up!'

'You're always wanting to start a fight. You just take a pride in starting a fight...'

October 1946

'Gillian, I don't mind your biting your nails. You'll have to get over that yourself. But if there's one thing I do dislike, it's your telling me lies about it. You cannot do anything worse in my opinion than tell lies.'

'But, Daddy, I could do something worse.'

'What could you do that would be worse?'

'I could steal, couldn't I? Anyhow, everybody tells lies.'

'That's no reason why you should.'

'You tell lies as well.'

'Do I?'

'Yes. Do you remember the other day when I wouldn't eat my meat?'

'Yes.'

'You said something to get me to eat it and it was a lie.'

'What did I say, pray?'

'You said, You'd better eat up that meat because your boyfriend, John Boucher, gave it to us.'

'Did I?'

'Yes, and that was a lie because he didn't do anything of the sort.'

'Well...'

'So that was a lie, you see. You told it. See?'

1947

The great flood
8 March 1947
Coming home from the Co-operative Hall in Worcester, where we had been to see a college play, we were caught in a heavy snowstorm, and had to abandon

the car on the corner of the road down to our flat. We did not know it, but we had got off lightly. We had merely been caught in the tail end of what was the worst blizzard of the century. Seven inches of snow fell on Worcester, but elsewhere there have been drifts up to fourteen feet deep. Dartmoor, the Cheviots, the Pennines and Lakeland are all under feet of snow, and sheep and cattle losses will be serious.

12 March 1947

There has been more snow in the country. Men have been working all night to keep rail lines open. Hedges have disappeared and in some places the milk-churn platforms and even the churns themselves are buried under the snow. There was snow on some roads even before the blizzard and many country bus services have been out of action for weeks. At Cradley a bungalow was completely covered with snow.

16 March 1947

The thaw has come and with it the danger of heavy flooding. All the rivers—Avon, Severn, Teme—are rising rapidly. The Severn is already over the North and South Quays and there are large lakes on Pitchcroft and the County Cricket Ground and all the old stories of floods—of the groundsman catching a salmon at the wicket—are being revived. The water is pouring fast through the arches of the bridge, piling up rubbish against the cutwaters. It is bringing down with it all kinds of debris—tree trunks, bales of hay, lengths of timber fencing, even drowned animals. The uprooted trees turn over and over as they are swept down river, like drowning men flinging their arms about in despair. The bankside trees are standing deep in water and rubbish is beginning to collect in their branches. I've seen men trying to hook lengths of wood and tree trunks out of the water for fuel. The swans have pulled out of the mainstream and are paddling about in the shallow water near the North Quay, waddling on to the wet roadway and looking long-necked and ugly. There are one or two boys riding their bicycles through the shallow water on the Quay, lifting their feet clear when they come to the deepest part. I saw an old woman in a house in Croft Road, shouting at lorry drivers to slow down as they passed her door because they were sending waves of water over her threshold. The cattle market is flooded and buses are having to splash their way into Newport Street bus station.

17 March 1947
The water continues to rise. They say the road between Eardiston and Tenbury is flooded to a depth of three feet. The direct bus route between Evesham and Worcester is impassable.

19 March 1947
The water has risen above the 1886 mark (on the wall of the old Water Gate). In Hylton Road the water is beginning to rise in the drains and sewers. The police are out with a van and a loudhailer telling everyone to boil their drinking water. The footpath in Hylton Road is under water, and people go from house to house by means of planks laid on bricks.

20 March 1947
The water has now risen above the 1777 mark. Tybridge Street and even the New Road are under water. The Fox at Bransford is completely cut off. Burnham's coaches have laid on a shuttle service along the New Road, and Nick Turnbull's little boy, David, has discovered that he can spend all day riding backwards and forwards through the floodwater without spending a penny. The only other link between this side of the river and the city centre is by rail. Crowds of people are queuing at Henwick Halt and Foregate Street Station for trains. The only way of getting to Tybridge House is by boat. They say the current at Diglis is running at 20 mph.

The flood produces strange illusions. All the houses by the river seem to have sunk, but the boats, riding high on the floodwater, look big and bulky. There is an ironic sign near the cricket ground standing just clear of the water and reading: NO CARS BEYOND THIS POINT. This is the worst flood in living memory, perhaps the worst flood of all time in Worcester. People are lining the bridge all day to look at the spectacle.

25 March 1947
The floods have receded. The mud and straws that collected in the branches of the riverside trees are drying and falling off. Women all along Hylton Road are bringing out sodden carpets and mats and hanging them out to dry on lines and over walls. The firemen are once more sluicing the filthy mud off the roads that were covered with floodwater, especially the South Quay and the path by the cathedral wall. Ironically the fields that have been under water look all the better for it.

It has just been confirmed that this was the worst flood in the history of Worcester.

1948

An incident on school practice
February 1948
'Now,' said the student, 'I am going to light this candle and put it under the jar. I want you all to watch what happens to it. What do you think will happen, John? You don't know? Well, just watch and see.'

He took up the candle in his left hand, and with his right he took from his pocket a lighter. 'Now I am going to light the candle,' he said. 'All you boys at the back, watch very carefully.' Then he flicked the lighter wheel with his thumb. The flint sparked, but the wick did not catch. He flicked the wheel again, and a third and a fourth time, but still the wick did not light. He tried again, and as he did so, a deeper silence came over the class. Failure is a more enthralling spectacle than success, and the class was caught in the suspense. In his agitation the student shook the lighter, twirled the wheel, shook again, struck the flint again—until at last a weak flame appeared at the end of the surly wick. The student's agitation was painful to watch. The hand that held the candle shook so violently that he could scarce bring it to the flame, but happily the flame didn't go out, and the candle caught. The experiment was saved.

Before I left him, I asked the student to come and see me after dinner, and I promised to give him some practical advice. He was so nervous to know what I had to say that he was waiting for me outside my study when I arrived.

'Am I too early?' he said, 'I couldn't wait to hear the worst about that lesson.'

'I have no worst to tell you,' I said. 'I promised to give you some practical advice. And here it is.'

I handed him a box of matches, and he was so relieved he burst out laughing.

1950

The hanging tree
19 February 1950
'It's a delightful house,' I said. 'I suppose you have a big garden.' 'Enormous!' said Miss C. 'Far too big, I'm afraid, for us. We have an old man who does a little for us now and then, and on some evenings we have time enough to do a little weeding. But you can't do very much in an evening.'

We had by now moved half way down the length of the garden. It was very untidy. Here lay broken tiles and half-bricks, and stalks and haulms that had refused to decompose, and there a rotted pea net hung from two leaning posts. Through the weeds there showed the red leaves of overgrown beetroot, and through a rusted bucket thrust a fleshy rhubarb shoot.

The bottom of the garden was overgrown, and rough grass choked the gooseberry bushes; but in a corner rose a beautiful pear tree, its trunk like charcoal, and its top branches drooping and falling like a fountain. It was very old and the weight of hundreds of fruitings had so overborne it that it leant at an angle to the ground.

'What a remarkable old tree,' I said. 'And there's a monument under it.'

'Yes,' said Miss C, 'It's to a man—a priest—with whom the tree is connected. He was a Jesuit.'

'You didn't put this up, did you?'

'Oh no, it was put up by a few Catholics who still reverence him. No, it isn't ours. But they asked permission to put up a little shrine, and I let them.'

'You must get visitors then, do you? I mean, to see the shrine.'

'Oh yes. On the day of his martyrdom they hold a service round the tree. They come in their robes and they chant, and they look very picturesque, although they sound rather doleful.'

'That's interesting.'

'Some Irish priests once asked me for permission to cut off some of the bark. They took it back to Ireland. And I think it was very highly thought of there.'

'I suppose it's a kind of Gospel oak, like one of those trees that early Christians—or even Wesley—were supposed to have preached under.'

'Not exactly. You see, Father Wall didn't preach under this tree. He was hanged from it.'[1]

Just at that moment a fluttering figure was seen coming down the garden path. It was Miss C's sister. She was dressed in a floppy old-fashioned light-coloured dress. She had lost most of her teeth but wore no dentures.

'Oh you're there, dear,' she said. 'Are you telling them about the tree. Isn't it a fine old tree?'

'Mabel, dear,' said her sister, in some embarrassment, 'Don't you think you'll catch cold running out like this?'

'I don't think so. I can smell the Spring long before you, you know. It's the same with Father Wall, you know. She can never see him. But I can. She's not as sensitive as I am in these things.'

'We'd better not go into that. You'd better go inside.'

'She never sees him. But I do, over and over again. In the house as well. Don't rush me.'

Gently Miss C piloted her sister back into the house. I followed her, and before we went in I looked back for the last time at the tree, bent and brooding. It stood like one that keeps its eyes on the ground, bowed and ashamed.

Heard in a café in Ludlow
March 1950

'I feel that I have to get out, because if I didn't, I'd fret. It's three years now since my husband died and my son died, one after the other, and left me all on my own in my own house. And I fret because he was so good to me when he was alive. He took me to Australia twice, and that's where he bought me this gold watch. And one day he called to me and he said, 'Come on, Pat, I'm getting engaged today. You lost my first engagement ring so come on and let's have another.' Yes, all the way to Australia, and we had good meals everywhere except in Italy. What do you think we had there? Boiled rice with a ring of water round it. 'Come on, Pat,' he said, 'We're having none of that', and he put his coat on and went out.

But I still see him, you know. He was a lovely pianist and I miss his tunes and his funny songs at night time. But I play his favourite hymns every Sunday night. And one night, I was just undressed and getting into bed, when he came. He came straight through the door. He was always a good-looking man.

I spoke to the Vicar about it, and he said 'Expect him again, because them that's lived as good Christians can come back to us.'

'And my husband was a good Christian. Every night he used to prop up his Bible and read from it. But he didn't like that rice pudding we got in Italy.'

Incident in Dorchester
I was walking along the West Walks in Dorchester, enjoying the shade, when there drove up beside me an old lady in an invalid chair. We had just come to a little rise in the walk and I asked if I could help her.

'Thank you, thank you,' she said. 'A lovely day, isn't it?'

'Yes, beautiful.'

'But I don't like the wind.'

'I love it,' I said, 'I never seem properly alive till I can feel it blowing.'

'Ah, but you see, it blows my hat off and I can't run after it.'

Now that was something that had never struck me.

A stormy night
September 1950
The sky darkened and darkened and the wind began to blow madly, as if it was angry with the world and meant to tear and savage it. It snapped in the air with a sound like the shaking of a big blanket, and threw the rain like gravel against the windows. The trees writhed and twisted in the storm, as if they were begging to be taken in, out of the fury of the wind. They flung their branches about, like someone trying to ward off blows. But there was no relief for them. They had to stand and endure the tempest. Indoors, window frames rattled, and every now and then a door would fly open, as if some ghostly hand had given it a push; but in the lulls the clock could be heard ticking steadily and valiantly away, as if to reassure the house that it, at least, was not perturbed.

October
The Principal, Mr Hines, has not been in the SCR this term. By the end of the holiday he was walking with difficulty. Now I hear that he is bedridden and not likely to live much longer.

December
Mr Hines died just before lunch yesterday.

The funeral
13 December 1950
St John's church filled slowly at first, then very quickly. Some of the girls wore hats but most of them were bare-headed. Some of the men wore signs

of mourning, but most looked as they would at any everyday service. Harold Shaw was the exception.[2] He wore a gown with a magenta hood and a little white bow fitted not too successfully over his black tie. Most of the students wore a respectful but neutral expression.

The church filled long before the coffin arrived, and there was a long, long silence before we heard, coming from the porch, the voice of Pearce-Higgins—I am the Resurrection and the Life... We rose and the sad procession filed past us. The bearers carried the coffin as easily as if it had been empty. There was nothing in it but the wraith of a man, white, transparent, no heavier than a child.

When the service was over the coffin was whisked away with great rapidity to the churchyard at Hanley Castle. Although I lingered only for a few minutes to pick up passengers I was too late for the last rites. The newly-dug grave was very deep, narrow and damp, with spade marks on its sides. Upon the coffin had fallen one chrysanthemum flower. The Principal had chosen this churchyard, partly because of his strong link with Pearce-Higgins on whom he depended heavily in his last months, and partly because the graveyard commanded a view of the Malverns.

Before the end he asked that no college activities should be cancelled when he died. Tonight the students are holding their customary Saturday night dance. He ordered the world to forget him, and it is not hesitating to do so.

A cold Christmas

Neither snow nor rain fell, but the sky was shrouded from morning to night with grey cloud. No sun, and not so much a wind as an invisible but menacing movement of air, like the steady pressure of a glacier, and so cold that it hurt to draw it in. The nostrils ached and the lips smarted. The trees stood tall, regal and stoical, but the bushes shrank and huddled together. The tall stems of old chrysanthemums were embrowned and ragged, with a discoloured flower at the top of them.

1951

A cold Spring

It is now mid-May, but the weather is still bitterly cold, with grey skies and chilling winds. We seem to have had no sunshine for many months and the winter has been longer than any I can remember. The blossom has been late and lasted a long time. Daffodils have bloomed for many weeks and the primroses are as fresh as they were in April. In spite of the cold weather—maybe because of it—we have had a marvellous primrose year. Around Wichenford I have seen millions—crowded in heavy clumps, full-petalled and long in the stalk. The violets too have been full and plentiful. On the road to Ockeridge there are banks and banks of primroses and violets, and the cowslips are a foot tall.

May 1951

When Ted went to hear the nightingales in Monkwood, he took a tin of anti-mosquito ointment with him.[3] 'My heart aches and a drowsy numbness pains my sense,' he quoted, solemnly and methodically rubbing the ointment into his cheeks and neck. He said of his wife, after the birth of his son, that she was very well, but a little sore 'in those regions that had been stretched'. And speaking to me about his baby son, he said, 'Of course we do not put him out in all weathers. If it is very misty or what I might call 'general humidity', then we don't put him out. But if the day is at all propitious, I wheel him round. Of course I do not leave him entirely covered. Perhaps I'll fold the oilskin back just a shade, nor more than perhaps beyond the first or second eyelet...'

'Tell me,' I said once to him. 'Is Bournemouth really pronounced as you say it—with two long syllables of equal weight? Is that the proper local pronunciation?'

'Well, I must admit that this is a little fad of my own. Perhaps I put a little too much stress on the second syllable. But you see, what really annoys me is the way people shorten names—Chelt'num, for instance. That's unpardonable.'

'But you don't mean to say that you pronounce it Chelt-en-ham, do you?'

'Not quite like that. But I must confess that I like to breathe a little on that 'h'.'

Later in the year

August 29 1951

The great horse chestnut, heavy with shadow, stood stock still, and round it and over it flew the martins, in loops and swings and circles and figures, turning their little bodies so that they were now black, now white. The other trees stood lonely, unvisited, uncomplaining, except for the black poplar that had been struck by lightning some time ago. Now it was nervous and shivered in the evening wind. Softly it fretted and complained, while its neighbours stood still, dour and uncommunicative. In the grasses insects went blundering from stalk to stalk in their green jungle, trying to take flight, jumping, hitting the stems of the grasses, clinging to them as swimmers do to branches and rocks in a rough sea.

Wichenford

I have grown very fond of walking around the small roads that criss-cross the country around Wichenford. This part of Worcestershire has very little to offer the conventional sightseer. There are no beautiful villages or fine houses to admire, no breathtaking views to enthuse over, nothing spectacular, nothing unusual, nothing one would dream of putting into a guide book. But it is this seclusion, this unspoilt charm that attracts me, the cottages, the farms, the turns of the roads and the modest vistas.

I usually walk these roads in the afternoon but today I went out after breakfast. It had been a cold night. There was hoar frost on the shaded corners of the roadway and ice in the ditches. It was such a morning as T.S. Eliot had perhaps in mind when he was writing Little Gidding.

> 'When the short day is brightest, with frost and fire,
> The brief sun flames the ice, in ponds and ditches...'[4]

Christmas Eve

Erica is sitting in bed with her many-coloured shawl over her shoulders. She is reading out aloud while I sit writing. This is a very real Christmas for her. She has been calling out 'Merry Christmas' to me for the last twelve hours. Now she has set out, on the window ledge nearest her bed, a beaker of tea (now cold of course, a candle in a stick, a plate of ginger snaps, a pen, wrapped up and labelled, a letter addressed to Santa Claus and a little note:

> Sant Claus
> Dear Sant Claus you hav got a pen for your Crisms presunt.
> I hop you lic it. I thinc you will lic it.

1952

6 February 1952

On this day the King died suddenly, and I had a dreadful quarrel with Jim Wilson about the enlargement of the Woodwork Room without my being consulted. The first I knew of it was a chisel coming through the wall of my study.

The college in May
Mid-May 1952
Noon. The voice of a tutor comes from the Science Lab, and the whirr of the mower from the far field where the groundsman wheels his machine dextrously round the corners.[5] A student is playing some record or other; and from the wallflowers rises a powerful smell. The flowers are dying but they still give off that heady smell.

It is close in the lecture rooms. The tutor, dark-suited and academic, rubs the blackboard cleaner vigorously across the board and the chalk-dust hangs for a moment like a little white cloud. The edge of the sunlight moves across the desk, a straight line moving slowly on and burning where it touches. The voice of the tutor goes on. 'And now we come to Gestalt theory...' Out on the field a student is training for some event. He runs across the vision, doing lap after lap, past the dark figure of the groundsman who takes no notice. He has finished mowing and is driving in pegs to mark the boundary. The lecture room is full of yellow light. A fly settles on the string that hangs from the light; and outside a blackbird cocks an ear, listens, then darts forward across the lawn, and attacks a worm, pulling it out like a piece of elastic.

I can hear the cleaners going down the corridor, banging their pails and dragging their brushes. The tutor goes droning on about the virtues of Gestalt theory.

Outside the air is still. The heat grows and grows. A few students have come out to sunbathe. They lie on the brown turf, some prone, some supine, browning like pieces of toast. Then the great trees begin to stir a little, like sleepers waking. Their branches move up and down, listlessly. And now, in the great heat the pines let fall their cones. The cones crackle, open and fall, some in the deep grass, some with a rattle on the corrugated-iron roof of a garage.

Now it is evening. The scent of the wallflowers is stronger than ever, and a beautiful scent comes from the mown grass. Bill Smith tells me that all that perfume comes from one little grass. Folk dancers have appeared on the green space outside the Hall. As the darkness falls, the lights from inside the Hall fall slantingly across the figures of the dancers. The sky grows milky and the stars assemble and look down on the dancers.

2 June 1952
Mr Thomas (who was then MP for Cardiff and is now the Speaker of the

House of Commons) came to address the students and was introduced (incorrectly) as the MP forWhen he rose to speak he said, 'I know—indeed, no one better than I—that Cardiff is an important city. I know too—again no one better than I—what cause we have to be proud of our city. But, ladies and gentlemen, never in our wildest flights of fancy have we dared to suggest that Cardiff includes within its boundaries the city of Bristol.'

12 June 1952
I dreamt that the students began to call up to the platform from the floor of the hall, 'Who is the Staff representative?' and I answered, 'I am sir!' and everybody laughed because my voice and my eyes were the voice and the eyes of a boy.

21 July 1952
This is a record of a brief but enjoyable holiday from which we have just returned. It will be a halting and badly written record because I have cut my thumb; and perhaps I had better tell first how I came to cut it. It was at New Quay, just south of Aberystwyth. I had walked into the water, thinking of having a swim, and had come across a broken milk bottle. I picked it up, knowing that Martin was disposing of two more that he had collected.[6] I called to Susan, 'Take this to your Daddy,' holding out the bottle to her with the broken neck in my hand. Susan, who is always impetuous, cried 'Give me that,' and pulled. The wet bottle slipped through my hands and cut my thumb in two places. It was not a bad cut, but after I had bound it with a hankie, I unaccountably fainted. I can remember knowing that I was going to faint, and then coming to, feeling unutterably sad, wondering with great agitation where I was—and then calling out 'New Quay!' with great relief.

Now that that little account is over, and I seem to be holding the pen a little more securely, I can go back to the beginning. Early on Saturday morning, Gwen, Erica, Gillian, Gill Lees (her friend) and I set off for Cwmtydu, a little valley just south of New Quay, where Pam and Martin had taken a furnished house. We ran into rain at Llangurig, ran out of it, were caught again at Devil's Bridge, ran out of it again, and after a tortuous chase through Tregaron, Llanarth and Synod Inn, we came to the cwm and found Pam, Martin and the children in high feather. We put up our tent in the hayfield and prepared for our first night in camp.

The cwm was deep and sheltered, with valley sides covered with bracken and the floor wooded with hazel, alder, and hawthorn, all riotously overgrown with honeysuckle, bramble, campion, bryony; and it led to a harsh little cove with a beach of grey shingle, twisted black-brown rocks with caves and ledges, and cormorants crossing the grey water. It had a hostile, savage look about it that did not go with the luxuriant cwm behind.

We had supper together in the tent, lit a camp fire and told a few stories, then all went to bed at ten. Then—irony of ironies—while I, the experienced camper, ought to have been fast asleep, the envy of all the novices—I found myself lying awake while Erica was without doubt fast asleep—and Gwen quite unconscious. Very mortifying!

We all slept well and woke at six, delighted with our first night under canvas. When I woke I turned to Erica. She looked refreshed, as Gwen used to look when I first knew her. She smiled and said, 'Daddy I like sleeping out.' That smile and those words were enough for me.

On the way home Gillian and Gill were gabbling in the back seat. When Gillian had delivered herself of one particularly incomprehensible sentence, I asked:

'What on earth did you say, Gillian?'

'Didn't you get it, Daddy?'

'I certainly didn't. Of course I know that you are good at languages, but I didn't think that you'd pick up Welsh in one brief weekend.'

Most of my family jokes are total failures but this, to my surprise, was a great success. (What a Pooteresque ring that sentence has!).

A week later
24 July 1952

Erica suddenly learnt to ride her bicycle. At four o'clock she couldn't ride. At five she cycled a hundred yards across the cricket pitch. Later, Gillian tells me, she cycled without accident to Henwick Grove and back. She is just a few months more than six.

30 July 1952

Last night in the Crown at Hallow I heard an old man talking about foxes. Foxes cannot carry shot, he said. Once a pellet enters them they're as good as dead. Every shot wound turns septic, and they die a cruel death. A fox can lead a dog into a wood then sit so close as to baffle it. It can sit very close and kill its scent. Are these things true?

The grave
27 August 1952
A year after the Principal died, I went to see his grave. This was an unusual thing for me to do, for I am not a haunter of churchyards and had no great affection for the dead man. Yet I went.

It was only with difficulty that I found the grave. There was an open patch of ground that sloped to the west and faced the Malverns, and it was there that I had expected to find it. I remembered those two wishes he had voiced before he died. The first was really the expression of a sentimental fondness for English village life. I call it sentimental because his spirit was essentially mercurial and gregarious, and the average English village would not have held him for more than a few months.

His second wish—to be buried facing the Malverns—was probably more sincere. He had been fond of hills. He had sincerely thrilled to the conquest of steep slopes, the exhilaration of height, the vigour of mountain air. The best photograph I ever saw of him was taken on the Malverns, on the summit of one of the Beacons, looking into the wind in a slightly theatrical manner, but with a look of genuine elation.

Yet when I found the grave I saw that while the less genuine emotion had been respected the more authentic had been ignored. The grave was certainly in a country churchyard, but it was thrust against a straggling fence, and between him and the hills rose this untidy obstacle.

There was a simple headstone saying that he had been Principal of the College from this year to that. I admired the simplicity of the stone and the reticence of the inscription. But how neglected the site was. The rough churchyard grass was pushing up the sides of the curb of the grave, and in the space between the weeds grew rank and high. I tried to pull some of the weeds up, and got hold of a big thistle; but it pricked me and I couldn't hold it without being scratched. I kicked the base of the big stalk. It bent and fell over, but its great ugly roots still clung to the gravelly soil. I put my hand to it again and pulled though the spines went into the flesh; and at last it came away, leaving an ugly hole.

I ought to have persisted, but I gave up and left the churchyard. I have not seen the grave from that day to this.

[*Editors:* The last two sentences have clearly been added at a later date, when Fred was preparing the text for publication shortly before he died. This occurs elsewhere.]

Plate 2: Fred held extramural classes in English Literature in Worcester and Welland. This photograph taken at the Old Palace in 1957-8 shows the Worcester group with Fred talking

25 September 1952
I have some remarkable characters in my extramural class at Welland. One old dear, who always joins the class late, when all the fees have been collected and paid in, walks over the fields with a primitive lantern and a screw of Barbadoes sugar for Gwen. 'Genuine stuff, my dear, not like that poisonous white stuff.' Mrs Mortimer, a relative of Lady Mortimer, comes on a corgi, a primitive war-time motor bike. Miss Docker, who really belongs to Cranford, lives in the Old Rectory. Her sister and her friend, who used to drive a governess cart around the lanes, were of the opinion that most of the animals in the world were underfed. They invariably took a bale of hay with them in case they came across a hungry horse, and corn to scatter on the roadway for sparrows. They had an old hen, which they called Miss Rose. They kept it in a little coop in the house, and when it grew too old to climb on to the perch itself, every night one of them would call out, 'Come along, Miss Rose. Come along, Miss Rose!' and lift it onto the roost *(Plate 2).*

The Clarkes had a shrew in their bedroom. Every few hours it ran downstairs, across the kitchen—under the very nose of the family cat—and outside for insects.

1953

Early in the year
18 January 1953
Gillian's guinea pigs are the joy of her life. She has just put Micky and Minnie together, and in a few weeks we'll have a brood of them. She collects twigs, boughs and buds and knows more about trees than I'll ever know. She is planning to build a hide near her bird table and take photographs from it.

Erica is learning to play the piano, but her greatest joys are her dollies. When Erica goes to bed they go too. They are laid out on a little pink chair at her bedside—the new doll whose name was once Céleste, but has been rechristened; and Coco the beloved puppet. The laying out of the dolls is merely part of an elaborate ritual. The bottle must be in the bed, the night light switched on, the beaker of water on the dressing table, the mirror tilted so that she can look at herself, the book ready to read in the morning, the hair in curlers and enclosed in a hair net. What a palaver!

23 February 1953
Gwen went to see the first production in this country of *Man of God* by Gabriel Marcel, and found herself sitting next to the great man himself who had come over to see it. He signed her programme for her.

An anecdote from Beryl Beer
1 April 1953
A mother, who already had many children and was expecting yet another, was speaking with a Headmistress. The Headmistress said, 'You shouldn't have any more children. You should speak to your husband about it.'

'Oh I have, Miss,' said the woman, 'but he says he is not going to have me pasteurised.'

A new car again!
I have sold my Austin 10—the car that Gwen never really liked—and now we possess a great Standard 14 (JUR 491), a lovely grey car that runs between us and our wits. It's a magnificent pantechnicon—so magnificent that we all go in awe of it. We hasten to put it in the garage if a shower falls. We wipe off every spot. We breathe on the chrome and shake our heads at a speck of rust. I go to it in the morning in a fever of anxiety lest it should not start.

An extraordinary mood of happiness

An extraordinary mood of happiness seems to have descended upon our house. Gwen is more contented than she ever was; at times she radiates a rare serenity. Gillian is engrossed in her school, and loves her work and her mistresses. Erica is less moody and less tearful. Best of all I now have the feeling that they really love me. I think they all have, at times, feared me rather than loved me; but I can now see that Gwen loves me, Gillian looks up to me and relies on me, and Erica will sometimes kiss my hand in an excess of fondness. At times the sense of fulfilment is so strong in me that it rises warmly to my eyes, and my eyes fill.

19 May 1953

A note on Ted—the occasion, Education Day at Birmingham—a service, a meal and then athletics. 'I heard some complaining about the service. How did you find it, Ted?' 'Well, I can't say that I found very much to complain about. I wasn't kept waiting very long for my food.' 'No—not that, Ted, pardon me. I meant the service in the cathedral, the religious service.'

21 May 1953

Sometimes I am in despair. I am utterly alone and utterly lost. Love is dried up in me, I cannot come near to anyone, I can neither understand nor be understood. Nothing enriches, nothing exalts, nothing fulfils. I am like a growing thing whose growth has been arrested. Somewhere in an unknown part of me, a process has failed, and nothing reaches my head, my heart, my blood. A flow has halted, a degeneration begun.

And yet joy is near. It is there; just beyond my reach, but there. I can hear it in that great tree outside that sighs and lays its long tresses along the levels of the wind, that sighs with its soft primeval sound and ceases and sighs and ceases again. It is there in a movement towards a face, in a caress, a caressing response. Oh it is near. And sometimes when I have closed my eyes, and put my head down, it touches me. Like a shy thing, beyond me, reaching out to me, it puts its fingers on my sleeve. That is all I am allowed: but the touch is real.

The Climax

23 May 1953

This was the climax of the year. On this day suddenly the sun shone with great and overmastering heat. The lupin spikes rose, stiffened themselves, and one by one opened their flowers. The hawthorn burst, white and red, and the whole hillside of gorse became gold, a glorious, dull, heavy gold, breathing a thick and nutty scent that rose and drifted like dust across the brow of the hill. Suddenly it was the climax. The first waves of May flowers turned brown and burnt in the heat, and the last flowers and blossoms opened to the full. The grass trembled and knew that its greenness would not hold out aginst the sun. The birds sang and knew that they could sing no more ardently, no more lyrically. This was the best of their best. The year had risen and risen, and was now at its full, steady quivering peak.

I sensed it was an event, a fulfilment, a culmination. If I could not perceive that in all its details, then I was missing the point, I was ignoring the great central act, the best symbolical gesture, the detail, the essence that was the significance.

And I missed it. Like a spectator who averted his head at the crucial moment, like a watcher who fell asleep just when the revelation occurred, I missed it.

Despair and hatred
28 May 1953
I have gone, am still going through, a period of great despair. I did not think myself capable of so much malevolence. Is it because I envy Gwen that I behave so intolerantly to her? I find myself inexplicable and hateful.

1954

Skating at Thorngrove
6 February 1954
Yesterday we went skating on the lake at Thorngrove—a lovely setting. At the lower end of the lake lay a little footbridge half-hidden in bushes and reeds, but above it a bigger bridge, three-arched, of weathered stone, and in the wintry light the emerald and ochre of the mosses glowed vividly. Under the arches the ice was black, glassy with bubbles caught at a depth of a foot or more, patterning the ice. We skated just above the bridge, sweeping in big circles, exploring the ice-bound punt, shooting the arches of the bridge and watching the winter sun go down into a mesh of twigs and branches beyond the parapet. Further beyond the space that we had cleared a fringe of large reed mace encroached

upon the pond, and a spit of land, well wooded, ran out towards the reeds, leaving only a little channel. We did not care to explore this channel. There the ice was clearer, apparently thinner. To approach was to send off a few cracks by the roots of the alders that ran down to the water.

So we skated near the bridge till the sun fell into the trees, the straw, spread out for the cattle in the pastures, glowed with a bright flame like gold, and a pink flush fell across the snow. Then quite late in the afternoon one by one we dared the channel and came out timorously on to a second lake, two hundred yards long, fringed with yellow reeds, backed by a copse of oak and sycamore, secret and unexplored. The snow that lay over it was virgin. No fox, dog nor rabbit had walked across, and the scribbles of our skates were the first letters to be written on this lovely page. It was with awe and then delight that we skated up and down this secret pond, our newly-found sea, and then through the perilous neck of cracking ice, home to the bridge. As we went, the far-off sportsmen fired and drove the pigeons high over our heads, out towards the sun low in the brakes. The cattle breathed little clouds of warm air. The geese, very high, flying in a wavering v more like a tick than an arrowhead, made off silently for the south. It was a lovely moment *(Plate 3)*.

A course at Cambridge
July 1954

This afternoon we were shown round Jesus by a fellow of the college, Dr Brittain, a corpulent bachelor with soft grey hair, and dark trousers supported by a broad belt that might have belonged to a ploughman. His rooms were littered with the biggest collection of cockerels in the world, china cockerels, wooden cockerels, even cockerels made of plaited straw and of coal. Every ledge and shelf was filled with these curious, not all beautiful, figures. Dr Brittain had the habit (common in dons) of parading his knowledge with a kind of whimsical conceit.

'I suppose you know,' he began, 'I suppose you know'—as all lecturers say when they have a shrewd idea that their audience really does not know, but consider the information indispensable to their talk... 'Two more things I shall tell you, one of which I can prove, the other of which I cannot prove. The first is that this collection is the best in the world; the other is that I am not mad.'

Nevertheless, he was very kind, and went to great pains to show us Q's rooms, decorated in a rather depressing terracotta colour, the ancient cold

Plate 3: Fred and Gillian skating, 1954

library, the skeleton in the cupboard, the hall with its portraits of Coleridge and Sterne, Henry VIII and Mary Queen of Scots.[7]

'There are three ways in which you can qualify to have your portrait hung in our hall—to be a distinguished member of the college and bring fame to it; to be undistinguished but have your portrait painted by a famous artist; to be neither but to be a benefactor to the college. Give us enough and we'll paint your portrait without a fee. Henry VIII, I am sorry to say, fulfilled none of these conditions.'

Then we were taken to the Combination Room and told of the ritual that had to be strictly observed there—to the right of the fire the Senior Fellow, to the left the fellow next in seniority and in the middle the Master or the Keeper.

'I like to call him the Keeper now and then. It is more in harmony with the atmosphere of lunacy that often pervades an educational establishment.'

Mid-August 1954

Last night I walked down to look at the Severn in the moonlight. The river was full but smooth, with faint wreaths of steamy air rising from it and being borne downstream by the fast current. The mist seemed to bank up against the cathedral, and spill over into the meadows. The meadows were hidden in the white woolly mist, the trees rising out of it black and heavy-leaved, the cathedral with its lower outlines hazed over and its upper structure silhouetted sharply against the brilliant moonlit sky. On the quay above the bridge sat the eel-fishers, with their gumboots, haversacks, stools, flasks and windcheaters.

'How long you stoppin', Ted?'

'I'll stop till mornin' mate.'

'Here, where does your missus live? She'll be a bit lonely tonight.'

'You never get near 'er. Us as got two good dogs, chum, as ull keep everybody off of that house, I can tell you.'

Their rods were pointed upstream, but the lines slanted away, taut and straight, down towards the bridge, with its cavernous arches and wobbling reflections.

> Now, like that single heifer that will not sleep,
> but blunders in and out of the dry bracken,
> the night will not compose itself. Below,
> the distant traffic thrums through the city streets,

and, high in the concave dark a headstrong plane
chases the fading day.
Nearer at hand, an owl
cries mouse and beetle warnings ere it swoops;
and in the pauses, apples and chestnuts, like
swimmers that can no longer hold on to the raft,
let go, drop into the docks and nettles.

Yet, from time to time, all will fall silent,
the stumbling heifer, the traffic, the owl, the chestnut,
and in the silence I can hear a fine vibration,
a high and universal sibilance.
It is the globe itself, like a prayer wheel, spinning
and whirring its way across the enfolding dark.

In a Worcester pub
19 September 1954
The room was crowded, with every seat taken and scarce space enough to get to the bar. The counter was wet with spilt beer, wet and frothy. There was a fearful din, with at least five different songs being bawled out. A woman tilted her head back and began to sing in a strong forced voice 'It's only... a shanty... in old... shanty town,' pausing at each phrase and shaking her head as if to gather new energy for the next attack.

Another woman in a green dress, below which hung three inches of flimsy petticoat, was on her feet, yelling. With her, but taking not the slightest notice of her, was a man with a tumour on his cheek, swollen, red, repulsive. Someone knocked into a chair and joggled the glasses standing there, making the beer run over the seat. The barman and the barmaid might have been deaf for all the notice they took of the hullabaloo. With stolid faces they slopped out the beer, rang up the money, and handed back sticky pennies for change.

In Gloucester Cathedral
7 October 1954
In the north aisle near the doorway to the cloisters there is a great coke stove—a black cylindrical affair that gives off great heat; and near the stove there is a stone bench, built up against the arcading. On this bench, out of the

rain and cold sat two old men. As they talked their voices rumbled through the cathedral and sounded like a priest intoning prayers. But they were not talking of religious matters. They were merely enjoying the privacy and warmth of the almost empty cathedral.

I went up to the stove, warmed my hands, and spoke to them.

'Enjoying the warmth?'

'The only place, sir, where we can sit and be warm and dry.'

'Yes, it's a bad day.'

'We don't like the rain, sir, but we cannot be choosers. I be 76 now. I seed it cold in my time. Once I was up at Birdlip, and I seed snow there up to my thighs.'

'And where are you living now?'

'Us is not living, sir, us is just lingerin', not livin'.'

I gave them half a crown to spend between them, and left them there, their voices rumbling and echoing in the great nave.

18 October 1954

André Maurois was the Chairman at a meeting in Cheltenham at which Christopher Fry was the speaker. 'I know that the function of a chairman is to be unobtrusive. In fact, I am going to suggest two maxims which might serve Mr Fry as two new titles—"The Chairman's not for Hearing" and "The Short is Long Enough."'

21 October 1954

Not far from us is a Headmaster whose passion is Roman History. And the great moment in his school year is when he gives his lesson on the Romans in Britain. At the end of it he takes from the cupboard the Roman standard he made some years ago, and sends the children out along the lane to the little stretch of Roman road that leads across the fields—a vague depression between the oaks but labelled 'Roman Road' on the Ordnance Survey map. His favourite girl carries the standard, and his favourite boy is the centurion. After them march the conquerors—three abreast, and at the end, the Head himself, proud and victorious in the autumn sunshine.

Notes

1 Father John Wall (1620-79), a Franciscan Friar serving in Worcester, who was martyred for his Catholic faith.

2 Harold Watkins Shaw was a musicologist and lecturer in music at Worcester Training College.

3 Ted Burrows was a mildly eccentric colleague and friend and the source of many an anecdote.

4 T. S. Eliot, *Collected Poems, 1909-1962*, 1975, quotation from 'Little Gidding', 214.

5 This Science Laboratory was next door to Fred and Gwen's flat in B Block on the college campus.

6 Martin Randall was a lecturer in Physical Education at the Training College and one of Fred's closest friends.

7 Q, Sir Arthur Quiller-Couch (1863-1944), was an undergraduate at Trinity College, Oxford; he became a poet, novelist, and anthologist. He was best known for editing the *Oxford Book of English Verse* (1900), and was subsequently elected Professor of English at Cambridge (1912), where he was responsible for developing the English Faculty.

Chapter 2: 1955-60

1955

The caravan

Just before Easter 1955 we bought a caravan. Our first holiday took us to Bourton-on-the-Water, Bath, Wells, Wookey Hole, Cheddar, and Stourhead. I think I have an account in an issue of the Caravan Club magazine. The whole holiday, if I remember rightly, cost us about £12 for a week. It was the first of a long series of caravan holidays—to Norfolk, to the Lakes, to Brittany and the Dordogne, to Frankfurt and beyond. I wrote most of them up for the Caravan Club.

5 June 1955

I did not enjoy going to Hellens, near Much Marcle. I found it all a bit squalid with its faded brocades, worn tapestries—an untidy irregular house, huddled and rather ugly. There are some fine things, but I thought it was the kind of house no self-respecting woman would choose to live in for a moment—cramped old beds in cramped old bedrooms—tasteless and shabby. A young man with a good voice showed us round but, like so many professional guides, was less of a guide than an entertainer manqué. Still, I liked the story of the tenants who took refuge in the cellars during an air raid (why should anyone want to raid Hellens?) 'Are there any expectant mothers here?' asked the lady of the house. 'Give us a chance, your ladyship,' was the reply. 'We nobbut been here five minutes.'

The Wind and the Book

'I don't know why people bother with this,' said the wind,
idly turning over the pages of the book
I left lying on the garden table.
'For my part I can see nothing whatever in it.'

On Berrow Green
September 1955

Out of a clear sky with a few thin white clouds like faint brush marks, the day suddenly produced a shower of rain like diamonds, a glittering fringed curtain of rain in which the wings of the flies caught in it shone like silver.

The wind went up and down, steeplechasing over the little hills. Jackdaws were sucked upwards as it reached them and grey birds thrown off the bushes. A bee, knocked over into the tangled grass, buzzed angrily till it freed itself. The wild clematis—traveller's joy—crowded over the hedges as if to peer at all that was passing, and the wind rocked the tops of the trees like cradles.

The water-diviner
18 September 1955
It was Peter Koutellaris, a Cypriot student who was doing some kind of course with us, who introduced me to the water diviner. Peter made the connection, and I supplied the transport. It was a reasonable arrangement.

The diviner came out of his cottage to meet us as soon as we drew up. He was puffing at a cigarette and coughing. He threw away the stub and, still coughing, took another from the packet and lit it. The diviner was a big man with a round face, rugged and marked with a big scar across his nose, but surprisingly babyish in features. He was wearing a dull yellow checked shirt, army surplus jacket and trousers, and farmer's boots.

He walked out over the stubble, holding the divining rod rather loosely and casually, with the ends pointing outwards and the prong of the fork away from him. He walked slowly till suddenly, as if he'd got an electric shock, he let go with his right hand and twisted his face, as if the pain had moved into his cheek. The stick looked as if it had suddenly become alive, and he had to leave go of it.

The diviner told us he had never been taught his craft. He had just gone in for it as a boy, and grown better and better at it. Now he made a living out of it, using four boring machines and employing ten men. He was so confident in his skill that he always worked on a 'no water, no pay' basis. He could divine not only where water was, but its depth and volume. To do these two things he had a complicated formula, which Peter took down in his notebook, but I have forgotten.

The diviner used mainly hazel rods, he said, but you had to try them out because some were good and some useless. It never paid to leave rods out in the open. They would lose their virtue. And he was a tracker as well as a diviner. He could find missing persons by wrapping something belonging to them round his right hand before gripping the twig. He told us how he had once gone looking for a young woman who was missing.

'Her'd been missing since early morning, and they asked me to look for her. They know'd she was up to no good. So I follered her and seed as how her'd gone down to the river, and stopped at every dip hole. First this 'un and then that 'un, as if she'd been considering. But her'd gone into none of them, I see'd that. Her'd changed her mind. She's agone back home, I said. She's athought it over and she's back where she started from. And so she had. When they got back, long after it were dark, they found her there, sitting afront of the fire.'

The diviner had smoked almost incessantly, and was lighting up another cigarette when we said goodbye to him. 'Don't you go amessing about with pendulums and things like that,' were his last words. 'You keep off wires and whalebones. You just stick to what I told you and get it to work. Then you'll be alright.'

Aunt Lil's story [1]

During the war I heard from one of my American cousins that a boy of hers was in the services and that he might be coming to Worcester. Naturally I promised to look after him as best I could, and when he came to see me I thought I'd try to show him the city's beauty spots. What a depressing day! I took this boy to the cathedral and tried to show him all the interesting items—everything that was likely to interest a young fellow of his age. My dear, he never uttered a word. He was chewing his gum, working away with his jaws as hard as he could, but not a word could I get from him.

At last I remembered the silly old story about the Danes who came raiding up the river. I told him that the people of Worcester had caught one of them, and how, just to make an example of him to any of his kinsmen who might have the same intention of looting the city, they flayed him and nailed his skin on the cathedral door. But he didn't even make a comment on that. So I took him out, his jaws still working on the dreadful gum, to see some of our famous old houses. Then, just when I was giving him up as a bad job, he spoke. Do you know what he said? He said to me, 'Say, aunt, do you reckon there's any chance of my having a look at that dead feller's skin?'

The cider maker

Yesterday when I was out walking near Doddenham I came across a cider maker at work. The sweet smell of apples piled outside an outbuilding lured me to look inside, and when I went through the doorway I came upon a sight that might have come straight from Hardy. To the right, in the shady windowless half of the shed was an old mill, a circular stone trough, a vertically set grindstone, attached to the mill a yoke, and in the yoke a young black horse. The man emptied the bruised and smelling apples into the trough; the horse went patiently round, pulping the fruit; and then the brown, rather unpleasant-looking yeast pulp was ladled out in preparation for spreading in the cheese or press.

'He's a good horse, this one,' said the man. 'He's never behaved himself badly for me. An' tidden' every horse that ud do a job like this. He gets dizzy, you know, just like we would. But he'll stop, just you watch him, he'll stop, not acause he's lazy, but just to settle his yead.'

Sure enough after every few rounds the young horse would stop and shake his head a little, wait till the giddiness had left him and then go on.

When the pulp was ready, it was lifted out, a pailful at a time and poured on to a square of rather dirty coco matting. The matting was then folded and squeezed in the press, like clothes in an old-fashioned mangle, and out poured a stream of muddy juice, running into a vat that stood on the ground below the press.

'It'll come up clear as gin, that will,' said the man, 'But I dare say it will be March afore we can bring it down.'

The horse shook its head disbelievingly, then pulled at its harness and started on more monotonous rounds.

A day in Ledbury
August

I started my walk from Malvern Wells, then went past the British Camp over the hot and dusty hills to Eastnor. Climbing was a labour. I went on down to Eastnor and on to Ledbury.

It was market day, and Ledbury was once more the unspoilt country town that Masefield knew—no tourists swarming over the streets, no coaches cluttering up the car parks. The farmers were drinking in The Feathers, one old fellow doing a deal in the bar.

'What do you think of he for 78, eh? O he'd cut up rough still if you'd of upset him. And by God, he's still that quick, you'd never see he coming.'

In his traditional place, under the black and white town hall, a loquacious potman was exchanging banter with his customers.

'Service after sales with this one, ladies. If you buy this lovely pot I'll come every other Thursday and dust it for you. No? Nobody want it? I'll put it away then. But speak up, ladies. Tell me what you want and I'll produce it. What? No offers? Blimey they'll be sending missionaries to this place soon. I'll tell you what I'll do. Here's a lovely dinner set—six plates, genuine willow pattern. The old man chasing a girl across the bridge with a beer bottle—all in lovely technicolour. What'll we say—7/6, 7/-, 6/6... Now I've dropped one. Well, they're no good to me if they don't break when you drop them. Here they are—the rest reserved for the Countess of Bosbury. Are you taking nothing more than your cigarette lighter out of your pocket, lady? Blimey, I thought you was reaching for your purse...'

Great fun. For a souvenir I bought a beautiful little cup and saucer for Erica.

1956

In The Fox, Monkwood Green
Easter Saturday, April 1956
The Fox at Monkwood Green is a modest little country pub, where on weekdays all the company gathers in the kitchen bar. It has a brown floor, bare-topped tables with dingy tops and brown-painted legs and brown forms for seats. On cold evenings there is a fire, glowing underneath but neatly banked with nuggets of black coke. There is an ingle, a dark dartboard and a 'ringer-board' with a single brass peg. On the wall ticks an ugly clock with ornate and barely decipherable figures on its mottled face.

Often the men play tippit, a simple guessing game, with three players ranged on one side of the table and three on the other. The 'worker' sits in the middle of his team, and with an elaborate and baffling play of the hands drops a farthing into one palm. Then the hands are all lifted and brought down so that they rest clenched on the table. Then one of the trio opposite begins to 'fetch', calling 'Take it away' or 'Take both away' or pointing to the hand which he thinks holds the coin.

A wrong call and the point is lost. A right call and the farthing changes hands. One of the players is an old man in a thick grey working suit, knotted scarf and heavy unlaced boots. He has a strange faraway voice and the men often speak to him in signs. He is a wonderfully deft 'worker' with surprisingly soft hands. He works very cautiously.

'Damn them as works in a rush,' he says in his strange barely audible voice. 'I likes a horse as'll work steady all day, not give up after he's done an acre.'

1957

An astonishing recollection
27 February 1957
Last night before I went to sleep, I had a few moments of what I would call vision, were it not that the experience was one of recall rather than clairvoyance. Suddenly, in such vivid detail that it surprised me, there came before me old Rushy Field that I knew in my boyhood—the slope that I climbed day after day when I was a schoolboy, where I would sit hour after hour looking over the valleys of the Wear and the Deerness. With a clarity that was almost a revelation I saw that field in all its detail—the stile that led into it, the water gurgling between the two posts of the stile (I could actually hear it running)—the very grasses of the field, the quaking grass, the woodrush, the coarse wild barley—the little hollows full of brown peaty rainwater, the curled dead leaves that lay beneath the water, the sodden reedy edges—the very contours of the ground, the shallow trench that sloped across the field and the little ledge or shelf on the higher side.

It was incredible that I should recall such detail. But there it was, complete and vivid enough to startle and fill one with a mixture of incredulity, awe and delight.

Donald Wolfitt
22 April 1957
A girl I met today once played Goneril to Wolfitt's Lear.[2] He was never on the stage till the performance. He directed the play from the stalls, and the rest of the players had to imagine where Lear was. She found the whole procedure very difficult, with Lear speaking his lines from the pit; but when she complained, he called out 'You must be rock firm, my dear! Rock firm!' All the moves were carefully laid down and he did not like anyone to deviate from them.

Eclipse of the moon
May 1957
First the lower left-hand edge of the moon began to darken—very faintly, so

that the full circle looked a little dented and misshapen. Then the roughened edge of the shadow began to encroach upon the disc, denting it more and more deeply. It seemed a short time only before half of the circle was obscured, but the part that was in shadow was still faintly visible, a vague umber shape. A vapour trail across the sky just above the moon showed very clearly, a chalky mark scored in a shallow arc. At eleven—or near that time—the moon looked like a ring, a thin silver ring with a single stone. It was no longer a solid disc but a circlet one could see through. The full shape was still visible, but a lovely dusky brown.

I came indoors to write this note, and left the students getting up tripods, taking photographs, talking together. Now the night is very clear and still, and every sound carries. Aeroplanes are going over with thunderous noises.

Now the moon looks as if a deep haze was rising from the earth to engulf it. The lower edge is already hidden in darkness.

Heath Chapel, Shropshire
17 May 1957
I was looking at the exterior of this simple little Norman chapel when Mr Lewis, who keeps the key, drove up with his wife. She was carrying flowers.

'Are you having a service tomorrow?'

'Two. The vicar gives a service on one Sunday a month. So we have a shortened Matins and Communion at eleven and Evensong at three. Have you been inside?' Mrs Lewis spoke very clearly and her accent was not the accent of a farmer's wife.

'Yes, but I'll come in again.'

I opened the door for her and she put her flowers down on one of the older pew benches.

'They're the smallest pews I've seen,' she said, 'but they're homely.'

'You've a job to see the parson when you're in one of them,' said Mr Lewis. 'But there's just six of us when we're all here. Just twelve houses in the whole parish. Them birds are a nuisance. They get under the eaves and knock the plaster down. I'll show you an old well if you'd like to see it.'

But when we were outside he pointed first to a little shed on one side of the field.

'We had a chap commit suicide there this year. New Year's morning. He cut his throat in that shed there.'

'Good heavens, was he out of his mind?'

'No, no. He was a good worker. He helped me to pleach that hedge over there, see? He was seventy-six. A stone cutter off the quarries. But he could do any job on a farm. Anything.'

'Why did he commit suicide?'

'He had that hardening of the arteries. Dizziness and a bad head as he couldn't get rid of. He said to me many a time he'd do away with hisself. I never believed him but he done it all right. I think if I'd ha gotten to seventy-six, I'd a stuck it out for the rest of my time, wouldn' you?'

I left him turning the car round for his wife.

'I'd shift that tree that's growing out of the wall there,' I said. 'It'll split the masonry before it's finished.'

'The new parson'll see to that,' he said. 'He's a bright fellow and he'll keep them birds out as well.'

A parson I met in Ludlow told me this anecdote about Dr Parry, Principal of Carmarthen Training College. A student had asked to see Mr Parry, and the interview began thus.

'I am at a loss to understand why you are here. If you had meant to make an enquiry about the administration of the college, I suppose you would have enquired for Principal Parry. About your studies—Dr Parry. About your spiritual welfare, Canon Parry. I am at a loss therefore to understand exactly why you wish to consult me, but no doubt you will enlighten me.'

Summer

17 June 1957

Tonight is one more glorious evening, the close of another day of real splendour. It is nearly eleven, and the colour is going out of the eastern sky, so slowly that the afterglow will last till long after midnight, and the stars will be pale all night. The dry lawns seem to glow in the half-light, as if they were giving off a luminousness of their own. In one corner of the field, under a wilting laburnum from which the dry seeds drop, the feathery heads of the uncut grasses are as white as blossom, almost incandescent. Beetles and moths go whirring upwards against the lemon-coloured west, and the flowers of the elder are like white clouds on the dark bushes. The air is still, as if in a trance. The lights from the students' rooms shine through the uncurtained windows, so that the college buildings look like illuminated ships becalmed in a still sea. We close the doors reluctantly, unwilling to turn away from the midsummer tranquillity; and all the small noises of the night are muted in the massive stillness and arching silence of this mid-summer evening.

Weather such as this comes very rarely—Elysian, Edwardian, the gift of a year that has made up its mind to be benevolent and golden. In this summer Gillian is seventeen, and in love. And since she will probably not make this note for herself, I'll make it for her.

November 1957

Today I was confirmed. I am afraid I have gone into it with a poor motive—largely so that I can accompany Gwen to Holy Communion, the service that she prefers. I noticed the chrysanthemums on the chancel steps, the precise way in which the curate twisted his mouth as he announced the hymns, the unfamiliar vestments, the touch of brogue in the vicar's voice, the yawn that the Bishop's chaplain gave halfway through the service, the cold brickwork of the church, the hole in the sock of the candidate before me, a touch of redness at the Bishop's wrists, the blue lips of the acolyte, the piercingly sharp voice of the girl in the choir, the puffy eyes of the candidate on my left, the different kinds of veil worn by the girls, the stamp of the cross on the wafer, the clear red of the Communion wine. Easy to see I have no strong religious convictions when I can be so easily and completely distracted.

Sunset from the Northbound Train

I clear the steamy window, and can see
the ridged and wintry fields,
the sooty palings round the black allotments,
the tins and cans of the tip,
and there, above the tilted colliery roofs,
the even outline of the slagheaps,
the geometry of the pithead gear;
and into the hazy valley-filling evening
someone seems to have cast
the purely rounded
newly smelted
guinea-golden
sun.

December 1957

Durham at dawn
20 December 1957
When I left on foot I found the morning enveloped in a thin grey haze. Everything beneath the sky seemed to have taken on a dove-grey colouring—the brick of the houses, the blue slates, even the odd figures that moved slowly along the shrouded roads. Against this sombre greyness the yet-unextinguished streetlights of the collieries for miles around glittered romantically in chains and arcs of blue and orange. But after a few minutes, in the east, cloud and horizon began to part, revealing the golden wedge of dawn, at first clear, then smouldering, then bursting into flame. By the time I had got to Durham the wedge of clear sky was wide enough to reveal the monumental outline of the castle and cathedral against a cyclorama of gold. Then suddenly a little cloud, far away in the deep opening, caught fire and hung motionless and bright as a goldfish in a pond.

From the frosty platform I looked down on the moist roofs of the city, from which a thousand spirals of smoke went up in softly writhing folds. Then another object claimed my notice—a bare thorn, every twig of its skeleton pencilled against the sky; and on a twig, a single bird. When the sun came up, it rose directly behind the thorn; and the last thing I saw before I went to catch the train was the hunched body of the bird outlined against the full disc of the sun.

1957

January	*The Emperor's New Clothes* by Nicholas Stuart at Birmingham. These plays are quite phoney, but have some attraction for children.

February	*The Playboy of the Western World* at Oxford. I love the play but did not think highly of this production by Theatre Workshop. Produced *Cockpit* at college. Not worth doing. *Frost at Midnight* by A. Obey will not live.
March	*Lysistrata* at the Oxford Playhouse with Constance Cummings. A jewel of a production. Never to be forgotten.
April	*O My Papa* at the Theatre Royal, Bristol. A very enjoyable show with Peter O'Toole and Rachel Roberts.
May	*As You Like It* at Stratford. *Le Misanthrope* at Birmingham—adaptation by Miles Mallinson. Adaptations of Molière are rarely successful. *Julius Caesar* at Stratford. Somebody wants me to produce *The Crucible* but I cannot raise any enthusiasm for it. For me it lacks variety.
September	*All My Sons* by A. Miller. Naïve, didactic, but gripping.
October	*Under Milk Wood* at Oxford—not a patch on that wonderful first production we saw in Newcastle.
November	*Long Day's Journey into Night*, a very powerful and moving play. *Summer of the Seventeenth Doll*—a very good play, with no literary graces, but continuously interesting. *The Tempest* at Stratford. Gielgud as Prospero. *Death of a Salesman*—a sombre but very moving play. *The Emperor Jones* produced at college. *School* by T. W. Robertson—musicalised at Birmingham Rep. *Saint's Day* a powerful, haunting but alas puzzling play by John Whiting.

1958

A phoney house
4 January 1958
Ghastly grey brick, with bilious yellow bottle-glass in all the windows, and stained glass in muddy purples and oranges in the hall; false beams supporting nothing in the bedroom and lounge; dim light from old police lanterns; a phoney electric fire with mock logs in the grate; two unused and unusable spinning wheels in the far corner of the lounge; a dining bench too hard to sit on; rows of unused pewter dishes; elm doors with trumpery country-pub latches, and inefficient radiators. How pretentious and ugly in comparison with my mother's old colliery kitchen!

The owner, who has created this unhomely home, has an old black dog of which she and her husband are very fond. It is hopelessly spoilt, and cannot be left alone unless it has a bowl of milk laced with whiskey, the fire and the television set switched on. Professor Allardyce Nicoll was equally fond of his old dog, which would eat only a special sort of chocolate biscuit (KitKat), sulked when left alone, and had a special travelling bed made for it on the back seat of the car.

26 January 1958
The other night I saw the Russian sputnik for the first time. I was looking for it in the northeast sky when suddenly it appeared going overhead like a fast moving aircraft. I ran in and called to Gwen and Erica to come and see it.

13 February 1958
Yesterday I went to the top of the cathedral to see the floods. All the County Cricket Ground was submerged, and all Pitchcroft except for a little green island. The meadows beyond Diglis were under water and the river was at least a mile wide. The landscape had a foreign look, houses low and small, and trees standing in the water like mangroves in a swamp. It was a clear day, and thin clouds were forming across the sky like trails left by a squadron of planes that had vanished over the horizon.

Later in the day, as the sun was about to sink, it shone on all the windows of Britannia Square, until they gleamed like the windows of a palace; and the light was reflected in the flood water. A marvellous transformation—Worcester turned to Venice.

An incident in Ludlow
29 March 1958
As I crossed the playground I could see that the boys were playing marbles. I stopped to ask them the name of the game.

'It's marbles, sir.'

'Yes, I know it's marbles, but what is the name of this particular game?'

'In the rig, sir.'

'And have you any special names for your marbles? For these small ones, for instance.'

'No, sir.'

'What about that big one? That one?'

I pointed to a big steel marble that the boys were using to throw into the ring, the kind that I would have called a 'penker'; but the boys simply sniggered. Thinking that they were doing so out of awkwardness, perhaps because no grown-up had ever before shown any curiosity about their game, I urged them to reply.

'You do give it a name, don't you?'

The boys began to snigger and guffaw again, holding their hands over their mouths to prevent them from exploding with laughter, and I was a little irritated.

'Come on, don't be silly... what do you call it?'

There was a pause, the boys looked from one to another signalling with their eyes to one of the group to answer. At last, containing himself only with great difficulty, he burst out. 'We calls it Baldy, sir.' And the group went off into more fits of mirth.

It was a moment of embarrassment I richly deserved.

The affair of the vicar
May 1958
The vicar, Malcolm Richards, is in hot water. Some time ago he obtained permission to move the 1914-18 War Memorial to a different part of the churchyard. While he was moving it he thought it would look better without the calvary that formed the upper part. Parishioners, finding the calvary removed, raised objections. Malcolm was summoned before the Consistory Court, admonished and told to pay the expenses of the enquiry, plus the cost of restoring the memorial to its original position and condition.

Last night in church he publicly apologised to the congregation for the unwelcome publicity the parish had had to put up with, and announced his decision to fight on! A former curate, the Revd Pilkington, went up into the pulpit and defended him. But just before he took his place there was a dramatic moment. The door at the back of the church opened, and down the aisle swept Mrs Pilkington, who is a very beautiful woman. No ally could have arrived at a more timely moment. It was almost as if Malcolm had stage-managed this dramatic entry.

In Spetchley Gardens
18 May 1958
Today Gwen and I went for a walk around Bredicot. It was a gusty yet somehow steamy afternoon in which we could scarce get our breath—the time of the year when the first greenness of Spring begins to dull and the air thickens. The grass in the hedge bottoms was tall, and along the Bredicot lanes the comfrey was high and profuse, its red and mauve flowers hanging limp in the warm afternoon.

At the last moment we decided to take a look at Spetchley Gardens. A great treat—square solid hedges of yew that Malvolio might have strutted between, walled-in spaces with shrubs trained up against mouldering brickwork. There was a Tennysonian beauty about the gardens—a toy landing stage, a tiny bridge across a weedy stream, lawns and cypress trees spreading up to the edge of an Arthurian mere, lily leaves lying flat on the water as if they had lately fallen there, coot and moorhen in the reeds, and through the trees, the blank façade of the great house.

In the conservatory we talked with an elderly man in cheap grey flannels, a frayed, knitted pullover, an old hat with the brim turned down all round, and a rough jacket with a much-used notebook in the flapless pocket. I learnt later that he was the last of the Berkeleys, the last untidy heir and survivor of the great royalist family whose effigies lie in the church nearby, and who gave to the city the almshouses that now stand in the Foregate.

11 September 1958
Gillian was made Head Girl of the Grammar School for Girls. This is her last year and Headmistress Miss Webster's last year.

1959

10 January 1959

At last we are under snow. Suddenly today the brilliance of the morning was dimmed and the snow came, first in small hesitant flakes, like white dust blown from a roof. Then the air began to thicken, and the snow fell so fast and so thick that it looked as if the air would become solid with snow—as if the spaces between the flakes were filling. The snow was coming from the northwest. All the trees were white on that side, and black on the other side, so that it was the black trunks and boughs and the wet brickwork of walls and outhouses that seemed to stand out.

Then the cloud blew over, and the sun went down, very golden, behind the thin screen of the bare twigs. There is something wonderfully beautiful about the winter sun setting behind the bare poles and branches of a wood.

Broadheath
May

Almost every day of this May has been glorious, and all the flowers and blossom and leaves have been welcomed with warmth and sunshine and stillness. A Springtime without disaster! The whole process of growth and flowering has gone on without check or setback. Tonight I walked along the road from Broadheath and saw the cow parsley breast-high, like clouds or drifts of whiteness. The buttercups are very tall, and their golden flowers seemed to be floating in the still air. The lilacs were brimming over with white and purple, the laburnum was hanging out its yellow flowers like clusters of grapes; and the evening sunlight filled all the downy globes of dandelion heads till they were luminous. All the wonderful varied display of Spring flowers was on show—stitchwort, may, dark bluebells in the rank grasses by the hedge, bugle, speedwell, cowslips, the malachite sheaths of the wild arum, Jack-by-the-hedge—none beaten down, none withered, none broken by storm or nipped by frost—all straight and perfect in this magnificent weather. This 1959 May was one of the finest I have ever known.

Tonight I went out walking in the dark. It was so still that the trees, black and furry, stood around me, immobile, dark, impenetrable, with every leaf motionless; and the night was so clear and open, with a high sharp moon in the south, and the horizon ringed with glittering stars, that the eye and the spirit were drawn up and up from the prone surface of the earth towards the illimitable vistas of the universe—upwards and outwards to the vast unpeopled space beyond. A boy was walking under the trees and singing, and his voice seemed to thin away as it rose into the listening skies. All the sounds of the night—the hooting of an owl, the horn of an invisible car, the vibration of the earth itself—all echoed and vanished into the limitless empty space that receded, milky and vast, beyond the scattered glittering archipelagos of the stars.

A coffee bar in Shrewsbury
July 1959
Every now and then as the cups are filled the coffee machine makes a noise like someone clearing his throat. The girls at the tables lift their feet as the attendant sweeps under them. A group of three men are talking, one declaring very emphatically that something (I can't catch what it is) isn't made nowadays as it used to be.

'They just don' make them good enough—that's the top and bottom of it.' His companions agree with him almost obsequiously.

'I agree, I agree.'

'Yes, you're dead right there.'

The two girls come to life as a young man joins them. They brush the crumbs off their table and make a clear place for him as they smile at him. I catch sight of the young man's thumb as he raises his cup to drink. There is a thick line of grease around the edge of his broad spade-shaped thumb. The machine clears its throat again.

'These fellers that smokes,' grumbles the attendant. 'They will keep on throwing their matches on the floor.'

The old man sitting near me looks up.

'Ah,' he says, 'They never throws their pound notes there, does they?'

Open Air Theatre at Stratford
15 July 1959
The Two Noble Kinsmen, given by Reading University Drama Society in the Open Air Theatre at Stratford, was not an epoch-making event; but the combination of a most beautiful natural setting, good verse and a lovely summer evening was irresistible. The play began in full evening light, and the players were alternately helped and hindered by several adventitious attractions. You

can see the river from the auditorium, and from time to time rowing boats and punts appeared quietly and became part of the backcloth. It was sometimes difficult to keep one's eyes on the stage lovers since real lovers in the meadows made counter claims on the interest. And the first part of the evening was diversified by the loud unorthodox comments of a gang of Teddy boys who climbed the wattle screen at the back and responded to the action in a refreshingly unorthodox way. Hippolyta was more than once greeted with wolf whistles. Two actors struggling under the trees were adjured to 'cut out the rough stuff', and a quick dash for cover by the rustics was helped by a raucous call 'To the woods!'

But as the evening wore on, lovers, Teds and even the river were lost in darkness, and the artificial light began to tinge the lawns, the garden walls, the imposing cedar. A thousand moths fluttered in the beams of the floodlights, and belated birds provided notes that at times outdid even the sweetness of the incidental music. The actors began to take on substance, their voices to grow stronger. Palamon and Arcite fought their duel under the trees. The jailor's daughter enacted her madness by the side of the river. We were all quite won over, and the magic of the perfect summer evening matched the mood of the play.

The Broken Heart by John Ford, was even finer. The play began slowly and progressed humourlessly, but incident followed incident—Ithocles in his torture chair, the coronation of Calantha, the fireworks, the displays, the music, the dancing with its succession of bad news, the capture of Orgilus, his death, ringed round by torchbearers—and the infinitely moving scene in which Calantha, now Queen, having disposed of all her responsibilities, dies of a broken heart over the body of her dear Ithocles. This was one of the most moving dramatic experiences I have had for a long time.

Ironic footnote. As you enter the open-air theatre you pick up your anti-mosquito lotion. It is as essential as a programme.

Sister Eucharia

It was Sister Eucharia, Headmistress of St Mary's Convent, Battenhall, who told me about the extraordinary romantic, the Hon. Percy Allsopp, who lived in Battenhall before it became a school. You can see him in person, once carved in wood and staring fixedly across the staircase at his wife, who romantically stares back at him; and a second time in stained glass, armoured in all the paraphernalia of an Arthurian knight, with the names of his fellow-Arthurians on scrolls around him (here his name has been modified into Percival) and neighboured by his wife, also in stained glass, surrounded by a multitude of little birds calling her equally Arthurian name—'Maud, Maud, Maud.' It is said that he was so devoted to his wife that he made himself a bankrupt for her.

Once she went to Italy and saw a house she admired. He built a copy for her in Worcester—and that is why the house with its balconies and columns and pergolas is still Italianate, a little bit of Tuscany that has found its way into the Faithful City. And inside it, in addition to the carved adoring faces and the stained-glass Pre-Raphaelite figures, there is a miniature chapel, a copy of a chapel somewhere in Italy that the Hon. Percy's wife fell in love with—dome, sedilia, lamps dangling from the ceiling, the lady's father's portrait done three times in wood, as a young man, an older man, and a bishop (he was in reality a bishop), mother-of-pearl on the altar, coats of arms on the floor, painted ironwork and a rosewood door—all in miniature, a small scale masterpiece of Victorian artistry.

'But isn't it a comedown, now,' said Sister Eucharia, 'to have to confess that all his money was made out of beer, and the lovely flag you can see on the school flagpole can be found on every bottle of beer his blessed firm turns out.'

Squire of Brockhampton

A Mr Browne from Hereford, who is in Holy Orders but has no living, told me an extraordinary story about an old Squire of Brockhampton. Mr Browne had been invited to preach the Harvest Festival sermon in the church which stands close by the Hall. He presented himself in good time, but was restrained by the churchwarden from beginning the service till the Squire had arrived. When the Squire did arrive he was wearing vivid yellow gloves and carrying a silver-topped cane; and he paused before entering his pew to look round, like Sir Roger de Coverley, to see who was present.

The church had been lovingly decorated, and Browne felt that he ought to begin his sermon by congratulating whoever had been responsible for the decorations. But there was one omission that puzzled him and he felt that he ought to comment on that too. 'How beautiful your church looks tonight,' he said, 'adorned and beautified by the glorious gifts of harvest fruits which Our Lord has plenteously bestowed upon us. It is all the more surprising to me that I have not seen, among these carefully chosen decorations, one ear of corn.'

No sooner had he finished his sentence than there came to him the sound of rapping. It came from the Squire's pew, and the sound was the rapping of his cane on the stone floor. Browne was so surprised to be so brusquely interrupted that he stopped speaking, and the silence that followed was filled with the bold confident voice of the old Squire.

'Excuse me, sir,' he said, 'There's some here.'

Hop-picking
Early September 1959
Today I went hop-picking with Paddy, the college night watchman. You take a crib, a kind of long cradle made of sacking slung between poles, and you are paid for all the hops you can fill into your crib. You may work alone or with a team, but all payments are recorded against the name of the crib-holder. Once you have a crib you are given a house, a section of the hop field, usually all the hops between two sets of large hop poles. You clear this 'house', having your work 'bushelled' from time to time—that is, the overseers come round, scoop out your hops into large wicker baskets, and record the number of bushels you have picked. Once the 'house' is cleared, you move on to another.

So section by section, or 'house' by 'house', the field is cleared. The pickers seem to nibble away at the hops, like caterpillars nibbling leaves, or locusts devouring greenery, and little by little, the bines are pulled down and stripped, and nothing remains but a bare field, stark with poles and wires, and littered with the stalks and strings of the gathered hops.

It is a pleasant job in fine weather. The work is not arduous, and people talk as they work, in a quiet sociable sort of way, if they feel so inclined. But I found the hop field anything but noisy. Children were playing and occasionally crying, but the pickers worked on assiduously and almost morosely, as if the act of constant picking had partly hypnotised them. Most of the pickers were women. Gypsies work at great speed and with great skill, but it is not easy for an average worker to earn a pound a day. As you work your hands become black, like a miner's; but the dirt washes off easily in a dark green froth.

On the Avon
7 September 1959
Today, in beautiful weather, Michael Lovatt and I took a canoe to Wyre and went up the river to Fladbury.[3] Anglers on the low banks of the Avon, the low

reed-fringed river, continually crossed and recrossed by moorhens, gardens running down to the river, red persicaria and faded waterflags, dragonflies riding the air, cattle ankle-deep in the ooze, chewing the succulent sedge, a heron rising like a puff of smoke and an old black horse taking fright and galloping over the sloping pasture, swans with grey cygnets, the cobs pure white, arrogant, hostile, the white distant vapour trails of aeroplanes reflected in the smooth cold September water.

We went upstream, passing a strange island-like retreat with a hut on stilts, and a landing stage all locked and shuttered, and came eventually to Fladbury Mill, like a fortress on its island, tall, shapely, built of beautiful pink brick, with white window frames and a sparse creeper, golden and blood-red, scribbled over the walls. The water was pouring steadily over the weir, thinning as it fell into a lacy fall, with froth twining and twirling in the pool below. On the weir stood two swans and five grey cygnets.

This has been a fine summer, but the long days of sunshine bring their problems. Tonight I can see fires spreading on the Malverns.

Great Tew
15 September 1959
During the course of a short holiday in Oxfordshire, we called at Great Tew, a remarkable village surrounded by evergreens. The woods are the creation of a gardener with a passion for box, cypress, holly, ivy, laurel, fir and cedar. A unique setting, dark, elegiac, sombre but very lovely.

On the church gate was this extraordinary handwritten notice: Since next Sunday is the 216th anniversary of the death of Lord Falkland, who received mortal hurt at the field of Newbury, and was brought here to be buried, there will be, in place of evensong, a service of remembrance for his death.

After 216 years!

The Gardener at Great Tew

Thinking that life was far too brief to bear
trees without leaves for one half of the year,
I chose to screen
these cottages, this church, with evergreen,
cypress and juniper,
holly and laurel, cedar, box and fir.

It was my hope that they might grow to be
green images of immortality;
but, being old, I know at last my trees'
adornment only fit for exequies,
and each undying leaf upon its stem,
waits but to celebrate my requiem.

20 September 1959

Fording the Teme
16 September 1959
Today I walked upstream from Bransford Bridge and did an unusual thing. It was a lovely walk along the dry river path. I saw a kingfisher within a hundred yards of the bridge. The views were good, the fields lying flat and fawn-coloured, and the low hills beyond Cotheridge blue and distinct. I looked at my map and found that if I walked about two miles upstream I would arrive at a point opposite Leigh Church and Court. If I could find a way of crossing the river at that point I could walk back to the bridge by way of the road. I didn't expect to find a ford, but I did. I cut myself a stick, took off my shoes and socks and got across the river with no difficulty.

The river at that point is fast and clear, and tumbles over rocks and pebbles with something like the vivacity of a northern beck. It is overhung with willows, but the afternoon sun falls on the water. There was a kind of ancient pleasure in finding a ford and crossing a river, like a mediaeval traveller, without the aid of bridge or boat. I scrambled up the bank on the far side and found myself in a hop field, where the pickers were far too busy to notice one more in their midst. Beyond the hop field was the deserted station of Leigh, and at the end of the lane leading to the station, I came to the road that led back to Bransford Bridge.

I suppose that most of what I saw will vanish soon. The hop pickers will be gone and their places taken by machines. The station will never be used again. Even that lovely figure of Christ on the church wall will erode and waste. Perhaps the river is the one indestructible thing.

Early October 1959
Gillian has passed her driving test and gone off to university, and the great drought has at last broken.

1960

January 1960

A heavy snowfall, a rapid thaw, then torrents of rain. The consequence—the worst flood since 1947. There is so much water on the New Road that there is barely room for the traffic to move along it. Pedestrians are crossing the flooded sections on planks raised on stone blocks. Crowds are hanging over the bridge, awed by the magnitude of the floods and vaguely waiting for some catastrophe. The water has flooded into the goldfish pond in Cripplegate Park and all the fish have swum free. There is a ladder allowing clients to get to the upper rooms of The Rectifying House, and a notice on the balcony—BUSINESS AS USUAL. In midstream the river is running angrily, sluicing through the arches, but in the flooded bystreets the water is calm and lake-like.

For some reason or other the captain of the big petrol barge that was moored near the power station at the bottom of Hylton Road decided to drop downstream, slackening the mooring ropes. Then he cast off, keeping however one hawser attached to the bows to prevent the barge from being borne broadside against the piers of the bridge. Then he dropped his boat inch by inch downstream, swinging the wheel continuously to keep her parallel to the river bank.

The skipper had chosen the near arch, and let the stern slide slowly down till it had entered the arch. The funnels were taken down, the side rails collapsed, and everything that was high or prominent was removed or lowered. Then the barge was allowed to slip further and further down, but at a critical moment she swung and wedged herself in the arch. The gunwales knocked off some of the bridge masonry, and the boat had to be eased upstream again. Then a cleat got jammed in the arch, but at last after a great deal of manoeuvring she was worked free and clear of the bridge.

An accident

4 February 1960

Two days ago a large chimney stack that had been very loosely built up against Winwood's warehouse in Sidbury collapsed and fell on the old White Hart Inn. Two men who were in the bar were hurt and a seventeen year old girl who was passing was killed by the falling masonry.

Read Beckett's new little play, *Krapp's Last Tape*, and very impressed by it.

April 1960
Fulfilled a years' old ambition by going to Avignon.

Provençal scene
Since this Provençal scene
Moved to idyllic praise the stern Racine,
It would indeed be rum
If it left me dumb.

Lovely May weather
6 May 1960
We are enjoying most beautiful early summer days, the kind of Maytime weather celebrated in folk song and ballad. We wake to lovely mild shining mornings, the trees in full leaf, and the new foliage so tender and fresh that the sun shines through it, filling the trees with a golden greenness. The bushes are loaded with flower and blossom. The lilacs are heavy and scented and the apple trees seem to explode with whiteness. When we were at prayers the other day, I could hear, even above the hymn singing, the bickering of the starlings that have nested in the spouting. We have never had so many queen wasps. They come veering down the corridors, peering in at closed windows, hovering inquisitively and then swing away again as if they found nothing to their liking.

Tenbury Wells on market day
23 August 1960
Everything is on a small scale here—the cattle market modest, the covered space for stallholders small and unpretentious, the streets uncrowded. But there is a wonderful feeling of space and leisure. The apples, pears, plums and blackberries set out on the tables give off a wonderful fresh smell, and the people are individual—the shepherd with his thick boots, miry trouser bottoms and crook; the farm wife with her few flowers and single chicken; the gypsy woman with her wrinkled face, Meg Merrilees hat, full skirts and necklaces. It is a warm day, and the country sun is shining on the half-timbered buildings and the creeper that almost covers the top windows of the Georgian houses.

Flood
6 December 1960
Late in 1960 we had another heavy flood. The summer and autumn had been very wet, and by November we had had five months of almost continuous rain, that left the fields saturated. The newspapers began to speak of 'the paddy fields of England.' The November weather was strange and sinister. A wild uneasy wind kept roaring, savaging the trees, and then falling into uneasy lulls, as if a series of spasms were coming over the upper air, making it strain and writhe and convulse. The swans, unusually white against the dark flood water, paddled out of the violent midstream of the river into new and quieter reaches and lagoons, and fed on the shoots of inundated hedges.

The water rose so high that it came flooding over Hylton Road near the Power Station, and pouring into the transport cafes on the South Quay. The door to one of them was left open and I could see a plank resting, at one end on the dry upper edge of a wall outside, and at the other on the stairway of the house. The lower rooms of these cafes looked abandoned, but there was a cheerful sign outside the Rectifying House 'Plenty beer upstairs'. People were standing on the shores of the flood water, looking wonderingly at the strange sight. On the fringe was the usual flotsam and jetsam—papers, twigs, straws, slices of sodden bread, apples. Two big barges were moored above the bridge, swaying dangerously in the strong current. The water was pushing up against the piers, piling up and splaying out, then roaring fiercely through the narrowed arches and swirling in dangerous eddies and whirlpools. Eventually the water began to form on each side of the New Road, until there was only a single lane for traffic. Police kept a constant watch, and a rescue boat was moored opposite the entrance to Cripplegate Park.

A few days later the New Road was so obstructed with floodwater that no wheeled traffic could get through, and thousands set off to walk to work, all flocking along the road, like some concourse assembling for a fair or a festival. For once, the monotony of going to work was relieved, and there was almost an exhilaration in the air. The liberation from routine, the pearly morning light, the faint sunshine after weeks of rain, the silence and serenity of the scene, the sense of sharing in a rare experience—all seemed to inspire us with energy and light heartedness. We looked with pity at the yawning frustrated drivers, and the spiritless passengers who persisted in trying to use the buses, and with pleasure at the rough workmen in wellingtons, who, with a new fellow feeling, helped old men and women and girls along the narrow insecure planks laid across the flood water. There was among us a spirit that recalled the camaraderie of the almost forgotten days of the war. The sun had broken through the clouds; the swans and gulls were riding at ease in the flooded meadows; the December air was mild and beneficent. It was a morning not to grieve over, but to remember with pleasure.

These were the sounds and sights and smells of the city by night: unimpeded traffic speeding down the High Street; the alleys dark and full of shadows; the warm night full of smells; of hops stored away in the quayside warehouses; of cabbages rotting somewhere over some wall; a whiff of apples from a shop; of elderflowers on the dirty old trees growing on waste lots, glowing like ghostly white lamps; scraps of paper turning over and over senselessly in the night wind; the light glinting on pieces of broken glass embedded in the pathways; great huddled lorries parked for the night, shrouded with tarpaulins; the stirring of drivers bedding down for the night in their cabins; drunken men moving, stopping, shaking hands, agreeing loudly with one another; people saying goodnight, lights snapping off in shop windows; ghostly suits with no heads, no hands, no feet standing rigid behind plate glass windows; lights going on in flats above shops; two men leaning out of a window high up in an old house, looking out over the sluggish tarry river.

A man and his clocks
7 December 1960

When I came out of the army my nerves were in a terrible state. I couldn't sleep a wink. It didn't matter what I did. Damned if I could drop off. It was the milkman that cured me. 'How's your Bill?' he said to the missus one day. 'He's in a terrible state,' she said, 'I think he's getting worse.' 'Get a grandfather clock', he said, 'and stand it beside the bed, that'll send him off.' Aye and it did. The first night I thought it 'ud drive me daft, but the second I felt better and, would you believe it, by the fourth or fifth night I dropped off and I had the best night's sleep since I was in the cradle. And since then it's nivver failed. And that's when I took to clocks, mister, becos I thought that if one would send me to sleep, two would be even better. An' they were. They all tell different times, mind, but that doesn't trouble me. If I want to know what time it is, I listen to the wireless. I've took a fancy to clocks, and I keep them like pets. Does ta know, once I went on holiday, but the place was that quiet I nivver slept a wink. I got straight on t'train, and come back here as fast as I could to get a bit of rest.

Notes

1. Aunt Lil' was aunt to Marjorie Whiteman, a friend of Gwen's.
2. Sir Donald Wolfitt (1908-68), English actor-manager, known for his touring productions of Shakespeare during the Second World War.
3. The son of a colleague, George Lovatt.

Chapter 3: 1961-69

1961

At an educational conference
February 1961
I sit in the conference room, watching the women light cigarette after cigarette in an effort to keep awake, to keep listening to the soft indecisive sentences of the man who is speaking. There is an air of unreality about everything. Nothing is real—except the sound of the engines in the station outside, preparing for departure, releasing sudden explosions of steam, their wheels shuddering and skipping on the rails as they strain to go; and the inexplicable outbursts of cheering from some children somewhere below us. The woman opposite presses one more cigarette into the steel ashtray, and I can see the marks of her lipstick on the stub. A fat man on the other side of her sleeps with his jowls resting on his soiled collar. And again in protest comes the slipping and shuddering of the wheels on the rails. I hate conferences. I surrender part of myself every time I enter a conference room.

Saw *Antony and Cleopatra* (which I do not admire) and *The Glass Menagerie* (which I do).

The Ruined Church at Edvin Loach

Sunken, swarmed over now by bush and tree,
ragged with rooted weeds in cranny and crevice,
its tufa quoins like sponge, the masonry
like the bones of a nibbled fish;
roofless, stripped and scratched
by the horny fingernails of bramble and briar,
littered with cracking slabs, blackening tablets,
and letterless inscriptions—itself almost
a tomb, with the green earth mounding over it—
this ruin lurches backwards in time,
reverting into grotto, sepulchre,
pagan cave,

now nearest to the close and airless cromlech
it once was dedicated to deny.

7 February 1961

Wet days in Yorkshire
7 April 1961

The sun was shining when we left Worcester for Draughton, and the cherry blossom was out; but soon after we had left Birmingham it began to rain. In Cheshire a thin snow was falling. In Lancashire it had thickened into a heavy fall, and the roads were becoming a little treacherous. Then we discovered that the village of Draughton, which from the brochure we had thought of as being tucked away in a secluded valley, was almost on the crest of the moors between Skipton and Ilkley—right on the roof of the Pennines. It was bitterly cold. The countryside was hidden in snow. The central heating system mentioned in the brochure was certainly in existence but it was not working. It had been turned off at the beginning of April. The fire in the sitting room was tiny, and the eight or nine of us who were guests for the weekend were wedged in a tight arc around those miserable few cinders. It was so appallingly cold in the bedroom that we had to adopt this extraordinary procedure. I got into Gwen's bed to warm it up while she had a bath in the steamy bathroom. Then she got in beside me, and as soon as she was warmed through, I had to get out and get into my own cold bed. A fearsome moment. My bed was like a vault, and it was impossible to close the window beside it. I slept in my underwear, pyjamas and a sweater; and surprisingly slept well. The next day the temperature rose a little and the snow melted. During the next few grey dismal days we saw Bolton Abbey, Haworth, Harrogate, the church at Hubberholme, Aysgarth and its falls, and Malham.

A bulldozer at work
14 April 1961

The driver drove his bulldozer at the tree. The sharp edge of the shovel bit into the bark, and as the driver accelerated, slid up the trunk slicing away the bark like skin. As it rose the two front wheels of the bulldozer rose and kept on spinning angrily. The tree was stripped but it did not give. The driver retreated, lowered the shovel and drove it at the roots, its wheels spinning and sinking in the soft earth. He withdrew for a third attack. The shovel bit again into the roots and seemed to hold. In a fearful gesture of rage, the machine burrowed forward, then rose like a stallion as if it meant to fall backwards and crush its driver. Then, at last, the severed roots began to give, and the tree heeled and fell.

Listening to a nightingale
24 April 1961
Tonight Gillian, Erica and I went to hear a nightingale. I knew where I could find one—in a corner of Monkwood. As it turned out the nightingale was shy, and we heard only a few brief trills. But what an astonishing variety of other sounds we heard as we stood listening—a cat fighting outside the pub, innumerable cars; a curlew uttering only one unmodulated note as it moved invisibly and restlessly in the open space beyond the wood; lapwings, as restless as ever; the immensely deep lowing of a cow, a fog-horning sound that seemed to fill the night before it lost itself in the wood; a chirring of magpies or nightjars, and the barking of dogs challenging one another from farm to farm. The night was full of sounds—too many for the timid nightingale that sang once or twice, very tentatively, and then held its peace.

Producers are beginning to play strange tricks with Shakespeare. The other night I was displeased to find the line:

Don John, the bastard, has fled

turned into

Don John—the bastard!—has fled.

Very busy with my book on Worcester, and several short stories for slow readers I am writing for Mary Worrall[1]. *Aidan and the Strollers* goes into paperback. *The Bonny Pit Laddie* has had very good reviews.

A fragment overhead
'I thanks my stars I never asked nobody for nothing, except a smoke now and then. If I's in a pub and my glass is empty I never says to nobody to fill it up again for me. But you'm always on the scrounge. If I owed as much as you do I'd be ashamed to walk about the streets. But I knows what your trouble is—you never goes straight.'

The Balcony, Hanley Swan

This is the home of Mr and Mrs Clive—a lovely old house. At the back of the house a trestle table is set out in front of an old plane tree (some blue tits are nesting in a crack in it). There is a path with yellow poppies growing on either side, and a homely little workshop with a stove. This is Mr Clive's den. He is a benign old man, puffing away at his home-made cigarettes (he spills the shag over his plus fours as he rolls them), talking about his redcurrants and the Ribena he makes, the policeman who chopped down a tree for him, and the old man who helps him with his bees. Mrs Clive was a member of my literature class at Welland and we have remained friends ever since. A remarkable old dear (Swiss by birth?) who will go anywhere and do anything without the least hesitation.

Macbeth at Ludlow
28 June 1961

A lovely, still midsummer evening. As the play begins the light of the sun climbs upwards over the battlements till it is gone, pulling the darkness after it. The swifts go screaming through the air, until at last the coming of darkness silences them. The light from the floods begins to strengthen and the castle masonry, the weeds, the flowers growing out of the crannies acquire a new beauty. An aeroplane goes past, its noise subdued by distance to a faint rumble. Its trail is left like a crayon mark on a darkening page. An owl hoots. Then I hear the sound of the river pouring over the weir, and the rumble of a train going up the valley to Shrewsbury. A lovely night, completely at variance with the passions and crimes of the play. But the words create their own dark world. The ghost of Banquo appears on the battlements. The soldiers swarm up long thin ladders and over the castle wall. The body of Young Siward is lifted high and flung from the battlements to land with a thump on the boards of the stage. It should not have landed there. If it had missed the stage we would not have seen the dust shaken out of the straw-filled dummy. The effect is so great an anti-climax that we cease for a moment to believe in the play.

Wide Load

A lull in the street. An easy midweek flow
along the pavement. It's the quiet time
between the sales and the fag end of winter.

No urgency. No haste. Almost an illusion
of a retreat in time—of space and safety
not often felt even in this slow city.
Then, from the north, the blurred and garbled voice
of the policeman in the black saloon.
'Pull in please. Pull into the side. Pull in.
Wide load approaching. Pull into the side.'
And we all stop and turn to see what follows –
a high cab, door held open, driver and mate,
aloof, bored, almost like maharajahs;
and then, behind, the fettered bulging monster,
the name of some far northern foundry stencilled
in yellow on its black and rusted sides,
a shameless statement posted on the back –
'This is the seventeenth load for'—somewhere or other.
Without apology, like a Hindu idol,
the trundling juggernaut, on sixteen wheels,
brushes the traffic sideways into the gutters,
sucks all the counter girls into the doorways,
rattles the plate glass windows in the shops,
and passes.

It leaves behind a wake of grumbles, protests,
incredulous stares, disturbance, indignation—
and yet—a sense of something less unwelcome,
something alien, odd but fascinating,
monstrous—but a highlight, and event.

June 1961

Summer

August 1961

During the course of a holiday together we went to Escomb, to the Gulbenkian Museum in Durham, Lanchester, Blanchland, Hexham, and home through Richmond and Malham. Later I went alone for my first visit to the Edinburgh Festival—a never-to-be-forgotten experience. I stayed with Mrs Tervitt, who looked after me well, and charged me 12/6 for bed, breakfast and tea and biscuits in the evening.

An embarrassing moment in Hexham market for Gillian and Erica
'Now what do you want, hinny? What do you want? Come on, speak up.'

'We don't want anything.'

'Ye dinna want anything.'

'We haven't any money.'

'Why, if ye hevvent any money here's a pea. There now, ye can alwes say ye had a pea in Hexham mairket.'

I don't think they saw the joke till they heard everyone around them laughing.

Last night, before going to bed, I went for a walk across the field. Low in the south the moon, uneven as a lemon, threw across the world its yellow light. The mid-sky above it was as blue as a beetle, dark and deep, and against its darkness the stars burnt and flickered. They were like the glinting fragments of some great explosion, the smithereens of a great detonation, jagged, spurred and white with heat. But no echo of that upheaval reached the autumnal earth. All was still and tranquil. The trees stood motionless, their shadows like discarded garments on the yellow grass. From time to time across the still air came the sound of a car changing gear as it pulled uphill, or a train entering a cutting, or a bird went overhead, heading through the silent air for the south and the sea, uttering an elegiac cry as it made its way over hedges and roofs, meadows and woods. But the air itself held its breath, like someone in a trance.

The last day of the year
We have been out (in appalling weather) to look at part of Joan Brierley's house, The Hermitage at Powick, but we shall not buy it. £3,750 is too much for a house that needs a great deal of doing up.

I am afraid I lost my temper in a shocking way yesterday. I was ashamed of myself, and have taken a vow never to behave like that again. I think we were both deeply disturbed by this outburst, and I could have wept with self-reproach. Poor Erica, with whom I had been working on Chaucer's *Prologue*, was still weeping when she went to bed. I can't restrain these dreadful fits of temper, though I hate myself for them. Thank God, we were quickly reconciled. If my children were to keep a diary I'd find in it a picture quite different from the one I give of myself.

1962

January 1962
Went to the National Union of Students' Drama Festival at Bristol in bitterly cold weather. I spent my free time going from store to store—thank God for Marks & Spencer, D H Evans etc.; and one of my favourite haunts was St Mary Redcliffe, where I went not for spiritual refreshment but warmth. It had a lovely stove and radiator—a godsend to vagrant and homeless drama-festival-goers. I saw *Draw the Fires* (not the best Toller), *Antigone* by C. Logue (a stupid play) *The Dumb Waiter* (good), *The Birthday Party* (which I dislike) and *The King* by Michel Ghelderode (good).

An odd comment
'You know my right foot has a totally different circulation system from the left foot. I don't know why it is but one is always cold before the other.'

The other day I saw a boy catch hold of the bottom of his jacket and lift it and his arms right over his head, so that it made a sail. He turned his back to the wind and let it blow him along the street, like a sailing boat.

Mr Browning's shop
Some time ago there was an old shop in Friar Street kept by a Mr Browning (his name is still to be found over the shop), who sold inexpensive antiques and second-hand furniture. He was an unmercenary dealer, content with modest profits and a quick turnover, and he spent most of his time in a cold little room, heated only by a stick fire (there was an almost inexhaustible supply of fuel in his backyard where he kept innumerable wash-hand stands, kitchen tables, chairs and old wardrobes in a fairly advanced state of decay). It was a squalid little room, but it had one distinction—a low plaster ceiling decorated with a pattern of strawberry leaves and fruits in rather dull colours. Mr Browning, who was given to repeating himself, told me many times that the pigment used for painting the ceiling was human blood. He said he had had it analysed, and the analyst had confirmed what he had been told. I saw no reason to disbelieve him, for though he may have been credulous, he was generally truthful. Mr Browning, alas, is dead now, and his shabby little room has been spruced up and turned into a sweet shop, but if you peer through the door or the window

of the shop, you can still see the strawberry pattern on the ceiling—one more of those obscure and little-known curiosities which make the city elusively intriguing.

Greyfriars

Almost opposite Mr Browning's old shop is the Greyfriars, the home of Mr and Miss Matley Moore. It is more than their home. It is a monument to their unusual sense of civic responsibility.

The story of the Greyfriars begins with the Grey Friars themselves, who came to Worcester in 1239, and settled just inside the eastern boundary of the city walls. They prospered, built a church and laid out a cemetery and then, towards the end of the fifteenth century, built the Greyfriars as a hostelry for travellers. Less than sixty years later, however, Henry VIII ordered the Dissolution of the Monasteries. Most of the monastic buildings belonging to the Friars were sold for building material, but the hostelry was only sixty years old and presumably in reasonable condition. It was let as a private residence, and from then on many different families lived there as tenants. Perhaps the most famous of those families was the Streets, whose coat of arms can still be seen carved on a wooden frieze in the main parlour.

The Streets lived in the house for a long time, but in the eighteenth century the house was split into tenements, and the land behind it built on. During the next century it went further and further downhill, and in 1930 the City Council scheduled it for demolition. It looked as if nothing could save the house, but it was bought by Major W. J. Thompson of Harborough Hall, and given by him to the Worcestershire Archaeological Society. For a few more years the fate of the house hung in the balance, but just after the Second World War Mr and Miss Matley Moore came to the rescue with a very generous offer. In return for the right to live in the house, they undertook to bear the whole cost of restoring and refurnishing it.

How brilliantly that work was carried out anyone can see, for the house is now in the care of the National Trust and is open to the public at certain times; and at all times visitors may advance through the high coach entrance and over the cobbles to the entrance to the beautiful garden which the Matley Moores have created. This was a long and expensive process, for it involved buying up the eighteenth and nineteenth century cottages at the back of the house, clearing them away and then designing the garden from scratch. The result is remarkable, a spacious English garden in the middle of a busy city, with an English lawn and English plants, from the early hellebores to the brilliantly autumn fruited crataegus, but with a secluded and enclosed and almost Andalusian appearance.

Wichenford

When Gwen and I were out walking today near Wichenford we heard something moving in a hedge bottom, and when I crossed the road I saw it was a pheasant that was trying to push its way through the chicken netting that had been put up on the other side of the quickset hedge. It had pushed its head through the mesh and was trying to force its whole body through. When I went over to it, it began to run backwards and forwards along the fence in a panic, but in the end it gave up and allowed me to pick it up. It was a beautiful creature, and very tame, making no attempt to peck me or to fly away, and showing no signs of terror. I held it for a few moments and then threw it into the air as I have seen men throwing pigeons. It did not fly away but came down and then ran off in a comical cowardly way, looking neither to right nor to left till it had got over the brow of the field.

I spent all January and some of February writing at great speed and with great pleasure a story entitled 'The Tower.' It was an unusual experience to be so continuously absorbed in a story. And I thought there were some good things in it. But it has never been published. Miss George of OUP didn't care for it and was so critical that I put it away and have never looked at it since.

The Middle-aged Poet

Leaving the car in the garage, walking again,
he sees the world he loved too long ago
come into focus. The tree trunks sidle past him,
the growing daffodils lift from the darkened grass,
the shadows of branches are veined on the road beneath him.
The smell of the world, the perfume of something loved,
neglected, then ignored, like a friend whose letters
he failed to answer, assails him with joy and guilt.
Ashamed of his dereliction, won again
by the undemanding charity of the moment,
he opens again the notebook of his heart,

and in letters of black, the strokes and stripes of his guilt,
he inks the words of his recaptured joy.

3 March 1962

Laurie Lee
28 March 1962
I met Laurie Lee in The Old Talbot yesterday.[2] He was wearing a kind of corduroy shirt, a pullover and an overcoat, as if he had a cold. He was pleased to see his friends and relations in the audience (one of the famous four *Cider with Rosie* uncles was there). When I came to the passage dealing with this uncle, he winked at him and drew his finger across his throat. He read a passage about his mother—expressively but not showily, and with a great sense of humour. But he read little and was reluctant to talk. He seemed truly shy, and determined not to show off. He spoke in private about Osborne, about a play he was writing for Peggy Ashcroft, about the difficulties of going back to Shepscombe where he has bought a house, and John Wain, whom he likes. But he dislikes coteries and cliques and does not like talking about his work. He enjoyed the programme we put on for him. I thought he was an unassuming and unspoilt fellow and took to him.

Motorbike Boys near Ludlow

In leather jackets, as slippery as seals,
these boys with crossbones stencilled on their shoulders
come roaring through the lanes,
making the world a happy, goggled blur,
and the April air as cold as outer space.
They brake for a moment by the country bridge,
but their legs are not made for walking any more.
This still picture of water and arch unnerves them.
They'd be more at home in a capsule twenty miles up,
strapped to a couch, in permanent radio touch
with a world that is blessedly invisible,
with day and night coming like shadows of clouds.
They kick on their starters, impatient for movement and noise,
strap on their helmets, white and hard as skulls,
and sprint away in search of catastrophe.

24 April 1962

A cynical remark at a college play
'If this is a morality play, I think I'd like to see an immorality play.'

Gillian's wedding
30 June 1962
The day began with a round of ordinary duties. Since Gwen, Gillian and Erica were all at the hairdresser's, I had to do the shopping. It was difficult to remember as I bought bread and marmalade that this was a wedding day. But by noon we were all assembled, even Mother and Father who had come over from Birmingham. We ate, neither heartily nor sparingly, and seemed in spite of all the auguries to have time and time to spare. Perhaps it was Gillian who set the tone. Gwen had a cold and was a little out of sorts, but Gillian was more than composed. She was serenely and continuously happy. Then the flowers arrived. Gwen took Mother and Father off to the church. Then after we had seen some friends go past, the taxi came for Erica, with the news that Colin and the best man were already in the church. Still time to spare! Gillian and I, left unnaturally alone, walked from room to room watching the clock.

At five to two, perfectly ready and apparently with no misgivings, we drove to St John's, past the friends and well-wishers who wanted to see us off. The church clock was striking two as in calm, but rather overcast weather, we walked up the path, pausing to let the photographers snap us, and again in the porch to hear the organist change to the tune that was to announce the bride's arrival. It was a good moment. I didn't expect to enjoy it, but I did. With measured pace we walked down the aisle, paused and waited for the vicar to begin. Was he wearing his famous eye-shadow? I didn't notice it. I was aware only of the solemnity of the church, the flowers, Colin looking steadily up into the chancel, the vast respectful congregation behind me, the fitness of everything. Gillian held my hand firmly and would not let it go. I tried at one moment to disengage it, but she held on.

'Who gives this woman in marriage?' asked the vicar.

'I do,' I replied, perhaps a little too loudly. Then I let go of Gillian's hand and stepped back.

I do not think I ever enjoyed a service so much. I even forgot my anxiety at having to make a speech later.

I was anxious because I did not want to let Gillian down by being indiscreet or vulgar or just inept. But all went well. I made one blunder, though I can't for the life of me remember what it was, and I heard Erica behind me laugh as I made it. But I believed in what I was saying and didn't say it too badly.

It was warm on the terrace overlooking the river. I could hear the shouts of the boys bathing just opposite, saw the Cathedral tower rising over the heads of the guests, heard noises from the King's School fête in the grounds next door. The world seemed full of happiness, congratulations, friendship.

It was a good wedding, and went without a hitch from beginning to end—except for Gwen's unfortunate cold, which took the gilt off the gingerbread for her.

Of the trials and vexations of the honeymoon that followed it is for Gillian, not me, to tell.

Edinburgh Festival
August 1962
Saw *The Doctor and the Devils*; an exhibition of Hartung and Soulanges; *Philoctetes*; *Paolo Paoli* (a very dull play by Adamov); the Tattoo; a Writers' Conference with L. Durrell (small and intelligent), N. Mailer (conceited and dislikable), Rosamund Lehmann (a defeated person who has given up writing fiction), Angus Wilson (impulsive, an impression of petulance, but charming), S. Spender (a very trenchant critic); Cambridge Footlights; John Whiting's *The Devils* (unforgettable); Ionesco's *The Killer* (completely forgettable).

Later saw a brilliant production of *The Comedy of Errors* at Stratford.

The night is immensely wide and still, with the sky like a great pacific ocean with soft clouds spread like archipelagos, and down the blue reaches of sky the stars dipping like the lonely mast-head lights of journeying craft, borne like some great and scattered fleet towards the milk-white isles. Beneath these moving lights and white hazy shores the earth itself, with its humped motionless trees and darkened lawns, looks humble, flat, prosaic.

29 September 1962
Tom Finnigan told an amusing anecdote about a naval officer who had an unusual way of dealing with the many shirkers and skrimshankers who came before him with heart-rending (and mostly fictitious) stories of family troubles.[3] His answer was to hand them a card on which was printed the following message—

> Your story has touched me to the heart. Please accept this as a token of my sincere sympathy.

But he very rarely granted the compassionate leave that was asked for.

November, 1962

Tonight I met John Braine, author of *Room at the Top* (which has made him famous and rich). I did not care for him much, finding him a rather coarse and mercenary fellow, in spite of his apparent modesty. 'I am really an insignificant person' he said, 'a kind of specialised organism, good for nothing except writing novels.'

Busy writing my own Worcester story and lecturing on the novel at Martley. And another story centred on Great Tew.

A moonlight night
December 1962

The night was perfectly still, with a moon scarfed round with lawn-like cloud, and the sky whitened on the horizon like water into which milk had been poured. The bare branches reached upwards against the still sky, like the antlers of a silent vigilant herd, and the stars glittered like the scales of fish. I stood on the edge of the field and looked wonderingly upward, my eyes drawn upwards like the reaching branches of the trees.

Winter Plate

No raging wind tonight,
no hunted moon
fleeing from cover to cover.
Unmoving, luminous, still,
the sky is overspread
with a thin film of cloud,
like an X-ray negative
thrown on a wide screen
in a dark and silent room,
patterned with light and dark
of bone and muscle and flesh;
and the hard round moon

bedded there like a telltale bullet
with a faint discoloured ring
to show where it entered and lodged.

A severe winter—1962-3

It began with a bitterly cold but bright day. Then on Boxing Day it began to snow. It melted a little and grew slushy, but by New Year's Day it had frozen hard. I went sledging on the Old Hills with Gillian and Colin. After that, a variety of abominable weather—snow, sleet, frosts more or less intense, two days of high bitterly cold winds and another snowfall. Power cuts. Frozen water pipes. One college boiler burst. Wholesale cancellation of meetings, concerts etc.. I have just called off a lecture to the Literary Society by Michael Innes. It is a strange coincidence that the first year of Gillian's married life should be as disastrous as that dreadful first winter of our marriage. One notable difference—in the winter of 1939-40 I skated almost every day. This winter I have not been once on the ice.

1963

A case for charity

I was kneeling, not praying but giving the impression that I was praying, pretending that I had come into the church with a pious purpose. My real aim had been to take a rest. I used to be a tireless walker, although now that I remember, the streets of London always fatigued me. I could walk all day if need be over the moors, but when I was a student, the hard unsympathetic pavements of London made even my young legs ache. St Martin-in-the-Fields was a welcome resting place. I sat for a few moments, then knelt. Kneeling rarely moves me to prayer—there is an obstinacy in my nature that prevents me from abasing myself in supplication—but it somehow liberates me, and gives a freer rein to my worldly thoughts.

As I knelt, I saw, out of the corner of my eye—an old woman going furtively up and down the pews on the opposite side of the aisle, and I think my first confused impression was that she was a pew-opener. But I told myself immediately that this was ridiculous. There are no pew-openers now. Pew-openers belong to Dickens and Mayhew. I must have been more sleepy than I thought, for when I am bemused and drowsy I often move into the world of books. I refocused my thoughts and looked at her more closely, and saw that she was searching for something, looking under the seats and turning back the thin carpeting that had been laid down to soften the hardness of the benches. She was very old and feeble, ready to trip over any little obstacle, hardly capable of mounting and descending from the one small step from the church floor to the pew. The peculiarly charitable atmosphere of the church, the famed refuge for the old and dispossessed and homeless, made me feel vaguely benevolent.

My benevolence was vague, because, even as I watched her, I remembered how gullible I had been when I first came from the north to live in London. I was then the complete gull, ready to be taken in by anyone. I remember once, in those days, being approached by a man who must have observed me staring in my too-obviously-provincial way at everything around me. He asked me where I had come from and told me that he too was an exile from my native land, and was trying to make his way back there where a job was waiting for him in the Consett Iron Works. He spun such a plausible tale, and his apparent anxiety to return to Consett so chimed with my own homesickness that I gave him a florin. I was pleased to be able to help him, but the first friend to whom I mentioned my charitable deed laughed in my face and warned me never to be taken in so easily a second time. Experiences such as that have hardened me, and now, when I think I am about to be touched by some mendicant, I stiffen and think I must be on my guard.

So I was relieved when the old woman seemed to find what she was looking for. I was ready to rejoice with her, especially since it now looked as if she was no longer in need of help.

'Have you found what you are looking for?' I asked.

'Yes, I found it.'

'What was it?'

'It was my purse. But it isn't all here. Oh dear!'

'What isn't?'

'My money. I've lost a ten shilling note.'

This was enough to dispel my concern for her. I saw her revealed, not as a feeble and genuinely unfortunate old woman, but as one more cunning beggar who had found a unique way to appeal to me. But as she stood there holding out her old purse, it seemed that she was directing against me, not an appeal, but an accusation. Could it be that she was implying that I had taken the ten shilling note?

I found the suggestion extraordinarily disconcerting. I am often mean, but I am not a thief. I can be astonishingly suspicious and vindictive, but some moral sense—perhaps a kind of cowardice rather than a form of honesty—has always prevented me from stealing. I was so disturbed by the implied accusation that I felt that I must somehow make good the loss.

But before I could collect myself the old woman spoke again.

'Oh I've had a bad week,' she said—and surely there were in her voice the genuine accents of unhappiness. 'Look what I did yesterday!'

She put forward her left arm, and I could see that it was in plaster.

'I fell down yesterday. I broke my arm. And now I've lost a ten shilling note. Oh dear!'

Now my composure was completely shaken. This could not be a lie. However devious you are, you cannot put your own arm in plaster; and even if you got someone to do it for you, would it be worthwhile, just for the sake of cadging a few shillings from sympathetic strangers? And if this was not a lie, maybe her loss too was genuine. Maybe some mean person had really stolen her ten shilling note.

And how much that loss must be to her! The loss of ten shillings would not be much to me, but even I would be a little upset. How much more would it mean to her—this shabby and needy old pensioner. The church, the gratitude I felt for the rest and shelter I had enjoyed there, her obvious need—all conspired to urge me to be generous.

But suddenly the memory of the man from Consett returned. I hesitated. My fear of being duped returned; and while I paused the old woman turned away. Perhaps it was a fear that by an act of restitution I might almost admit myself guilty of an act that I had not committed that made me let her go.

I ought not to have done so. I missed an opportunity to be kind, and do not easily put out of my mind the sight of the old woman with her empty purse and arm in plaster.

April 1963

Today I met a woman who talked like this:

'Oh but I don't think—you see—sixteen to eighteen is, isn't it?—and if there is one time in a girl's—well it is, isn't it?—that's when they need, don't they—so I think that even if a teacher—it isn't much good without help, is it—especially when—because this is just the period in everybody's—it's really too much to go on like that, without any consideration at all—not that I don't believe in training—I do—but if they can't at school, where can they? No I can't say that I agree at all—to my way of thinking—that isn't the way of going on at all.'

Today *A Severnside Story* was published and I saw *The City Madam* by Philip Massinger, revived by the Birmingham Rep. It is worth reviving.

Potholing
27 July 1963

We were lured into going on this expedition by an assurance from the student who was our guide and mentor that the cave we were to explore, which had a name sounding something like Fun and Thee (Ogof Ffynnon Ddu), was no more than a 'walk-in' cave, and no serious exertion on anybody's part would be called for. Unfortunately the official guide for Fun and Thee was not available, so we were switched to another cave, which we were assured, was just as suitable for beginners. But to my horror, I found that this cave had to be entered by descending an incredibly narrow pipe. You had to use a tricky steel ladder to get down it, and there was a vicious double bend in the pipe about half way down that called for the skill of a very practised contortionist. While I was stuck, in complete blackness, feeling for the rungs of the ladder with trembling legs, I had the feeling that I would hang there, utterly immobile, until my muscles would give way and send me plummeting down heaven only knows how far.

Eventually I managed to reach the bottom of the pipe, and had time to look round and get my bearings. Those of us who had already made the descent were gathered in a dirty cave, totally devoid of any interest, with not a stalactite or stalagmite in view. I spent most of the time speculating glumly on what the next move would be. There were two exits—one reasonably wide and inviting, as big as the opening into a big cupboard, the other a mean narrow gap in a corner, like an enlarged rathole. Clearly we were to move on through the larger exit—but to my horror, when the last man had dropped out of that dreadful fissure, our guide began to squeeze himself through the mean wet rathole in the dirty corner of the cave and instructed us to follow him. I hated the progress through that hole, scraping my chest across the sharp flints, seeing nothing but the boots of the man in front of me and finding the strain on my shoulders almost intolerable.

Once finished with that painful and humiliating crawl, we encountered a short chimney, and then entered upon what our guide called the 'sand crawl'—an appallingly narrow winding passage, where it was too low to go on hands and knees and the only way to make progress was to dig one's elbows in the sand and work one's way along like a seal, dragging itself by its flippers. It was hot, it was exhausting, it was pointless, and it seemed endless. But rescue was at hand. To my great delight, a very fat young man who was ahead of me, suddenly called out that he was stuck. The only thing for him to do was to unwedge himself, turn around and retreat. Joyfully I called out that I would go back with him and, more joyfully still, heard a few more voices calling out in the darkness, saying that they too had had enough. So the retreat began. It was arduous enough—sand crawl, chimney, rat crawl, and then the fearful acrobatic climb up that vertical exit. But at last we were out—in the open air, in the sunshine, on terra firma. I could have bent down and kissed the earth we stood on, so relieved was I to escape from the horrid underworld.

This was my first and last potholing adventure.

Madresfield Show
5 August 1963
What did I see at the show today? Lovely trees, a Victorian mansion, lawns, ponds, a moat, a Victorian dovecote, dogs in the show ring, jazzmen on the bandstand, people with infuriating portable radios, listening to one stream of music from the bandstand and another from their transistors (the announcer pleaded with them to turn down their radios so that he could make himself heard), beautiful roses, obedient dogs, people watering their pets from polythene buckets carried in their cars, huge cows, even huger bulls. The air was heavy with heat and fragrance from the trees, and the smell of trodden grass in the marquees.

Inga from Sweden
17 August 1963
Inga is blonde, alarmingly egotistic, and very critical of England, which she finds dirty and old-fashioned.[4] 'Maybe in ten years you will catch up with us,' she says condescendingly. I have never thought of England as being inferior to a potty little country such as Sweden, but she may be more right than I give her credit for. She is a disagreeable girl, who smokes incessantly, helps herself

to everything in the house (fruit, matches, cosmetics) and spends lavishly on herself—on records, clothes, nail varnish etc.. She is mawkish, sexy and as dull as ditchwater until some young man comes on the scene, content to spend her days lolling in idleness, and totally devoid of any desire to explore or learn. She is a frightening phenomenon, promiscuous, voluptuous, spoilt, with an alarming rapacity of temperament. Yet we must learn how to deal with creatures such as Eva, for I feel she is a real portent.

Edinburgh Festival
August 1963
Today we went for the first time to the Traverse Theatre which is housed in a tenement near Gladstone's Land. You enter the theatre by a narrow spiral staircase, and find yourself in a tiny auditorium, with totally black walls, thirty raked seats on one side and about thirty more on the other, and in between a very small acting area. In this pocket-handkerchief theatre miracles are performed. We saw two memorable productions—*Ubu Roi* by A. Jarry, and *Comedy, Satire, Irony and Deeper Meaning* by Christian Dietrich Grabbe, an astonishing play to come out of 1822 Germany. Grabbe struck me as being the German equivalent of Thomas Love Peacock, and his play is witty, sensitive, inventive and dramatically effective.

In this festival we saw Ibsen's *Little Eyolf*, Shaw's *St Joan*, which impressed me enormously (far superior to Osborne's *Luther*), Walser's *The Rabbit Race* (to me a failure), Miller's *A View from the Bridge*, and Strindberg's *The Father.*

Of the poets whom I heard in Edinburgh, I thought George Macbeth a remarkable mixture of cleverness and silliness (his 'fin du globe' game is pretentious and inept); Norman MacCaig a true poet, balanced, humorous, homely and sincere; Peter Porter, a tough Australian, a formidable answerer of questions but not a poet I thrill to; Martin Bell and George Wightman relatively unimportant.

I heard Levin running down Brecht, Arden defending him, and Adamov making an eloquent plea for the later plays of Sean O'Casey (in vain, I fear); Wesker avowing his socialistic principles; Shaffer behaving in a civilised and sensible way, unlike the mercenary and small minded Mankowicz. Kopit, the American dramatist, sounded an ass. I wonder how many of these prominent figures will survive?

In the last few weeks have seen: *Sergeant Musgrave's Dance*, *The Fire Raisers*,

The Recruiting Officer, and *The Wings of a Dove.*

Border Landscape

The field-grey clouds retreat across the frontier,
ragged, disorderly, loosing random salvoes
of sharp metallic rain to cover their flight.
In the short intervals of their withdrawing
a random and transfiguring sunshine falls
on the soaked feathery grass,
the ebony cattle in the shining rushes,
the glossy wings of the crows, the brilliant burns
splintering over the boulders in the clefts of the hags
and the gaunt acres of moorland, stained
with the memories of battles.

A talkative guide at Ripon
Late August 1963

One day the Dean said to me, 'Somebody smoking here.'

There's nobody smoakin' in this place, I said.

'But I can smell it, verger.'

You may be able to smell it, but it iddn't here. And I know it iddn' here 'cos I've looked ivverywheer in the place.

But we traced it in the end. A feller had lit up at the bottom of the stairs just before he went up the tower.

'You'd better go up and stop him,' said the Dean.

I'm not stoppin him, I said. I didn' want to go climbing up all them stairs just for that.

There's nowt against a chap smoking up there in the fresh air if he wants to. If you want him chasing, chase him herself. Your legs are a sight better 'n mine. And so they were.

Landscape of the Civil War

On the green leafy awning of the lane
the rain peppers with the sound of musketry.

Fireweed slopes in the lane like blooded pikes
of ambushed militia whose wounds have bled
on the wild arum berries in the nettles,
and I see, beyond the screens of wet foliage,
the puffs of cloud, the smoke of salvoes fired
from invisible cannon, ranged and embattled there
under the black wall of the thundering sky.

17 August 1963

Growing Old

Now that I am growing old, I often feel
like someone at the end of a bad summer,
wondering why the sun failed so often to shine,
why all the journeys, planned and looked forward to,
never took place,
why so much time was spent looking out of the window,
with the beaches empty, the rivers high and cold,
the moors misty and sodden;
why so much time was ticked away by the clock,
and why the flowers in the garden were always weeping.

But even as I write, I look up and see
Beyond the orchard. where the leaves are falling,
The autumn night unclouded, and hung with stars.

Autumn Poem

The morning mists, like ghosts, dissolve and thin.
Stiff with rigor of the midnight frost,
the threadbare trees, slanting their bony wrists
towards the pale disc of the autumn sun,
prepare to suffer one more day of parting.
The icy links, the last cement to hold
the yellow foliage on the wrinkled twigs,

melt in the warmth. The curling leaves
gather, slip from the boughs, and fall like tears.
Somewhere before the dawn their summons came.
Waking in darkness, I too felt the touch
of valedictory frost upon my face.

October 1963

The boy from Woolwich

Mr S, an HMI, who came out with me on school practice, told me a remarkable story of a London boy whom, on the prompting of his son, he had befriended. The family gave up more than half of their own holiday to befriend and entertain this thin undernourished twelve year-old from Woolwich. Although he was twelve he was no bigger than an average eight year old. He had no notion where he was, even where London was (he had never been out of Woolwich in his life), was astonished that anyone could be expected to take a bath every night, didn't at all like the idea of having a room to himself, let alone sleep by himself. He wouldn't drink milk until it was disguised as a 'shake', was disconcerted at having no streets to roam around late at night, and thought Mrs S's home-made fish and chips very inferior to those you bought from the shop in Woolwich. The family fattened him up, took him to the zoo, found that he was not totally illiterate and encouraged him to read, discovered that he had a real fondness for wild flowers which he loved to collect and press. They found him exhausting, but they grew fond of him, and he became attached to his new home. At the end of the fortnight he didn't want to go back to Woolwich. 'Can I come back here?' he kept saying. Mr S said he could not help wondering whether, under the guise of helping him, he had merely unsettled him.

What extraordinarily good people these S's are! I can never get within a hundred miles of selflessness such as this.

I wrote up this episode in a longish short story called 'Poor Tony'. It has never been published. I have never even tried to publish it.

1964

15 April 1964
Gwen was talking to me tonight about the death of her brother, who was killed in the mine—or rather I was asking her about the event, because she would never willingly revert to it. I stopped when I saw she was on the verge of tears.

15 May 1964
A wonderful May evening, with a new moon, a thin paring of silver in a clear sky, and close to it, sparkling (as Gerard Manley Hopkins said) like a silver rowel, the planet Venus. All around, the glorious trees in their Maytime greenery, with not a brown leaf in sight, their green cloudiness fringed at the foot with stitchwort, cowslip, bugle. There were four nightingales singing together in the thicket, and two cuckoos, one near and loud, the other replying from the distance like a muted echo. The air was still but not warm, almost with a threat of frost before the coming of morning.

Whitsuntide

Two things happened this Whitsuntide.
You may not believe the first, but it is true.
I could name the place, and tell the cause
for which the village
organised teas on the lawn, sold pottery,
fabrics and vegetables in the village hall,
saw that the gardens of the local squire
were open to visitors, the church tower accessible.
I could describe the lilac, the laburnum,
the rhododendrons, the fields of buttercups,
the teacher behind the cake stall,
and the wealthy man whose house and lawns
were ours for the price of a florin to the cause.

Most would smile,
and think this rural idyll came from the pages
of a phoney brochure from a dubious travel agent.
They'd be more ready to credit the second picture
of lawless youngsters fighting on the beaches,
driving the children from the sands before
a shower of bottles and stones,
their pockets full of missiles and easy money,
greedy for blood, disgrace and punishment.

Whit Tuesday 1964

An adventurous young man
1 June 1964
S, who is a member of my extramural class at Martley, is clearly not unintelligent, though he has contributed little to our discussions. If he has developed it is in a curious way—he has grown more and more grimy week by week. But apparently his father, for whom he works, is a silversmith, and it is the buffing compound that gives silversmiths their dirty hands and grimy complexions.

We had hints before the class ended that S was preparing for an unusual adventure. He was planning to see the great statues of Abu Simbel before they were flooded. And he did what he planned. He set off, with £100 which he had saved, to get as far as he could. And since then he has been not only to Lower Egypt, but to Japan—hitchhiking all the way.

Surely he must go down in the list of extraordinary characters whom Gwen and I have met in extramural classes—dear old Mrs Clive, Mrs Mortimer and her Corgi (motorbike not dog), old Miss Matthewman and her Barbadoes sugar, Miss Docker, Mr Mainprice, David and his famous tea service that belonged to Thomas Hardy's first wife, Mrs Cammie the friend of P. H. Newby, and her husband who used to cut Shaw's hair.

1967

Aidan
(at one and a half)

Little tottering man, with a gait like Chaplin's,
lurching to dangerous edges, one foot in the air,
of steps, of pavements, of little concrete ramps,
he takes a dozen knocks in a single morning
from table tops, chair arms, the frames of doorways,
falling into ruts as enormous as craters,
tripping at pebbles, swarming up flights of stairs
as huge and steep to him as the Eiger face.
His world is a world of switches, furniture
on castors, knobs on cupboards and wireless sets.
He starts at the crow of a cock as at a fanfare,
and a Jersey cow looms big as a dinosaur.
His achievements are
naming his nose, his hands, his eyes, his mouth
and huge jumps from a hearth two inches high.

24 March 1967

1969

Christmas Day

Mild sunny weather, very still and spring-like. The countryside brown and green and golden in the unclouded light. A countryside of small fields, and plentiful hedges and woodland. No signs yet of anyone grubbing up hedges to make larger fields. The country roads narrow and unfrequented. Nothing has passed me but cars taking people to morning service at Wichenford church, and one big milk transporter going to Colkitts Farm. No cyclists. No other walkers. Bullfinches loping along the hedgerows, wood pigeons making a clatter as they go up from the fields or break out of the trees. Sparrows, robins, wrens, plovers. A hunter fires a shot or two, and dogs bark from faraway farms. Partridges skim the ploughed fields, and a pheasant or two get up and make for the woods with that strange throbbing note they make, like water gurgling out of the neck of a bottle.

The bell of Wichenford church has a flat sound, as if the bell was a poor one, made of inferior metal. Some new houses have gone up in the village (if so untidy a straggle can be called a village), but all the farms are old. There is no such thing in this countryside as a modern farmhouse. The big open haybarns give off a lovely familiar smell; and the weather is so mild that there are roses out in some of the gardens. There has been some rain and the brooks are full, running fast along the ditches and gurgling down the drains. The mistletoe gleams green on the orchard trees, and the ragged nests of the rooks are visible in the tops of the trees. A beautiful fairy-tale countryside, unspoilt, quiet, with russet leaves still on the oaks, and the outermost twigs of elms and limes and ash reddening and purpling a little already.

Notes

1 The Worcester book was later published as *A Severnside Story*, 1964.

2 Laurie Lee (1914-97) was an English poet, novelist and screenwriter who was brought up in the village of Slad, Gloucestershire. He is known for his books *Cider With Rosie* (1959) and *As I Walked Out One Midsummer Morning* (1969).

3 Tom Finnigan was College Bursar.

4 Inga is a pseudonym

Chapter 4: 1970-73

1970

24 July 1970
Gwen's birthday. We went to the Swan Theatre and heard my poem 'Cricket at Worcester' set to music—and very nicely too.[1]

Cricket at Worcester

The afternoon is warm and languorous.
The fingers of the clock are nearing three.
The lulled spectator under the pavilion
Settles his cushions, yawns and longs for tea.

Muted applause greets yet another maiden.
Towards the hour the minute fingers creep.
His eyelids flutter down; he tilts his trilby
Forward upon his nose, and falls asleep.

A burst of clapping wakes him. What has happened?
Kenyon has reached, at last, his century;
And the cathedral bells, in acclamation,
Break out in loud and unreligious glee.

To waking eyes the lovely view assembles—
Pavilion, sunshine, wicket, bats and bails.
The scoreboard flickers as the scoring quickens.
The leather smacks against the boundary rails;

And, over all, there rises the cathedral,
Jubilant, eulogistic and serene,
Adorning and approving with its music
The famous, fabulous, familiar scene.

My notebook for this year is filled with passages from my new book *Young Tom Sawbones*, and plans for a one-man show—'The Diary of Francis Kilvert'.[2]

[*Editors*: Fred's children's books were all originally handwritten into his diaries, especially in his most successful years 1960-72, and to a lesser extent after his retirement in 1972, when two more books were published in 1976 and 1978. In some years the record in his diaries was necessarily curtailed to make more space for his creative writing. After *The Bonny Pit Laddie* in 1960 virtually all his books were published by Oxford University Press.]

August 1970
I have just returned from a Conference on Children's Literature in Exeter. I was deeply impressed by Russell Hoban (a man of some profundity) and Patrick Dickinson, a quixotic, brilliant man; but many of the others, Leon Garfield, Edward Blishen, Helen Cresswell and others, are far too complacent and conceited for my liking.

Night Poem

Late, listening, listening late, waiting and listening,
light in a pool, from the lamp on my desk,
the fingers in light, the pen, the hands, the wrists,
the elbows in shade, the shoulders,
the brow in darkness. Sit in the pool of,
watch the fall of, listen to the revving
of cars that say,
I am coming, I am here, I am passing, I
go off into the darkness, the stillness,
like images that swim, come upward,
surface, break surface with bubbles and rings
and ripples, and
sink, dwindle, still themselves. We come,
we approach, we announce ourselves, name us,
quick, quick, give us a name, find a word
before we...
silence, dimness, loss, departing, gone.

30 October 1970

Lucky Man

Every day
I wake in expectation of good fortune –
the morning's letters will bring a wonderful offer,
those indeterminate stirrings in my mind
will form themselves by nightfall into a poem
everyone will acclaim.
I dream of great discoveries -
beautiful lonely landscapes found by me,
neglected mansions going for a song,
honours, privileges, maybe wealth.

Of course, I never find those bargain houses.
Those landscapes of delight are on no map.
Scribblings are all my yearnings turn into.
Follow me on the pools and you'll go down.
Nothing is real but my expectations.

I am a very lucky man.

16 November 1970

26 November 1970
The other day John Preston, who used to keep a shop in Oxford and from whom I have bought many a fine piece of pottery, inexplicably shot his wife and two children, set fire to his cottage at Callow End, and then shot himself. A fearful and incomprehensible crime. Gwen and I went to the funeral at Powick—a quadruple funeral and a cold, callous ceremony if ever there was one.

1971

This is Your Life

I meant to, and didn't.
I promised, forgot.
I sought and rejected,
ran cold, ran hot.

It was love, it was hate,
it was hope and despair.
It took shape and vanished,
was dark and then clear.

I rejoiced, I regretted.
I reached, I fell short.
I thought I was free
but felt I was caught.

I pushed on, full of yearning,
sat back and lay low.
This my day, this my life.
No, yes, yes, no.

2 January 1971

A strange scene
3 February 1971
Tonight I went to a concert of poetry and jazz in the JCR. A few chairs had been set out, but most of the floor was covered in mattresses and squabs taken from chairs and settees. The jazz 'combo' had a low little dais in the corner. The room was half full of pale, nice-looking girls, attractive but a little sad, and rough boorish young men, long-haired, bearded, in cheap jeans and dirty crumpled blouson jackets—a dirty unhandsome crowd. The student in charge said a few words before the music began.

'We're all ready now for the most disorganised event of the week. So just sit around and make yourselves at home. Smoke. Drink. Copulate if you like—nobody will take any notice. So off we go with the New Orleans Jazz Group, the finest jazz group in the West of England. So here we go, folks!'

I don't know how the evening finished. I came away, a bit stunned by the overloud music, a bit sick of the sloppy poetry, deeply anxious about the pale submissive girls and the dirty oafish men with their salacious looks, their vacant libidinous faces, a band of ugly satyrs working themselves up to some sordid orgy.

These young people are almost beyond my comprehension now. What an innocent crowd we were in the early days of the college, putting on our best suits to dance 'La Rinka' and 'The Gay Gordons'. The students and I have drifted apart, and I am too old to be in charge of them now. I do not mean to stay in college much longer.

Students

I watch them in lectures and in seminars,
young men in threadbare jeans and flimsy plimsolls,
with serious bearded apostolic faces,
and girls forever parting the casual hair
that falls in sad disorder over their eyes.
They seem to sit like captives, their brightness blurred
by the exhaustion of their lovers' quarrels,
by love's fulfilment, or by midnight frenzies,
stunned by the pandemonium of their music,
tormented by the penance of their living.
Anxious to help, but helpless, I sit among them,
but mine's the language now of meaningless fervour,
my private happiness a flippancy,
and my pedantic discipline a tiresome
played-out recipe nobody believes in.

Perrycroft
20 February 1971

This land is inexhaustible. Today I found Voysey's great house, Perrycroft, which he built in 1894 on the west side of the Malverns. As soon as I saw it I had an upsurge of exaltation and delight—a long low white house with a majestic view over the British Camp and the Herefordshire countryside beyond, and finely designed rooms enriched with Voysey ornament. Isn't it strange? I have often dreamt of such a house, and there it was. Alas it has been bought by some organisation which is busy making tasteless alterations. I shall never possess it, but I envy it.

Paul Scofield
17 April 1971
Today I had the great pleasure of seeing Paul Scofield in *The Captain of Köpenick*, an amusing but serious play about the devotion of the Germans to people in authority, especially if they are in uniform. In a way the uniform that the 'captain' borrows, and which he wears when he makes his daring swoop on the bank, is the hero of this play. I have been watching Scofield now for fifteen years—I first saw him as Don Armado in Brook's famous Stratford production of *Love's Labour's Lost*, and now look upon him as one of the best actors of our time.

During the same brief stay in London I also saw the film *Death in Venice*. I found it a moving experience.

Sister Meinrad
23 April 1971
This month we made the acquaintance of Sister Meinrad of Stanbrook Abbey, Callow End, a gifted artist whose work I first saw in London. This remarkable woman, a trained artist, who has lived in America (she is an American citizen) has voluntarily chosen to live in this enclosed order and dedicate herself and her talents to the service of Christianity. We had to converse with her through a grille. I was ashamed that I had lived so long within a few miles of the Abbey and had never heard of her work.

Stanbrook is a silent remote building, not beautiful, but with a Victorian stillness about it, with a façade of red and beige brick, a striped building that reminds one of Sienna Cathedral, adorned with rather lifeless carvings of heads of saints and kings cut in stone. It was silent but not unwelcoming. Although we had to speak through that barbarous mediaeval grille, and it was in many ways like visiting a prisoner, there was no sadness in that visit.

Sister Meinrad was delighted to know that the great world from which she was for ever cut off was finding pleasure and edification in her prints. It was her desire to present the word of God in a way acceptable to present-day families who might want to beautify their walls with them. Hers is a deeply and genuinely spiritual nature, though she is capable of an outburst of worldly rage against the slower moving 'externs'—the sisters whose job it is to mind the door and look after the abbey shop.

Later we went to see Dame Hildelith, who told us the story of her association with Siegfried Sassoon, who had been converted to Catholicism late in life and entrusted her with the task of printing his last poems. It was with the publication of these last poems that the Stanbrook Abbey Press had made its name. Sassoon's family did not like his becoming a Catholic and did their best to keep his conversion a secret.

I went inside the church at Ombersley to have one more look at that good Victorian interior, and surprised a tramp who had clearly been taking a nap on one of the benches. He rolled off the bench, fell on his knees and grabbed a prayer book. 'I was just havin' a bit of a read, guv'nor,' he said. I walked on, looking round the church, and he slipped out.

Dr Somer, of Porter's Mill, told me the other night how, when he was a young man, he used to ride into Worcester on his pony, leave it in The Butts, perhaps at the stables and kennels there, and go to the cinema in the Arcade, near St Swithun's, and then ride home again. He used to drive to cricket matches at Ombersley and Hallow in a pony-trap. Later he acquired a little Morgan. It had no doors. You simply stepped into it over a kind of sill.

May Day in Hallow
1 May 1971
Today I went to see the children of Hallow keeping May Day in their traditional style. It was Saturday and fine and warm. A local farmer had cleared a space on the green and provided a cart for the throne. The tractor that stood by it ought to have been incongruous but it wasn't. It was a telling symbol of the coexistence of the old and the new. Some of the dancing was done by Morris Men, practised veterans of the art of folk-dancing, a bucolic crew with gartered trousers, fluttering handkerchiefs and straw hats with bands of flowers, going through their galumphing paces.

The children, accompanied by their teachers, the parson and the parson's wife, were pretty and unselfconscious. But what really caught my eye was the May Queen, with her rather elaborate crown made of auriculas and primroses, her attendants and a little boy in a dark velvet suit and a wig, holding a branch of greenery. Around them crowded mothers with prams, a man with a yappy dachshund, the women with their voguish hairdos and the men with their twentieth-century equipment, movie cameras and tape recorders—and in the middle of everything that little boy with his green wand.

With his velvet suit, knee breeches, white stockings and incongruous white wig—looking like a travesty of Bubbles, a comical village Little Lord Fauntleroy, holding upright a green shoot wrapped in silver paper—he could not know that he was the unconscious descendant of those village lads and maids that, ages ago, woke early on this May morning, and went foraging and rollicking and making love in the woods that grew more thickly then around the village than they do now.

I forgot the cars parked on the verges, the whirring cameras, the mums in their bleached hairdos, and looked only at that incredible link with the past and the branches of living foliage heaped on the green, as they had been heaped there century after century, the living emblem of the never-defeated summer.

11 May 1971

Have just returned from giving a talk to the Library Association at Liverpool. In the last few years I have spoken about my own writing to audiences in Bath, Barnsley, Madeley, Birmingham, York, Worcester, Cheltenham, Stourbridge.

A strange scene in Birmingham

1 June 1971

In the middle of Birmingham, in a green space with the benches filled with tired shoppers and young men and women stretched out sleeping and sunbathing on the grass, a woman is preaching—an elderly white woman, with white hair, pallid skin and fanatical eyes—preaching to the tired shoppers, the old people taking a rest, the tramp-like figures with heavy ragged clothes, smoking fag ends and swigging from beer bottles. 'Herod was a bad man. A violent man. He was the one who gave orders that the children should be slain. And the blood! And the crying of the children!' By her a West Indian man, in an incongruous hat of shining black straw. When she had finished they began to sing together

Yes, Jesus loves me,
Yes, Jesus loves me...
The Bible tells me so.

Verse after verse. Then dourly he began his sermon—as rambling and meaningless as hers. And when he had finished they began on one more song—she ecstatically in a high excited voice, he in a dull bass second.

Old Teacher

Her voice is thin,
and her right hand shakes.
She remembers what happened
decades ago,
but cannot recall yesterday.
She says, 'Stand up, John,'
and sees his father
rising from his desk.

19 June 1971

A Wet Night

The trees were drenched in rain.
Walking in the dark, I kept blundering
into the drooping branches.
The raindrops fell on me in showers,
drenching me,
and the trees shook with laughter
at the joke they were playing on me.

20 June 1971

Mildenham Mill
3 August 1971
Not far from the city, very close in fact to the motorway link, is a house that is a remarkable survival even in a county such as ours. It is a mill, a delightful brick building on the Salwarpe, about a mile below Porter's Mill, with a millrace, and machinery that will still work; and it is still lived in by the miller, old Mr X and his

wife. The mill is not easy to find. It is not signposted and it is easy to miss it, but once you've found it you are sure of a kind welcome. For Mr X and his wife love their mill, and think only of the day when it will be in full working order again.

Mr X's father owned the mill. Unfortunately it ceased to be a paying proposition some years ago, and Mr X was compelled to close it, but he has been working ever since then, with no outside help and no labour but his own, to put it back in working order.

'There was a big mill pond here,' he said, 'and we could swim there under them weeping ashes. But it's all silted up. Once the mill stops working everything goes wrong. The millpond has all filled in, see. And there was two wheels working here once. But I ent got the second one working yet. I'll set this one working for you.'

He turned on the wheel. The clear water from the Salwarpe began to flow down the race and the great wheel turned.

'There's plenty power here,' he said. 'I get up to ten horsepower out of this. And it don't make much noise. Come up the stairs and you'll see the machinery working.'

We went upstairs and he showed me how you could shake the grains of pink corn gently into the grindstone and see the flour swept out through a little hole into the bin below.

He showed me the vast array of fittings and tools that a miller needed to understand, and know how to use. He told me about the skill needed to shape the millstones and score them and fit them together with a thin layer of plaster of Paris. He said he loved to show people round his mill, and he did it for love. It had never entered his head to charge anyone for looking round the mill, although all the work of restoration was being done at his own expense.

I was impressed by him, and his wife who insisted on our going into her parlour and looking through her album of mill photographs. There is a serenity and a courtesy about both these old people which I find very touching.

Roger Alma was so impressed by the mill that he recorded a conversation he had with the miller, and wrote a fine little poem about a former millhand who had carved his initials on a millstone, which I printed for him on my printing press.[3]

6 August 1971

Heard Professor Pevsner lecturing on the accuracy of the eighteenth- and early nineteenth-century classical architects, who knew exactly what they were doing, and the lack of precise knowledge on the part of the early Gothicists, until the arrival on the scene of Pugin and Barry.

10 August 1971
The Sealed Knot staged the Battle of Worcester today in the grounds of Croome Court. I gatecrashed and watched part of the battle from the top of the church tower. Standing there I was aware of a strange noise—the loud brushing noise of the feet of people walking across a stubble field towards the scene of the battle. The noise reached me with astonishing clarity.

London via Oxford
19 August 1971
A strenuous day. Got up at 6 am and left for Oxford by car at 7. Caught the 8.54 am for Paddington, visited several galleries, and saw two plays (*Enemies* by Gorki, which I liked, and *Danton's Death* by Büchner which I did not); caught the 11.15 pm from Paddington to Oxford. Got to Oxford at 1 am (a maddeningly slow journey), drove from Oxford in a thunderstorm and got home at 2.30 am.

At this time of the year I sigh and swelter in the humid Worcester heat. I look up at the sky and see it covered with clouds as grey and dull as old blankets. Nothing stirs or moves, and as the morning moves into the afternoon the heat grows more and more oppressive. The rooms in the house are airless, and even when the windows are thrown open, I cannot breathe and feel a great listlessness overwhelm me. I long for July to pass and for August to be over, waiting almost unendurably for the first crisp mornings of the autumn to come, for the skies to clear, the air to begin to move and the first dry leaves to come slanting down. The noise of dry leaves skidding over the terrace is music to me. They tell me that the long oppressive trance of summer is passing at last, that the earth is turning over, the air freshening, and the longed-for coolness of September and October is beginning to repossess the land.

Edinburgh Festival
Late August 1971
Once more in Edinburgh for the Festival. Our dear friends, the Sills, whom we called upon when we were in Durham, were rather down. Luke Curry is

dead. Martindale is dead. Georgina Richardson was found dead in bed... The next day when we drove on to Edinburgh the weather was appropriately wet and gloomy.

Saw a very interesting exhibition of Belgian Surrealists, and was greatly taken by the haunting pictures of Roger Delvaux. La Gare Forestière is a very fine painting. But I did not care for the work of Jim Dine, and found it meaningless.

Just as meaningless was a rubbishly play called *Lying Figures* by Francis Warner, who is a friend of Samuel Beckett—vague, inexplicit, semi-intelligible stuff which is supposed to be fruitful and significant. I am not unsympathetic to avant-garde drama, but my goodness the door has been opened recently to a lot of rubbish. Strange, isn't it, that the words of a retiring eighteenth-century bachelor like Thomas Gray should have infinitely more depth and poignancy than the contemporary utterances of Francis Warner. Michael Burrell's one-man show on Gray elevated and delighted us. *Lying Figures* saddened us.

This was not the most enjoyable of festivals, but we appreciated a straightforward *King Lear* in the Assembly Hall; Michael Burrell's recital on Gray of Gray's Elegy; the Belgian Surrealists; a programme of short plays by a group of very talented young actors from Keene State College; a wildly amusing *Comedy of Errors* (one of the first 'pop' productions of Shakespeare); Gonzalez in the Museum of Modern Art; and a programme on McGonagall—and, on the way home, a memorable picnic at Smailholm Tower, so beloved of Scott.

19 September 1971

Glorious autumn weather. Keats's 'Ode to Autumn' day after day.

Conker Time

All the summers of my life
seem to end like this—
September sunshine, the world held in a trance,
and boys stoning the chestnut tree on the corner,
tearing down branches, hurling brickbats and sticks,
to bring down the conkers they covet,
swap, prize, throw away.
It will give them all they want if they'll only wait.
And the scars will heal.

It will flower next year, as bountiful as ever,
come Dick, come Harry, come stick, come stone, come Winter.

21 September 1971

22 September 1971
Peter Nicholson would like to buy Knightwick Station, enlarge it and live there.[4] I wrote this little poem for him after we had been to see it.

Knightwick Station

It was never much more than a halt,
smallish, red brick, blue slate,
one platform, one siding, a yard and a weighbridge hut.
Now the track is up, the windows shattered,
the doors off their hinges, the panelling stripped for firewood,
and the black urinal almost choked with weeds.
There's only a gap where the bridge once crossed the road.

One day, when things have run down even further,
some latter-day Camden will maybe nose it out,
swarmed over with vegetation like a jungle temple,
but no inscriptions, no tablets, no tell-tale idols,
only a corroded pump, a weighbridge platform,
and stained urinal slabs.[5]

24 September 1971

In the footsteps of Francis Kilvert
Saturday 9 October 1971
Today Gwen and I (with Lee Harrod, his wife and little boy, Jonathan, slung on Lee's back like a papoose) had a wonderful walk across the Radnorshire Hills from near Llanbedr to the Rocks of Aberedw. Lovely hills, some farmed and green almost to the summit, others 'horse-back-brown', and covered with bracken and heather, the lower stalks of the latter encrusted with a grey lichen-like growth, the flowers dry and purple. The turf was spotted with the dark turds of the sheep, twisted hawthorns leaned away from the wind, the mountain ponies stood up to their fetlocks in water in the shallow mountain pools,

and crows and buzzards wheeled round the crumbling shaly rocks. I loved this walk, one of the finest I have ever done.

Upland Country

The sheep slip like ghosts in and out of the bracken.
They don't like my company.
Nor do the wild ponies,
looking up from the pools
where they stand up to their fetlocks.
They toss their heads and wheel off over the rim of the moor.

But the buzzards keep on tracing black circles
against the grey clouds.
Eyes search for rocks, crumbling walls,
long views,
while legs drag through the leprous sticks
of the dying heather.

22 October 1971

Today I saw an exhibition of very beautiful prints by someone called Hella Basu.[6] I must try to make her acquaintance—a superb calligraphic print-maker.

Formulating a great desire to write a little book about Francis Kilvert and his world.

Newman College

25 October 1971

Gwen and I went to Newman College (now Newman University, Birmingham) to hear a lecture by A. L. Rowse. He used his lecture, a eulogy of the achievements of the Elizabethan age—all the more astonishing because the total population of the country was under 5 million—to castigate our own degenerate and incompetent age. His address was not bad-tempered or vitriolic. It was rather an urbane performance, amusing and good-natured. He is a clever lecturer—old-womanish perhaps and pedantic, with a tendency to avoid difficult questions, but displaying a masterful control of his audience and, although arrogant, not offensively so. This is how he appeared to us today, but I daresay he was on his best behaviour.

27 October 1971

Gave tonight—or rather—produced John Hencher in my dramatised version of Kilvert. He was extremely good, and the occasion was more successful than the first performance, which was held in our own sitting room and which seemed to upset David Lockwood. It was rather tactless of me to end the recital with the death of little Davie so soon after the death of David's own daughter.[7]

A day in London

30 October 1971

A beautiful October Saturday and a day filled with good things. I went first to Helen Bradley's exhibition, and found everything sold, though the prices went up to £400. A year ago, when I first saw her work, I could have bought a small picture of hers for £28. The biggest and most ambitious were a little over £100. Lucie Rie has an exhibition at the V&A, and seeing her work there made me think that Gwen has some fine things in her little collection. I also saw a Klee exhibition and bought a book of Hockney's paintings and drawings from that lovely shop (Erasmus) in Cork Street. After tea we went to the Haymarket to see *Voyage Round My Father* by John Mortimer. No four-letter words, no nudity, nor pornograpples—simply a delightful affectionate tribute to a remarkable old man. Alec Guinness gave a superb performance. The whole day—train fare, play, taxis etc. cost us no more than £4 each.

I have just learnt that there is a Bernini in the V&A—the only one outside Italy (can this be true?). I must go and see it on my next visit to London.

Have bought a copy of *Les Grandes Heures du Duc de Berry* (we already have *Les Très Riches Heures*) and *Séjour*, a special edition of a recondite work by Samuel Beckett (signed).

4 November 1971

I have sent in my resignation to the Governors of the College and it has been accepted.

1972

A conversation with my grandson
5 April 1972

How old are you, Grandad?
I'm over sixty. Nearly sixty-two.
Will you die soon?
Not yet, I hope.
You could die today, couldn't you?
I could but I don't think I shall.
You'll probably die when I'm not there, won't you?
Possibly, but I think I'll last till you're about twenty.
Oh not as long as that!

Two for the Price of One (for Gwen)

You forget the names I remember.
I can't recognise what you recall.
What together we did turns to something
that never happened at all.

We differ on people and places.
Can't agree on the where and the when,
my June turns into your April,
your six is more often my ten.

But, in an amusing manner,
zigzagging by different ways,
we seem to get somewhere together,
and meet at the end of the maze.

And it seems, after all, better fun
to have two versions of living than one.

5 May 1972

Iain Ball's story
10 July 1972
When his wife became the Headmistress of the village school, Iain Ball thought he had better start attending divine service. He was not in the habit of going to church but he thought that he ought to give her some moral support. So he chose to go to a Carol Service. He knew that all eyes would be upon him, because this was his first public appearance, so to speak, and he tried to avoid notice by squeezing into one of the back pews. He was appalled, however, to find Major Knight, the churchwarden coming up to him, and saying, 'Take the sixth lesson, will you, there's a good chap. Micah, Chapter 5 verses 2-5. After Hark the Herald Angels. It will be all ready for you.'

Before he could protest the Major had gone, presumably in search of another victim. He began to look around him to see if he had overlooked the service sheet he was supposed to have. But there was no sheet. No one had a service sheet. There was nothing for him to do but wait for 'Hark the Herald Angels'. It never came. The fifth lesson came and went, but no 'Hark the Herald Angels'. Instead the congregation embarked upon 'In the Bleak Midwinter.' When it came to an end, he sat down thinking that perhaps the whole service was topsy-turvy and with luck he might not be needed at all; but to his horror he saw the Major signalling him to go to the lectern. He tried to signal back that it wasn't his turn, but the Major was not to be denied.

He went up to the lectern, and looked at the open Bible. It was not open at Micah but at the previous lesson. Where was Micah and what exactly was the lesson he was supposed to read? He had forgotten the exact chapter and the exact verses. In a state of great uncertainty he turned and bowed to the vicar, asking him in lip language, as best he could, 'Which is the lesson?' Unfortunately the vicar was not only hard of hearing but short-sighted as well. He merely bowed back. Iain went through the motions again, but the vicar, thinking it was a new and altogether enjoyable ritual, bowed back a second time. Since Iain was clearly getting nowhere, the bowing and counter-bowing could have gone on for ever. The deadlock had to be broken, so he broke it by marching down the aisle and asking Major Knight point blank which lesson he had to read.

With staggering self-assurance the warden said, 'Isaiah 65', as if he had never heard of Micah. Iain went back to the lectern and after some mis-shots found Isaiah, only to discover that all the chapters were numbered with Roman numerals. What was 65 in Roman numerals? Then followed one more dreadful hiatus in this nightmare service, until at last he remembered that L was fifty—so LX stood a fair chance of being 60 and LXV might quite easily be 65. He was appalled to find that it contained no less than 25 long verses, and it became increasingly evident to him that none of them had the least bearing on the Nativity. But he gritted his teeth and went on to the end. He left the lectern with the sound of Hark the Herald Angels ringing in his ears and sat down in his pew to watch the Major take his place at the lectern and confidently and unrepentantly announce 'Micah, Chapter 5 verses 2-5.'

Erica's wedding
29 July 1972
Erica and Nick were married yesterday in St John's Church by our friend Malcolm Richards. It was a very happy occasion. Erica was married in a dress of her own designing. No one wore morning dress. All the young people were in modern clothes—Nick had a very smart beige suit—and looked relaxed and free in a rather admirable way. Gwen wore a blue dress that suited her. The whole affair was simple and not too protracted, though Erica and I, through no fault of our own, kept the congregation waiting longer than we should have done. The reception was in College, and I did my best to make a sincere and eloquent speech. Erica behaved with great modesty and composure, and we were very proud of her.

So Gwen and I enter a new stage in our lives. But the prospect of being alone in the house by no means daunts us.

11 November 1972
I am just home from an extraordinary week in Nottingham and Nottinghamshire, during the course of which I gave no fewer than 21 talks to schools and societies. I found it very hard going and nearly went under, but was rescued by a true Christian, whose name most ungratefully I have already forgotten, who stood by me and helped me to end my tour on a note of exaltation and triumph. It was after midnight when I got home. Gwen did not waken and I got into bed without disturbing her.

One little boy asked me how long it took me to write a book.

'Maybe a year. Sometimes two. Do you think that's a long time?'

'Oh yes. Don't you get any time to watch television?'

Seagulls on Ploughland

Lopsided, one wheel riding in the furrow,
A tractor, from here no bigger than a toy,
Goes up and down, finding the fallow hessian,
Leaving it corduroy.
I find its noise in place. More alien sounds
The cry of the gulls plundering the landlocked acre,
Filling the inland air with sounds of rock,
Cliff, shoal and breaker.

17 November 1972

23 November 1972

Dr Chafy of Rous Lench did not like Methodists. He had this message cut in stone on the side of the school at Church Lench:

From all false doctrine, heresy and schism, Good Lord, deliver us.

The inscription is still there.

My life is full and absorbing, though I no longer have to run an English Department. I work steadily at Kilvert and from time to time write a little of my proposed book on him. I walk almost every day, keep up a heavy correspondence and lecture every Thursday evening to my extramural group. On Saturday Gwen and I go to London to see the Rossetti Exhibition and next Friday I am due to speak at the Doncaster College of Education. I shall have to set off at 6 am but that will be no hardship. My days are filled with study of one kind and another. It is a very pleasant existence.

Funeral in Wales

27 December 1972

Today Gwen and I went to Bangor to attend the funeral of my friend, Professor John Danby, who died last Thursday. It was a cold almost impersonal funeral. I expected to see Helena Mennie, Fay Pomerance, Tom Danby and others. They were not there. There were very few of us—one of his students, two members of the English Faculty (there was no one else, to my surprise, from the University of North Wales), Winifred Cawley and her husband, Professor Cawley from Leeds, John's daughters, of course, and a handful of others.

There was a cold service in a gloomy little Welsh church, without a single mention even of the name of the dead man. It might have been the funeral of a pauper. It was bewildering in its anonymity. The body, in a dark coffin, was buried in a little cemetery on a slope facing a wood. Gertrude and her daughters were stoical almost to coldness. I threw two booklets of my own verse into the deep dark grave; and so said goodbye to the man who was the greatest influence on my life, the man in whose shadow my early manhood was spent.

I did not feel grief so much as a sense of enormous waste. No one told me what John died of. The supposition must be that he died from excessive drinking. I felt almost angry that so gifted a man should have brought about his own death.

We drove nearly three hundred miles to attend this sad occasion, setting off in the dark just after 7 am and getting back at about 6 pm. A bewildering, almost infuriating experience.

1973

A visitor
31 March 1973
An old man, a stranger, in a long raincoat, with a woolly scarf under it. He put his hat down on the table and took off his glasses. When he took them off you could see two red marks on either side of the bridge of his nose; but his face was very smooth and his complexion waxy. He had a grey pamphlet in his hand.

'I hope you don't mind my calling on you,' he said. His voice quavered a little but his diction was clear. I thought he must be an old schoolmaster or a retired parson. There was an apologetic note in his voice.

'I am told you are sympathetic to writers,' he said. 'Very good to young poets. But I can't call myself that. Not at 73.'

I could see the title of his pamphlet. It was 'The Strangest Story of My Life.'

'I sent this poem to the editor of the local paper' he went on, 'but I think he must have forgotten about it.'

'I am sure he won't overlook it.'

'Do you think so. Would you look at it? I would value your comments.'

'Will you let me buy... You are selling copies, aren't you?'

'Yes. Twenty-pence each'.

Rather a large sum for a short poem, I thought but I gave him the money.

He took out an old-fashioned purse and popped it in with some alacrity. I had the feeling that only one thing of any importance had happened to him in his life—this unusual rapport with a sparrow—and that he had only ever written one poem—on this experience.

A parson in a train
It's a funny thing but all the people in my parish have something wrong with them, physical or mental. You'd be surprised how many of them book me for their funeral. 'I want you to do it,' they say, 'if you haven't gone before me'. And after twenty years the people you thought you couldn't stand have turned into your best friends. That's odd now, isn't it?

Craig Pwll Du (a walk with Roger Alma)
5 April 1973
We drove to Erwood and then set off up the valley of the Bach Howy from the road that is in places built on the line of the old Hereford, Hay and Brecon railway. We chose the left side of the stream and made a false start, having to climb up through a plantation of young conifers. It was on this road that Roger, bending down, picked up a discoloured penny or halfpenny. When we looked closely at it we found that it was a George III coin dated 1806. How long had it lain undiscovered on that lonely path?

We thought we could hear the noise of the fall, but all we could see was the stream itself twisting and turning through its defile. The descent to it looked steep and perilous, but clearly one would never see the fall unless one got right down to the bottom of the valley. So Roger went ahead and came back to report that though the way down was difficult, it was not impossible, and we decided to risk it. With no more than a few alarming moments I got down to the lowest ledge and dropped from it on to the stones in the river bed. The fall was still invisible, and it was clear that we'd never see it till we got to the far side, so I took off my socks and shoes and waded across. Then it occurred to me that since I was in the water I might as well wade upstream as far as I could. The water was not impossibly cold and it was not too difficult to keep one's footing.

So at last I came close enough to see Kilvert's famous waterfall. It was not as high a fall as he had made it out to be—nearer thirty than forty feet in my estimation—but the water as it came over the fall was astonishingly white, like a bridal veil. Perhaps this whiteness is all the more striking because the rocks that make the jaws of the gorge at this point are black, and so hidden by the bend in the valley that no sunlight falls on them. Those slopes where plants could get a footing were green with hart's tongue ferns and wild garlic; and the long spindly tottering trunks of willow and sycamore reached upwards for light or, exhausted by the effort, lay prostrate in the ravine. The water in the pool below the fall was black and peaty, with twindles of froth turning and circling in the space dammed by the boulders and roots and broken trunks that had been swept over the fall.

Craig Pwll Du (Grappledee as they call it here) is a wonderful secret place that few know about and even less reach (though some initials have been cut in the rock faces in the valley). We climbed out of the gorge on the far side, and found the return journey relatively easy.

I was nearly 63 when I did this trip. But I could not have done it without Roger.

A riposte from Veronica
6 May 1973
'Veronica, for God's sake, don't talk so loudly. Don't yell and shout.'

'Well you don't want us to go round whispering, do you?'

What my grandchildren argue about
Why should you always get into the car first?
Why should I have to sit behind the driver?
If you have the torch on the way there it's my turn to have it on the way back.
He shines it more than I did.
It's my turn to sit in Grandad's chair.
Veronica was frightened to go up a ladder.

An outing with the Kilvert Society
10 May 1973
Last Saturday we went on an excursion by coach past Eardisley, Kington, Stanner (where a little nineteenth-century railway station survives) to Newcastle Court, the home of Daisy Thomas's father when he was Vicar of Gladestry. Father Thomas must have been a man of means to maintain such a house. From here we went on to Pilleth (the scene of the battle in which Mortimer

was taken prisoner by Owen Glendower) and Llanbister. Llanbister has a beautiful and unusual church, commanding a marvellous view. It has a tower at the east end, a baptistry (to lure back Baptists to the fold), and a good rood screen. Further on we came to another church with a superb rood screen, Llananno. The valley of the Ithon is one of the most beautiful in Britain.

On this rather wet and stormy day, Sunderland from Division 2 won the FA Cup by beating Leeds 1—0.

Have just finished reading *Two on a Tower* to Gwen—one of Hardy's poorer novels. It has many faults but there were some things about it that we liked.

David Lockwood's cottage at Llowes
14 May 1973
This cottage, in which we stayed for a few days, is an attractive stone-built house, rather than a cottage, with thick walls, a roomy parlour with window embrasures, a reasonably sized dining room, a big hall, a kitchen and four bedrooms. There are several fascinating features: a bread oven, stone floors, a new stairway that shivers as you go up and down, and one new window which is a smaller version of the pointed window in Ashbrook House.[8] We spent all day at Capel-y-ffin and Llanthony, then after supper went out for a walk to, as I thought, Moity and Maesyronnen; but I missed a turning, and after many miles we found ourselves on the road to Cwmbach and Glasbury. There was no point in turning back, no alternative except to continue to Glasbury and on down the road to Llowes. We walked without a break for nearly three hours and did about ten miles in all. I am so tired my hand is shaking as I write—and my legs feel as if they are dropping off. Gwen still has energy enough to get the beds ready, but all I can do is make these few notes.

Things seen in Radnorshire
Sheep and lambs straying on the roadway.
A man dragging a great load of brushwood behind a tractor.
High hedges crowded with flowers.
Wild ponies among the bracken and gorse on the hillsides.
Cuckoos calling in the evening.
Lilac in flower in the gardens of Glasbury.
Men gritting the narrow road over the Gospel Pass.
Pigs roaming free on the commons.

A few dirty farms, littered with abandoned farm machinery, old drills and worn tyres.

Water Break Its Neck
15 May 1973

The water falling not sheer as at Grappledee but in a series of leaps, with no deep pool at the bottom of the fall. A wandering approach to the waterfall, a huge tree almost uprooted, hanging over the falling water, held by a single root. Below the fall two dead sheep with their faces eaten away. The sides of the chasm deep like a grotto, with green watery plants growing in tresses on the sides of the gorge.

Bredwardine and Clyro

Bredwardine is no more than ten miles from Clyro, but it is a different world. Clyro is very much a border village. Behind it rise the hills of Radnorshire. In the space of a few miles one finds oneself on the great moors. The parishes that border it, especially to the north, are lonely and wild—like Glascwm where old Mr Marsden could live an independent, unsupervised life. 'I am the Bishop here—come and see my cathedral.' And there was in Kilvert's time a wildness in the lives of the people who lived there—tinkers and gypsies and travelling folk. This is a region where an eccentric such as the Revd John Price, the Solitary of Llanbedr, could live his incredible life, and Father Ignatius seek to give substance to his wild visions.

But Bredwardine is closer to the rich plains of Herefordshire. The church is almost buried in orchards, the hills around are lower and covered with trees. Instead of rooms in an austere stone house by a brawling mountain stream, Kilvert has a large capacious vicarage, white-washed, with gardens reaching down to the peaceful Wye. He is better off. He has risen in the social scale. But a certain mystery has gone out of his life.

May 1973

Edward Lowbury has written a few moving poems about the last years of his father-in-law, Canon Andrew Young.[9] Old, a little infirm but stubborn, he announced his desire to go to Brighton for a change, and to see the haunts of his boyhood. He was put on the train, but before he got back, he died. A postcard he had written home was received after the news of his death. And this is the theme of Lowbury's poem 'Postcard from Eternity.'

Veronica and Aidan have been with us for a week. We went by train to Hereford—I think it rather scared Veronica—fished for newts in the college pond, saw a snake attacking a toad, and played football. In the same week Erica moved into her house near Gheluveldt Park. It cost £8,500.

17 June 1973
Am in the process of reading aloud to Gwen Hardy's *The Well-Beloved*. The novel is free from some of Hardy's vices. Its plot is less involved, its style less tortuous, and it is held together by a metaphysical idea which acts as the core of the book.

Today we attended a Kilvert Commemoration Service in Brecon Cathedral. On the way there we called at Llanigon, the home of the Thomases, and passed Llangorse with its lake. Mr Prosser was very annoyed because we did not picnic in the place chosen for us. It was a good service with an excellent address by Willie Price from Lampeter. As always I was in a bit of a stew about my little talk on Kilvert's literary background, but I got through it satisfactorily. William Plomer read the account of Kilvert's visit to Brecon for a church conference and, at his request, we called on the way home at Llansantffraid where he read for us the Siegfried Sassoon poem 'At the grave of Henry Vaughan.'[10] I did not have much talk with him but he told me about Benjamin Britten's serious heart condition. He did not mention his own, but he was clearly tired and found the occasion rather exhausting. He told me that Siegfried Sassoon was very disappointed that the world thought so little of his later religious poetry.

21 June 1973
My sixty-third birthday. Went to see Victor Hext (a former colleague) at Doncaster and to lecture to his students. Made great friends with Katie, who is a real little Yorkshire lass.

'Do you like your new school, Katie?'

'Yes.'

'Is it nice?'

'Yes. You get two fish fingers for dinner. We just got half a one in the school at Malvern.'

2 July 1973
Veronica's astonishing tantrums! Yesterday because she could not have her

blanket (why is she so attached to this?) she kicked, screamed, beat and kicked in the car, yelled, blubbered, fought and said she would cry until she got what she wanted, and threw her clogs away. An astonishing performance—but probably no worse than Maggie Tulliver's outbursts in *The Mill on the Floss*.

15 July 1973

Today Geoffrey, Nick's father, gave me a bundle of old letters to look through. They belong to an old lady in Bridgnorth. Some are from a young man serving in the Peninsular War, and one actually describes the death of Sir John Moore at Corunna. I mean to set to work transcribing them.

24 July 1973

A visit to Rochdale. I had to give a talk to parents and children in the Whitworth School, and took the opportunity to have a look at the astonishing Town Hall. What a wonderful building, with its imposing processional staircase, high painted wooden ceiling, organ, elaborate platform and stained glass windows of kings and queens of England culminating in Victoria and Albert. A treasure house of Victorian craftsmanship, tremendously impressive in all its details. There is a story somewhere behind this building.

2 August 1973

Gillian and Colin have spent a week at Aberfeldy where they had good weather, and a second week at David Lockwood's cottage at Llowes. The children have greatly enjoyed living in the country. When we were there the other day they were very happy dangling their teddies out of the upstairs windows, catching grasshoppers, reading the tombstones, playing football and paddling in the stream. They all look well and fit. I am preparing to give a talk to the Archaeological Society on the Park Ornaments of Croome.

An anecdote about Capability Brown: 'I hope I die before you, Brown, so that I can see Heaven before you start improving it.'

Dodington

8 August 1973

A superb Regency house by Wyatt; house, dower house and church combined in one superb ensemble. Wyatt was a great designer—witness the library and its furnishings, and the octagon room with its four cunningly placed doors and the remarkable family tribune with its fireplace and elevated position. A house full of brilliant things. An early nineteenth century masterpiece. I was bowled over by it.

Woodchester
In 1951, when we first went to see the famous mosaic floor, there were very few of us—just a small group from the Archaeological Society. Now thousands visit it every day, and there is a huge field churned up with cars and coaches.

13 August 1973
Have finished reading *Dr Wortle's School* to Gwen, and with few expectations have started *The Hand of Ethelberta*.

17 August 1973
Have given up on *The Hand*—a worthless novel.

19 August 1973
Troubled by an unsolicited visit from Jane who invited herself to stay overnight on her way to Taunton. She has left her car here and proposes to spend one more night with us on her way home. A cool and disagreeable piece of effrontery on her part. She knows we are setting off on a holiday in Bath but simply will not recognise how much she is inconveniencing us.

23 August 1973
In Bath saw the American Museum, and exhibition of the Saxon Kings at Holburne of Menstrie Museum (kept afloat by Robertsons, the jam people). I did not realise that the museum was once Sidney College where Kilvert's sister and brother-in-law lived.

Widow

A dry leaf, arched like a crab,
skids over the terrace slabs.
She lays her hands face down.
The brown age-spots are running together now.
She says, 'I heard a man say on the radio,
when you give up your job you should live dangerously.

I'd like to do that now that I'm free.'
In the hanging basket over her head,
the alyssum's finished, the lobelia dry and dead.
The edges of the geraniums are brown,
like the back of her hands.

5 September 1973

Tramp

A man, on a bench at the crossing,
back to the dirty wall,
cold chips in a paper bag by his side,
and a bottle of something at his feet,
standing upright like a skittle.
People walk past carrying shopping,
cross when the pips bleep.
The cars go round endlessly, like toys in a fair.
He talks to himself silently,
like a man on TV
with the sound turned down.

5 September 1973

A lovely summer
15 September 1973
August and September have been months of almost continuous sunshine. The ground is hard and dry, and gardening is difficult.

Molly Holden
17 September 1973
I met Molly Holden at her home in Bromsgrove today.[11] She cannot move from her sofa, but the upper part of her body seems flexible enough. She can turn, reach for things, write, and shake hands. I hope we did not stay too long and tire her. What a courageous woman she is! She has a photograph of Hardy on her wall and tells me that she had written a poem about him for the *Critical Quarterly*.

22 September 1973
I have just seen a note in *The Telegraph* reporting the sudden death of William Plomer. He was only 69. Gwen and I are deeply grieved to hear this news. She

was fond of William, and he took to her.[12] The last time we saw him was at Brecon. He seemed tired and disinclined to talk to anyone. I wonder if he completed the transcript of his Kilvert notebook which he promised to do for me.[13]

A Victorian afternoon
1 October 1973
Today I spent a most interesting and fruitful afternoon in a far corner of Worcestershire finding, with great pleasure, the Poet's Stone (near Leysters old church) where Wordsworth and his wife rested to admire the view of the Clee Hills; the fine Victorian church of St Michael's Tenbury, built by Sir Frederick Gore Ouseley; and Brockleton Court where Kilvert was entertained by Capt. Prescott Decie. The weather was superb and the countryside paradisal.

A coincidence
When, during the course of a talk at Malvern today, I was reading from *Under the Greenwood Tree*—or rather after I had finished my talk—a woman came up to me and told me that her mother had been the schoolmistress of Fancy Day's school at Upper Bockhampton and had lived in the very house Hardy had described. She had known Hardy well. What a coincidence!

At the end of the talk I was given a sealed envelope. I was impatient to open it because it seemed a gathering of reasonably well-heeled ladies, and I thought they might have done me proud. I had certainly taken a great deal of trouble over my talk to them. It was a book token for £1! I had spent hours preparing the talk, had cut an Archaeological Society committee meeting to give it, and spent a whole afternoon delivering it. Since it cost me at least 40p to get there and back, my total remuneration for a highly professional lecture was 60p!

The Blackberry Year

Every year something is chosen to excel,
to be abundant above everything else.
I remember the apple year,
when the world was full of Laxtons,
Blenheims, Bramleys, Coxes, Golden Delicious.
And the primrose year when the fields were yellow with flowers.
This year is the blackberry year.
So many a starving people might live on them.

Who knows? One year, my fortune
may be the year's target.
A finger points this way,
and a voice says
'Prosper and flourish!
This is your year.'

10 October 1973

A Kilvert Service at Llanigon
14 October 1973

The sermon had just begun when the door of the church was pushed open and in came a strange couple—a not unhandsome young woman with a two-year-old girl. She was dressed in a long brownish skirt, old and dirty shoes, and her long hair hung down her back. The man with her was pale and nervous in a curious rig—a long loose ragged sweater, brown woollen knee breeches loosely fastened below the knee, thick green stockings and dirty ploughman's boots. I didn't know who they were. The churchwarden ushered them into a back pew, but they had not been there long before the child began to get restless. The parson was doing his best to praise the unspeakable Mr Thomas who would not allow Kilvert to propose to his daughter Daisy, when strange gurglings and protests were heard from the little girl.

The congregation was polite but could not resist turning and shooting reproving glances at the strange couple. The child grew more and more restless, and almost every sentence from the pulpit drew some sound from her—a gurgle, a cry, a groan, semi-intelligible sounds that seemed like loud denials and contradictions of the parson's claims. He was a little put out—but worse was to follow. A loud cracking noise came from overhead and looking up, I saw that someone had switched off the electric fires attached to the roof, and as they cooled they crackled and snapped in a disconcerting way. The preacher did his best to seem unperturbed but he must have been greatly put out as each eloquent, rhetorical phrase, each telling sentence, was ruined by the noise of the child in the back and the fires overhead.

It soon became clear who the thoughtless parents were. Half an hour later, we assembled outside Ashbrook House in Clyro to unveil the new plaque to Kilvert. We were all called upon to thank and compliment the stone carver who had cut the plaque—and who should step forward but the slatternly, bohemian young man who had almost ruined our service!

24 October 1973

Have just seen a most moving performance of *The Changeling* at the Birmingham Rep. I was almost moved to tears by the sight of the doomed pair in each other's arms. They had attained a kind of love of their own—all the more poignant since their next step was death.

Gwen and I have had more than thirty years of play-going together. It all began nearly thirty-five years ago when I took her to see *Much Ado* at the People's Theatre in Newcastle.

Conversation with a Croome estate worker

October 1973

A man on the Croome estate talking to me about Mr C: 'He was a good man and he did his best to get the church filled, but he was very mean, if you know what'm gettin' at. We raised £9000 for this church and he never gave a penny. You know what he said, he said 'I'm not giving anything to this fund because I'm giving my services free.' Damn me, that's the first time I heard he was workin' here as our parson for nothing. He was getting paid plenty, I can tell you. You know, he had a family livin' with him in the vicarage, paying him board. And one day he seed the woman givin' the boy an egg for his breakfast. 'How often do you give him that for his breakfast?' he said. 'He gets one every morning,' she said. 'Oh I can't have that. I'm the one paying for that, you know.' Well, damn me, fancy him talking as if he couldn' afford an egg for a lad's breakfast. And you know how much he left when he died? Fifty-four thousand quid.'

1 November 1973

After a frost the chestnut tree at the bottom of the garden lost all its leaves in an hour. One hour it was thick—another it was stripped bare. So many leaves fell that the children made a huge heap of them and played with it.

A story told to Gwen by Nancy Stratton

12 December 1973

A wealthy old lady, recently widowed, was exercising her little dog in the park when someone came up to her and said, 'There's a man in the bushes over there, exposing himself.' The old woman walked over to the man, looked at him and said imperiously, 'Put it away, man, put it away. I buried a far better one last week!'

Crisis
13 December 1973
Country facing a serious crisis. Miners are on go-slow, train drivers working to rule, and oil supplied from the Middle East has been cut off. There is a serious shortage of petrol, derv and paraffin. Factories are to go on a three-day week. Probably the worst crisis since 1939.

The Laodicean
13 December 1973
I have been trying to read this aloud to Gwen but have given it up. It is probably the worst novel Hardy ever wrote—worse than *Ethelberta*.[14]

The year ends with a production of a dramatised version of *The Bonny Pit Laddie* by a school in Faringdon.

22 December 1973
A gloomy Christmas—a petrol shortage, industrial disputes (miners are going slow and power hands are working to rule). It looks as if everyone will have to go onto a three-day week. Trains have been cut and are unreliable. Some shops are without lighting. None of this stops people from spending on a record scale.

24 December 1973
At Midnight Mass the parson spoke to us about the cold and dark days ahead. It seemed that we were all standing there like a doomed and beleaguered people, obedient and submissive, but totally at the mercy of that other body of people who were not present, the cynical, the greedy and the alien, to whom we and all that we stood for were irrelevant. Two women squashed themselves into our pew, and I had so little room I had to sit slantingly on my seat. It was out of the question to kneel. Gwen, of course, had the giggles and could hardly hold herself in.

Notes

1 The Swan Theatre is in Worcester.
2 *Young Tom Sawbones* was published by Oxford University Press in 1972.
3 Roger Alma was a colleague of Fred's at the Training College and a poet.
4 Peter Nicholson was a colleague and potter.
5 William Camden (1551-1623) antiquarian, historian and topographer; author of the first survey of the British Isles and the first detailed historical account of the reign of Elizabeth I of England.
6 Hella Basu (1924-80) was born in Germany but became naturalised British in 1964. There is a collection of her calligraphic prints in the Victoria and Albert Museum, London.
7 Revd David Lockwood (1925-2006), vicar of Hanley Castle and Hanley Swan near Malvern (1964-81); married Dr Wilhelmina (Willy) Mom 1956 (1925-2017). Revd Lockwood was Vice-President of the Kilvert Society 1970-1990, Chairman 1990-99 and President 1999-2006; he published two books dealing with Kilvert: *Francis Kilvert* (1990) and *Kilvert: The Victorian* (1992). Dr Lockwood was an Hon. Life Member of the Kilvert Society.
8 Kilvert lodged in Ashbrook House, Clyro.
9 Edward Lowbury (1913-2007) was a distinguished medical bacteriologist at the Accident Hospital, Birmingham and a published poet. Andrew Young (1885-1971) was a Scottish nature poet and Canon of Chichester Cathedral.
10 William Plomer was the editor of *Kilvert's Diary* in 3 volumes, 1938, 1939, 1940, and this was an important meeting for Fred as the future author of *Francis Kilvert and His World*, 1982. The grave of Henry Vaughan (1621-95) was visited by the war poet Siegfried Sassoon (1886-1967) in 1923, and gave rise to his homage, 'At the Grave of Henry Vaughan,' which Plomer proceeded to read to Fred and Gwen in the churchyard at Llansantffraid.
11 Molly Holden (1927-81) poet and author of children's books.
12 William Plomer gave Gwen a copy of his three-volume *Kilvert's Diary*, 1960 'Inscribed for Gwen Grice with all good wishes, William Plomer, Worcester, 7 October 1972'.
13 William Plomer did indeed transcribe his own copy of the Kilvert notebook in Durham University Library for Fred, who photocopied it for his own use. Plomer's copy has subsequently been published as *Kilvert's Cornish Diary*, (ed.) Richard Maber and Angela Tregoning, 1970.
14 Fred read to Gwen in the evenings as she got on with her embroidery; this was the pattern throughout their retirement.

Part II

In the Footsteps of Francis Kilvert

Chapter 5: 1974-75

1974

1 January 1974
We went playing football on the college fields and were troubled by the stockman's silly dog, which always runs after the ball. While we all stood hesitating, not quite knowing how to deal with it, Veronica rushed at it, stripping off her anorak and, whirling it round her head and uttering wild cries, went for it. It did not take the dog long to realise it was dealing with a very superior adversary. It put its tail between its legs and fled. Fog, frost, not a glimmer of sunshine, rime on the grass and trees all day long.

I began the New Year with a cold, which as usual I neglected. Then yesterday I had a strange attack. My temperature went down alarmingly. I could not keep warm but sat in front of the fire wearing two cardigans, with a hot water bottle in my lap and a blanket over my knees. I smouldered there for a few hours then went to bed, feeling like Shadrach, Meshach and Abednego all rolled into one, slept soundly and woke cured.

6 January 1974
Met Marilynn, Peter Nicholson's new wife, an American and a silversmith. I like her very much. I began the New Year in a mood of great economy, and spent hardly a penny during the first week. But I fell from grace the other day when I bought three new shirts at two pounds each from Simon Armstrong.

We are reading together *Felix Holt, the Radical.*

Colonel Awdry
28 January 1974
Today I met Colonel Awdry, who lives at Coters, Rowden Hill, Chippenham, a rather gloomy, cluttered Victorian house. He is a tall strongly-built old man, probably once an athlete and given to talking in cricketing language. When he was talking to me about the Awdry family (who figure so largely in the Wiltshire passages of *Kilvert's Diary*), he kept using phrases and sentences such as these—'This one, you see, lived for a long time. She got her hundred—but

the sister didn't quite make her century. It was a very large family but I can see that two them didn't bat.' He is a fine old man, knew Lord Methuen of Corsham and possessed several of his pictures, and has a son who is MP for Chippenham.

I enjoyed the day, though I had to drive through a furious rainstorm near Malvern on my way home.

Still reading *Felix Holt, the Radical.*

1 February 1974

My commonest dream is of being unprepared. Last night I dreamt I had to give a lesson in a girls' school somewhere. I was late. My car was parked in a bad spot, and I could not lay my hands on the poem that I needed. More often I dream (a) that I am producing a play and have not the faintest idea where the setting and the costumes are to come from, and (b) that I am expected to take a part, but not only do I not know the words—I don't even know what the play is. When I do find a copy I cannot understand it and keep turning over the pages looking in vain for my part.

A remarkable surprise

14 February 1974

Before he died William Plomer promised to make a transcript of his Kilvert notebook. When he died so suddenly I was afraid he had not had time to do what he promised me. I feared the notebook might be lost for good. But Sir Rupert Hart-Davis, William's literary executor, who has been most cooperative and helpful, found the transcript—about 90 pages in William's own remarkable hand—among his papers, and has sent it to the Kilvert Society. I have made a photocopy for my own use.

18 February 1974

Daffodils, prunus, flowering cherry—all out already this year.

A girl with a fondness for her working-class relatives

21 February 1974

'When I think—honest when I think of my little grandmother, who's never had anything in her life—she's 80 and she hasn't even a house of her own. No, at 84, 85—not a penny in the bank. And if she came and I had nothing to give her but a cup of tea and a piece of cake, she'd be so appreciative! And Bob and Olive that would do anything for you. And then when I think of this woman with her cutting remarks. Doing her damnedest to make us all feel uncomfortable and unhappy. Setting herself out to make me and her own son, whom she's supposed to adore—to make us feel small. I think she's malicious. And thick. I haven't much in the way of brains myself, but I'm beginning to think she's plumb unintelligent. I get the shivers every time she comes. And he's worse. He gets them worse than I do.'

'Let it wash over you, love.'

'I wish I could.'

28 February 1974
Veronica and Aidan are with us all this week—playing football in the afternoon, beetle in the early evening, reading *The Railway Children* and watching all kinds of TV after tea.

Conversation in a Brandon bus, County Durham
7 March 1974
Tha's a Brandon lad, isn' tha?

Aye.

I thowt I kenned tha. Mick Parkin's lad, eh?

Aye.

I knew thy father, man. I've had many a drink wi' him. And I'll tell tha summat else. I knew thy uncle Billy.

Geordie.

That's reet, George Dixon.

No, Geordie Pybus.

Aye, that's reet, Geordie Pybus. And I'll tell tha summat else. I knew thy grandfather, Peter.

Peter the Sinker.

Why aye, I knew him. He went to Trimdon? didn' he?

Mainsforth.

I ken all thy family, man. Where's thy da livin' now?

Sleetburn.

Dis he lad? And I'll tell tha summat else. He was my marra once...

After coming back from Spain in April I spent a great deal of time writing my booklet of Kilvert, and making endless notes on my boyhood in Brandon.

Out of my brooding on Durham in the 1920s came *Nine Days' Wonder* which OUP published for me. Not my best book, but by no means unpopular.

September 1974

Probably our last visit to the Edinburgh Festival. We saw *Father Ignatius*, the Mummenschanz Mime group (very good), *The Sting* (an overrated film), a programme on Dylan Thomas by Jack Pointing of Bristol, Abbotsford and Kelso, and a very good Klee exhibition. Gwen bought a Sanyo portable radio for ten pounds.

Visit to the Tanners

19 September 1974

We went to Kington Langley to meet Robin and Heather Tanner, friends of Graham Sutherland, Geoffrey Grigson and Lucie Rie.[1] They live in an intriguing house designed by Heather's uncle Vivian Goold who was a disciple of Voysey. There are two interesting stories connected with the house. The first is that, unwittingly, they constructed it on the site of the mausoleum built by one of Kilvert's ancestors, and never knew till they read the diary and did a little research. The other is this. Robin is a good calligrapher, and a seedsman to whom he sent an order once, struck up a bargain with him. If he, Robin, designed material for him—letterheads etc.—he could if he wished be repaid in kind. So many plants and shrubs and trees were sent to him that the grounds are almost completely overgrown—their house is like the home of Sleeping Beauty, almost lost in shrubs and trees. Robin, who was an Art HMI, is planning to leave his fabulous collection of fabrics etc. of the twenties to a museum in Bath.[2]

30 September 1974

In *Evelyn Waugh and His World* Lady Dorothy Lygon tells how, before the war, Evelyn often stayed at Madresfield. He was in the process of learning to ride and his tutor was a Malvern man, Captain Hance. Madresfield seems an unlikely starting point for *Brideshead Revisited* and Lord and Lady Beauchamp were not in any sense like Lord and Lady Marchmain; and while it is clear that Brideshead is a Palladian mansion, Madresfield is largely Victorian. But

Waugh always maintained that Madresfield was the starting point for his novel; and there is one feature of the house that Waugh incorporated into his fictional Palladian manor—the late nineteenth-century chapel which Lady Beauchamp had made in 1902 for a wedding present to her husband the seventh earl. Pevsner describes it as an exceptionally complete piece of Arts and Crafts decoration of its time.

Sister Meinrad

Today we paid another visit to Stanbrook to see Sister Meinrad and some of her latest drawings. She met us in the big parlour, wearing fur-lined boots of a very old-fashioned style, and a cardigan with a hole in the sleeve. Her hands were very cold. Her drawings in charcoal are mysterious, symbolic, evanescent, in which images of birds, trees, roots, springs, mountains, male and female bodies are vaguely and provocatively (do I mean evocatively) conjured up. Apocalyptic drawing with a hint of the later Sutherland, even Hieronymous Bosch. I gave her the Edinburgh Klee catalogue and a little book of poems by Canon Andrew Young. When we shook hands at leaving her fingers were very cold.

But, thank goodness, in the few years we have been coming to Stanbrook those prison-like grilles have vanished from all the parlours.

Sudden Shower

The sky darkens like a bruise,
and a sudden shower of hail
smacks the top of the trees,
hits the back of my head
like an undeserved slap.

The hailstones pepper the roadway like grapeshot,
bounce, fall again,
dissolve.
When the sun comes out
the light flashes on the wet trees
like wings.

3 October 1974

9 October 1974
Went to Sheffield to give a talk on my work to the Board of Studies. These talks are a chore and I like them less and less as time goes on.

Ilston, Gower
13 October 1974
To Ilston in the steps of Francis Kilvert. A charming little church with a plain homely interior and a rugged battlemented tower attached to a nave of grey stone. Set in a little valley, with a stream, a ford, stepping stones, lost in trees. Above the church, a well-proportioned, whitewashed parsonage. Wynford spoke about Kilvert in Gower, Willie Price about Kilvert in Wales, and I on Kilvert as a traveller.[3]

1 November 1974
This morning, while Gwen and Gillian were shopping, Aidan, Veronica and I went into the workshop to make rafts—toy rafts made out of squares of plywood, with short lengths of broom handle for tubs and barrels, and shorter lengths of thinner dowel rod for logs, and a pair of cut-out balsa wood steers-men, coloured in with felt nib pens. We were finished by coffee time and just after eleven we took them down to Laughern Brook. It was a warmish morning and even though it was November the water was not too cold. The brook was low but clear, and running fast enough to carry the rafts downstream at a fair speed.

We kept the rafts floating out of reach by lengths of nylon string. The water was running fast between the stepping-stones and breaking into miniature rapids. We ended up by letting the rafts float free down through the toy gorges. I stood in my wellingtons well downstream to rescue them—retrieve them. Aidan kept fairly dry and clean, but Veronica got her trousers wet and dirty. On the way back we saw a dog chasing a pony in a field, and then the pony turning and chasing the dog. Before Aidan and Veronica went back home to Liverpool we cast the rafts from the bridge into the Severn. We watched them as far as the Water Gate and then left them to their fate.

7 November 1974
Last night we were privileged to hear a fascinating lecture on the Bromsgrove Guild by a Mr Pancheri, son of an old Italo-Austrian woodcarver who came

to join the Guild. This story ought to be published but for some reason Mr Pancheri will not allow it to appear in print.

Storm

This is the threatened gale.
The television aerial on the roof
clicks in the wind, tapping out distress signals.
The trees slap like rigging—
and look at the moon—
a small white craft rounding the horn of the night,
plunging from roller to trough,
breakers of cloud thundering and smashing over her.
I rock in the crib of my bed,
waking to peer at the binnacle clock.
Wildly off course we flounder together—
the house in the storm,
I in the tempest of all my fears.

11 November 1974

Whitley Court

A faded photograph revives the scene.
Dinner is over. After a day with the guns
the wealthy guests assemble on the steps.
A signal from the host
reaches a nameless and invisible servant,
and the glittering plume of water springs into the air.
Perseus, with lifted arm,
the dragon writhing in death,
Andromeda swooning at the moment of rescue,
are as the Gorgon would have had them be.
But it's the fountain that the guests applaud.

We know the secret of the spectacle—
the cistern in the hills,

the hidden machinery under the pool,
the maze of passages the workmen used
to keep the pumps in trim—
the whole elaborate apparatus
built for a lord to stage his expensive trick
for the diversion of his blasé guests.

One night the house itself went up in flames.
There were no guests to watch that spectacle.
They blame a negligent servant for the blaze
that left the house in ruins,
the pool dried up, the fountain at a stop.

My own force nearly spent, with little left
except a curiosity to pry
into the hidden springs of diminished powers,
I found, by way of a hole in the overgrown garden,
and a rusty ladder,
a way into the clandestine passages
beneath the fountain.

Nothing but darkness there.
Damp walls, derelict cistern, broken pipes,
and sealed-up corridors,
a silent labyrinth of impotent gear.

10 November 1974
We have just bought a most beautiful facsimile of the Book of Kells (it cost £25). And I am writing my story about the General Strike of 1926.

Hilda and Joan
Never use the word 'screw' dear.
Why not?
It has a rude meaning now.
What?
Well—sex you know. So never say anyone had a good screw.
But I've said it many a time. Who tells you these things?

Midwinter Day

A sharp report somewhere, a shot,
like the snapping of a twig,
and the peewits spray upward from the green pond of the field,
tremble, glitter like drops in air,
fall, settle.
The sky is isinglass.
Rooks strut and stab for worms in the meadows,
bullfinches flash along the hedges
and, among the antlers of bare oaks,
the globe of the winter sun hangs like a lantern.

Am reading *Ravenshoe* with Gwen—a very exciting novel—worth better critical notice than it gets.[4]

Snake

Sleeping, I knew
something had given, something outside and in me,
a gathering and bursting,
splitting of mummy bonds.
Wriggling past forks of twigs
I resurrected myself,
drew off the slack glove of my skin,
lay tender and breathless.
Turning to look at myself, I saw
brightness and brilliance,
but still no arms, no legs, no wings.
Still my fate to crawl between sticks and stones,
to dread the boot lifted over me,
and the stick that breaks my back.

4 December 1974

Elizabeth Barrett Browning
20 December 1974

Ruby Cottage, where Mr Boyd, Elizabeth Barrett Browning's friend and mentor lived, still stands near the Essington Hotel on the road to Little

Malvern—a modest place, with whitewashed, pebble-dashed walls and rather gloomy black window frames, substantial enough to boast a little drive. Hope End, Elizabeth's home, is harder to find.[5] Maybe it is best approached from Wellington Heath Post Office. The house, not the one that Elizabeth's father built, is now empty. Down in a hollow one can just glimpse the remains of the pseudo-Moorish stables; but there are guard dogs on the prowl, and I did not dare to stray too far from my car. A pity—dream palaces (if I can use so grandiose a word) such as the Royal Pavilion at Brighton, Linderhof, Neuschwanstein, Sezincote are fascinating to me.

24 December 1974
I am just waking up too, to the neglected beauty of Malvern, which now seems to me to be a treasure house of Victorian architecture—Priory Park, Great Malvern Station and the Abbey Hotel.

1975

Kilvert Conference
9 January 1975
Gwen and I spent a happy few days at Attingham Park taking part in a Kilvert conference. At the end of it I was authorized to edit the proceedings of the conference; this subsequently appeared under the heading *A Kilvert Symposium*.

A most mysterious member of the conference was Mr Jelfs—a handsome man, well-built, well-dressed, smiling and affable—with impressive and expensive equipment, a good camera, a very unusual portable recorder, his volumes of Kilvert expensively bound in leather tooled in gold. What is his trade or profession? A man who seems to have been many things in his time, but a man wearing a mask? We don't know.

Davenham—Malvern
15 January 1975
Davenham strikes me as a beautiful house, sited on a little plateau or terrace, commanding a fine view over Worcestershire, and just far enough from the hills not to be overshadowed by them. It is an irregularly composed house built in excellent Malvern ragstone with tooled limestone quoins. The exterior is adorned with a wealth of good stone carving, heads resembling those

of Batsford and Great Malvern Station, and delicately-cut capitals, mediaeval in spirit and quality. The porch is modest but adorned with a number of fine capitals with heads of mediaeval kings, princes and queens with two small stained glass windows—as you enter read WELCOME on one, and as you leave FAREWELL on the other.

It has a generous hall with a fine wooden ceiling, a main drawing room, a library with superb bookcases, a ballroom with gallery and apse, and a beautiful staircase with stained glass windows representing virtues such as Love, Prudence and Industry. The first architect of the house was Elmslie who also built Great Malvern Station, the County Banks of Worcester and Hereford and the Imperial Hotel (now Malvern Girls' College). Perhaps James Forsyth, the great Victorian sculptor, helped him.

Masterpieces of Victorian architecture in and around Malvern
Great Malvern Station, Malvern Girls' College, Davenham, Chapel of the Convent of the Holy Name (by Ninian Comper), Newland, Perrycroft, Memorial Library of Malvern College, Stanbrook, Pugin Room at Eastnor, the Council House at Great Malvern.

A mild Winter
23 January 1975
It is not yet the end of January, but snowdrops have been out for a fortnight, aconites are nearly over and there are a few daffodils in the gardens. The roses have not yet stopped blooming this year. They have flowered continuously since June. So far we have had only two nights of frost and not a single flake of snow. I think this must be one of the mildest winters in living memory.

A curious story
24 January 1975
An old man died, leaving strict instructions about his will—where it was to be found and the importance of carrying out its stipulations to the letter. When the son and heir found the will, he was dismayed to find that he was to inherit only half the estate. Half of the money—which was stored away in ten- and twenty-pound notes in biscuit tins—was to be buried in the coffin with the dead man.

The son was appalled at the thought of wasting all this money—but the will was proved and there was no getting around it. 'Anyone can get a copy of anybody's will,' he said to his wife. 'The grave will be robbed.'

'Leave it to me,' said his wife. 'Put all the money in our account. And don't ask questions. Promise me not to look in the coffin.' After the funeral, he asked her if she had done what the will had said he ought to do. She reassured him that she had. Sometime later a grave robber opened the tomb. He found there a cheque made out for the amount to the dead man.

The corset shop
27 January 1975
Yesterday we had the chance to look round this old house in Broad Street, Worcester, a narrow vertical house of four floors at least, with large cellars reaching out under the street; and on the very top that intriguing little room said to have been a synagogue, octagonal with four gothic windows and four alcoves or niches, domed and plastered over with crudely elaborate cuspy designs *(Plate 4)*. Off it opens a little room which may have been a vestry of some sort or a retiring room for the rabbi. No one seems to know much about the rooms and their purpose. Down below there are still corsets and corset-making machines.

A sad story
8 February 1975
Some time after his wife had left him George N remarried. His second wife, for whom he has still considerable affection and whom he would take back, came from a restless family. Her father and mother had parted. Then the sisters left the mother to live together—and they also parted. Although he spoke affectionately about the second wife, I had a picture of a discontented woman who disliked almost everything he did for her and gave her. The house was cold and it was not furnished to her taste. She disliked the city, his connections with the theatre, even the holidays they took, although he left her to choose them. She lied to him, even buying a car without telling him. Then one day he came home to find she had gone, leaving no letter, no address, no explanation of her conduct. And only a few weeks before going away she had bought a new carpet and new furniture that had cost him over £600! He has not seen or heard of her since.

He has suffered a shattering experience that has left him nervous, unable to sleep, lonely—with nothing to hold on to but a job that exhausts him, unable

Plate 4: Fred and Gwen on a Worcester Civic Society visit to an old synagogue on one of the upper floors of a former corset shop in Broad Street, Worcester, 1975

to face the chores of a large empty house. I could not but feel sorry for him as he unfolded the story of her deceit and betrayal. How can a man continue to love such a woman? Yet, incomprehensibly, he hopes she will return, and is prepared to go to any lengths to find her.

A not-so-merry widow overheard

My dear, what about Mary? She marries a man with plenty of money and she hasn't been married for more than two years when he dies of a thrombosis and leaves her everything! She enjoys herself for a few years and then gets a proposal from another fabulously wealthy man. And before she knows where she is, he pops off as well with a heart attack and leaves her a second fortune. Honestly, it's not right, is it? Fabulous luck! She picked up two fortunes for nothing. She never had to nurse either of them. Not a day's trouble! When I think of what I had to go through—all those years of nursing and worry and not a penny for them in the end. And here's a woman, both of her husbands snuff it without a day's anxiety and she ends up with two fortunes.

But isn't she lonely now?

Not a bit of it. Already there's another wealthy old boy knocking at the door. Another fortune, because from what I can see of him he won't last long either. Do you know, I think she wears them all out in a subtle kind of way. It's magic. It makes me sick. And here am I, as lively as a cricket and not a penny piece. As poor as a church mouse. Life's unjust, isn't it? Can you blame me for not going to church anymore?

You could have married Joe if you'd wanted to.

I know I could. But one weekend he came to stay with me and after lunch he went to sleep on the sofa. I kept looking at him slumped there, and I said to myself. No, it's no good. I can't marry a man with a nose like that. Honestly, Gwen, it was criminal of him. He had a son a surgeon and he didn't do a thing about that nose. I can never forgive him for that.

What about the man with the bungalow you fancied?

Oh my dear. I saw him the other day. He didn't look too bad from the back, but when he turned round, he hadn't his teeth. Well, I mean, you can't think seriously about a man who goes out walking with no teeth in, can you? No. I went off him after that. Completely.

Disserth Church

This old church, cold as a vault,
was once parcelled out in pews as rectangular as fields.
You can still read the names of the tenants
painted on or cut in the unplaned doors
loose on their broken hinges.

When the men and women moved out
the bats moved in.
Entry was easy for squatters as small as these.
They hang upside down from the rafters,
grinning like gargoyles.
All that collects now on the pew seats and benches
is their black droppings.

2 February 1975[6]

18 March 1975

Earlier this month Beatrice Clift paid us a visit that turned out to be an extraordinary disaster. She lost her watch, had to take her dog to the vet, drove her car backwards over the roses then forward into our neighbour's shed. Two hundred pounds' damage in a few moments!

20 March 1975

This winter I gave two extramural courses—one on 'Diarists and Letter Writers' at Hagley, and one in Worcester on 'European Literature'. Too heavy a programme to repeat.

13 April 1975

I am preparing two volumes on Kilvert—a Kilvert Symposium for the Kilvert Society, and *Kilvert, Priest and Diarist* which I shall publish at my own expense.[7]

17 April 1975

Went to speak to a group of children and a group of parents at Ratcliffe near Nottingham. I hated the drive but liked the people I met *(Plate 5)*. On the way home, in Stratford, I saw Judi Dench shopping, Professor Allardyce Nicoll (he has had two heart attacks and now looks frail) and Tom Goodlad, an old

Plate 5: After Fred retired in 1972 he continued to write children's stories and to talk to children and teachers on school visits. Here he is in Jarrow a decade later

student who used to be fond of Erica. I have made a serious start on my story about the General Strike.

May 1975

Early this month we went on our first holiday to Austria. In the course of a week we saw Seefeld, Innsbruck, Neuschwanstein, Linderhof, Salzburg, Maria Taferl, Melk Abbey, Vienna and Munich.

Home Thoughts

There is talk at breakfast of our ailing currency.
The courier declines to exchange our old green notes.
We feel almost apologetic
in this composed and orderly land.

I walk out after breakfast
to enjoy the sunshine and watch
The mist rolling assuringly from the valley.
This is a pilgrim church, or was so once.
Are these pilgrims, these women in drab skirts,
boots buttoned up to the ankles, sober head-coverings,
and these men in dark almost Victorian suits?
Can such a word still be used seriously?
A priest is with them.
He lifts his hand in a blessing.
They follow him into the church, to Mass and confession.

Behind the altar, at the top of a stairway,
is a treasury of sorts.
Behind glass, a golden crown,
trinkets, rings and even silver watches,
and a chasuble made from a royal wedding dress;
on a shelf, a ripped boy's book,
souvenir of a hayfield accident,
and a note of thanks for his safe recovery;
and a knife that a farmer's wife had run into her hand.
She too gives thanks for her recovery.
From here you can look down into the church,
and see the women waiting to confess.

The meadows below the church are starred with flowers,
forget-me-nots, blue anemones, oxlips, gentians.
A grass snake suns itself on a woodland path.
I have to touch it before it slithers away.
And a cuckoo, almost a stranger to me now,
calls from the hillside.

I return to this soiled country,
the city I once admired,
to find that the riverside seats have been vandalised,
and new pornographic graffiti on the lavatory walls.

(Written after returning from Austria) *May 1975*

17 May 1975
A magnificent tour of Gower with Wynford Vaughan-Thomas as our guide. A terribly exhausting day—we set off at 9 am and did not get back till midnight. I have never met a man exactly like Wynford—the most eupeptic of men. He does not know what it is to be depressed, unhappy, worried, unwell. He bubbles over with bonhomie, and his good spirits are immediately infectious. He was on great form today and kept us all in good humour. But he also taught us a great deal about Gower.

The church at Mansell Gamage
20 May 1975
Just over a hundred years ago Kilvert attended a service to mark the reopening of the church after its restoration. Now it is redundant and has been for some time. A young man from the Bulmer family (the cider people) is converting it into a home. I saw him at work today. He is living, rather roughly, in the chancel which now houses a big untidy bed, a big table, his wife's dresses, his children's toys, and cupboards which he made out of the church fittings. The tower is to contain the bathroom and bedrooms; and he has built a big platform out over the nave. The floor of his living room is partly paved with memorial slabs. The garden is the graveyard, with tall weeds growing up over the Cottrell tombs. A strange Hardyesque—even Kilvertian—scene.

22 May 1975
Gwen is not quite herself. For the first time in her life her skin is giving her trouble. Ever since she housed a few indoor plants from Marilynn she has suffered from a kind of rash and a peeling of the skin. She has clearly developed a kind of allergy.

June 1975
My life is so interesting that I think I shall feel aggrieved when I come to have to leave it.

A visit to Durham
13 June 1975
I have been busy writing my book on the adventures of a boy in Durham during the General Strike of 1926. We took a break to go north and see Tommy and Lila Watson at Ferryhill.

One day I walked up to Kirk Merrington and sat for a few moments on a bench with an old miner who told that me that what he liked best of all was watching birds. 'And I'll tell tha how it all started. I used to work at Cornforth, and to get back to our house I had to come through Doggy Wood. And one morning after a night shift I was coming back through the wood and I seed the bonniest big yellow bird I've ivver seen. It went off through the trees and it give a queer sort of sound.'

'It must have been a yaffle—a green woodpecker.'

'I thowt it was mair yellow than green but I daresay that's what it was. Lad, it was lovely and ivvery day I used to look for that bird. And that's what set me off. Now, the wife and me—we'll gan anywhere to look at birds, man. And I canna think of owt nicer and better.'

Father Lomax
14 June 1975
Gwen told me about Father Lomax of Ferryhill. He was a rich eccentric parish priest, who used to live like a hermit in his large vicarage. It was his duty to keep a strict eye on his parishioners, and he would come down from his pulpit, still carrying on with his sermon, to reprove sleepers or couples holding hands. In opposition to the Salvation Army (and to show that he could outdo them at their own game) he would parade his choristers in their surplices around the village green (greatly to their embarrassment). Alas, he married a bossy schoolmistress who put an end to his eccentricities.

20 June 1975
We have spent the day (the eve of my sixty-fifth birthday) entertaining Professor Jim Morley from Albuquerque, a very amusing man with a passion for Gertrude Stein.

The BBC are contemplating a TV series of Kilvert, and I have met many of the people working on it. I fill my notebook with drafts of passages for my new book on the General Strike. I have been exploring with great pleasure the landscape around Tenbury—St Michael's, Leysters, the Poet's Stone and Bockleton Court. We are suffering from a fierce and prolonged drought. Raspberries are small and stony this year; one of our roses has died already and there is a shortage of milk. I have issued my first Kilvert publication—*A Kilvert Symposium*.

Eastnor Castle
1 July 1975
The house is in general badly kept, badly furnished, and cluttered with a great deal of miscellaneous rubbish. But the Ballroom or the Gothic Drawing Room (it seems to have two names) is a masterpiece of wholly satisfying Victorian Gothic—magnificent doors with lovely handles and hinges, superb fan tracery of great delicacy, a fine fireplace with a family tree, and a stunning chandelier designed by Pugin after one in Nuremberg Cathedral. At his best (here and in the House of Lords and in Cheadle Church) Pugin is one of the greatest designers.

Wightwick Manor is another fine nineteenth-century house—the best Pre-Raphaelite house in the country. The great parlour is a lovely room. I'd like to go and see this house again.

The hot summer of 1975
From early June till now, well into August, we have had hardly one drop of rain. Day after day of intense heat—climbing at times into the 90s. On occasions I have slept with nothing over me but a sheet. I haven't done this since I was in Khartoum in the war years. Trees and bushes are dying wholesale. One of our rose bushes seems past reviving. The winter-flowering prunus and the climbing hydrangea are turning brown in the heat. Tender shoots and buds have been burnt to a cinder before they could flower.

A new story
14 August 1975
This week I began work on my story about the boy who finds an early flying machine.

On a Kilvert expedition to Wiltshire, I went to Hullavington Church, Kington St Michael (with the Prodgers window), Kington Langley, Langley Burrell (especially the school which was built by the Ashes and has a portion set aside for living quarters for the teacher), the Rectory (outside only), Maud Heath's Causeway, Kellaways Mill and church, the Moravian church and manse at Tytherton, Chittoe, a cold unwelcoming church, and the beautiful church of Nonsuch where Ettie Meredith Brown lived. Chittoe is close to Bowood, the great estate of the Marquis of Lansdowne.

27 August 1975
I received the first copy of my booklet on Kilvert. I gave it to Gwen of course. 800 copies have been run off. Can I sell 800?

4 September 1975
Went with Roger Alma to Stourhead, mainly to see the wonderful gardens; but we went to see the house as well. I noticed on the library table a signed photograph of Thomas Hardy, and was told that he was a frequent visitor. Then I spotted—or Roger did—that the shelves were full of what were clearly early editions of the novels and the poems. Wondering if they were signed, we asked the attendant if he would take one down and let us look at the flyleaf. He reluctantly did so and to our surprise we saw that the book was not only signed; fastened inside with a rusty paper clip was a letter apparently in Hardy's hand. And this little discovery was the beginning of an investigation into Hardy's friendship with the Hoares that provided me with some of the happiest hours of my life. But more of that later.

11 September 1975
Coming back on the train from Oxford, I found myself in the same compartment as Peter Kemp, who used to run Stratford's Theatregoround. Seeing him reminded me of those exciting days, not so long ago, when I brought to college Michael Jayston in *Agincourt*, and Susan Fleetwood and Sheila Allen in *Under Milk Wood*—now all great names in the theatre world.

Routine
September 1975
I rise fairly early—not long after seven. I'm at my desk by 8.30 am—type, write, make notes, answer letters till coffee time. Then Gwen and I do a crossword puzzle. I work on in a desultory fashion till lunch at 12.30 (we eat very little for lunch). I walk or garden till 3.30 pm, have a smoke and a rest. High tea is at 5.30 pm. Then we watch TV or I read aloud to Gwen while she does her cathedral embroidery. I do a little more writing and smoke three or four more cigarettes before turning in at something past eleven.

I have read *Mansfield Park; Pride and Prejudice; Persuasion; Felix Holt, the Radical; The Moonstone; The Woman in White; The Dream King; The Spoils of Poynton; Kilvert's Diary;* and am now busy on Angus Wilson's book on Charles Dickens.

Langley House—the home of the Ashes
Late September 1975
A large square building in yellow brick, a mid-eighteenth-century house set in a largish estate with a private gate leading to the churchyard. A large hall of fine size and generous proportions with two arches through which one passes to reach the staircase (good but by no means outstanding). The walls (how long since they were redecorated?) are a dingy brownish-green, a depressing colour, repeated in the large dining room. The walls are hung with portraits—an eighteenth-century Ashe in military costume, and the egregious Squire Ashe, looking rather severe, but not bearded as in his photograph. The interior is generally depressing, but there are many fine articles of furniture and fine objects in cases, and good baroque/rococo mirrors. The large dining room on the first floor is just as dingy but the small drawing room is cosy and habitable.

Major Scott Ashe was in carpet slippers, waiting for his doctor. He is a sick man, with ulcerated legs. He gave an appearance of timidity but were there, beneath the surface, traces of his grandfather's irascibility? His brother, Arthur, an unassuming man, whose passion is looking after the churchyard, gave me a letter to copy. It was from Lucy Ashe about Kilvert's farewell sermon. Obviously there are Kilvert documents in the house, but will one ever be able to see them?

Mrs Scott Ashe gave us some sedum cuttings and they have all struck.

Nonsuch
From Langley Burrell we went to Nonsuch, the home of Ettie Meredith Brown, on the invitation of Mrs MacNeile, a Kilvert Society member who lives there. A beautiful stone- built house, with a handsome entrance and a spacious hall with walls covered in leather (Spanish or Indian?—no one knows). In the grounds are the famous larches, among the first to be planted in this country, still alive but twisted into strange shapes. There is a field walk from here to Chittoe Church. The MacNeiles were very friendly and hospitable and we enjoyed meeting them, although we had been warned that Mr M was rather blimpish. There is a lovely view of the Downs from the house.

2 October 1975
Set off early to get to a school near Wigan to give a talk to 50 or so sixth formers; and from there went on to Durham via Bowes. Saw the lovely El Greco and

an interesting series of Victorian photographs by a Revd J. Pattison (Seaton Carew and Weardale).

Three days in Durham
3 October 1975
I have had a strange three days here. Durham is a far more exciting city than Worcester—far more exciting than it was when I was an undergraduate there (actually I was a graduate)—more bookshops, more concerts, more performances, more public events, more museums—even *son et lumière*! I walked around Old Elvet, over the new footbridge and called on Dr Doyle to give him a copy of my little book on Kilvert. I have felt unable to be of much use to my mother. I am a poor son to her. But she is content with so little—a few words, the minimum of attention. I put my arms around her to kiss her goodbye, but she almost pushes me away. Why? Was it just a northern habit of disliking an open show of emotion? I found her reactions slightly puzzling.

My sister Mary has two remarkable neighbours. They no sooner meet—they are sisters—than they begin to quarrel violently. At the height of the quarrel the visiting sister takes refuge in the outside lavatory. She sits there until she has cooled, then returns to the house—only to begin quarrelling again with even greater virulence. They cannot be together without quarrelling—even fighting—but they cannot endure to be apart.

11 October 1975
In the steps of Francis Kilvert once more. Bredwardine, Mrs Kilvert's grave, Miss Newton's house, the Knapp, the Upper Cwm and Fine Street where Kilvert's churchwarden lived. Merbach Hill where K had a picnic, and then to Pope Place, the house that Pope built for himself after his marriage to Miss Money Kyrle.

23 October 1975
The service at Newchurch, David Lockwood giving the sermon *(Plate 6)*. There was a curious stain on the wall behind the pulpit that moved me to write the following poem.

Plate 6: Group at Newchurch, Radnorshire, for the Kilvert Service—sermon given on 23 October 1975 by the Revd David Lockwood (clergyman on the right of the picture)—with Oswin Prosser, Hon. Sec. Kilvert Society, to his left.

For a friend preaching the Kilvert Sermon at Newchurch 1975

Topping the rise, we see the humble church,
as grey as slate, adrift in a green trough,
between the breakers of the hills;
but, entering, we find it crammed to the doors,
a pilgrim ship, laden with souls.

Behind me, an old man, tone deaf,
groans out the hymns, but shrill Welsh voices
rally the singing.
Bare nave, bare chancel
ring to 'Jerusalem my Happy Home.'
If the sheep, scattered like stones on the green hills,
are bleating, no one can hear them now.

My friend, poet and priest,
mounts the cramped pulpit, speaks
of that other poet and priest who, a century ago,
stumbled by candlelight through his forgotten sermon.
Behind him the yellowing wall
is stained with damp.
The stains have formed themselves
into the shape of a head, the profile
of some romantic spirit—I think of Kean –
with thrusting head, eye on fire,
hair streaming behind him,
silhouette of the preacher dead and the preacher living.

When the church empties the image is still there.

October 1975

20 November 1975

We are watching a superb TV programme—'The Spirit of the Age'. Mark Girouard's contribution on Victorian architecture was a masterpiece. Now I am eager to see Thoresby Hall, Cheadle Church and the Natural History Museum at Oxford.

18 December 1975

My friend, Jim Siddle, has had a stroke. Two years ago John Danby died. George Westgarth is dead—and Bill Warner and Chas Hall—Jim Wilson, Martin Randall, Edith Harrison, Fred Shatwell, John Goodyear, Audrey Rogers... What a sad roll-call. But mother is 88, and in spite of having fallen and broken her wrist, is in excellent spirits.

Corrie Hodgson—a remarkable old dear who seems to make a living lecturing on Peru and Chile. Every now and then she sells something and sets off to see what is happening in South America. She travels rough, hitch-hiking as often as she can. She has no fear of being mugged—she has nothing worth taking; or of being raped. 'You know the coils of rope they have on board old ships,' she said to us. 'Lovely—just plant your bottom in one of those and lean back. And you'll have the sleep of your life.'

Christmas Day
The *pièce de résistance* this year was a series of 29 presents that Nick had prepared for Erica—one for every year of her life. A wonderful assortment of presents which had to be taken out of a box one by one. As usual I was the least convivial of all the gathering—I invariably feel off colour in December. Perhaps it was the thought of all the lectures I have to give that was making me anxious—and I have inexplicably lost the ring that Gwen gave me.

Vespers at Stanbrook
27 December 1975
The church is so clean and bright you would think it newly decorated. The tiles of the sanctuary are polished and a strong light—almost a spotlight—makes the altar gleam. One sister is at her place at the organ. Then, on the stroke of the bell, the nuns come in, two by two, turn and genuflect, and take their places. There could be forty or fifty. As soon as they have taken their places the singing of vespers begins. I follow the service but do not understand the significance of what happens.

The monstrance is brought in and covered. After a few minutes of sweet but repetitive singing the abbot appears. He brings forward the monstrance, now uncovered, displays it, then spoons incense into the censor. The strong, slightly disagreeable odour fills the sanctuary, and flows out through the side grill of the chapel to the five or six of us who are on this side of the screen. We are supposed to sing a hymn, but if it comes I miss it. The abbot is helped into some vestment and swings the censor. We stand and sit when the sisters stand and sit.

There is no communion service as we know it. The holy wafer is shown, then withdrawn, removed from the monstrance, then put into a little receptacle and covered. I have no idea what it all means—no idea why the service should end when it does, and the sisters withdraw, two by two, as they came it. It is all solemn, ceremonious and confusing. This is part of our friend Meinrad's life. It does not stultify her. On the contrary, when I talk to her I am aware of being in the presence of a profoundly religious and searching sensibility. Her life, and the strange fascinating but bewildering pictures that come from it, are alas beyond my comprehension.

Notes

1 Robin Tanner (1904-88) and his wife Heather (1903-93) were both members of the Kilvert Society; Robin was an artist, etcher and print maker, and Heather a writer. Following Robin's retirement in 1964, he collaborated with Heather, illustrating her topographical books, such as *Wiltshire Village*, for which she supplied the text. Dame Lucie Rie (1902-95), was an Austrian-born ceramicist, famous in Britain for her delicate hand-thrown pots, bottles and bowls in Modernist forms.

2 Her Majesty's Inspector (schools).

3 Wynford Vaughan-Thomas (1908-87) was a Welsh newspaper journalist and radio and television broadcaster of national importance. After William Plomer, the founder of the Kilvert Society, died Wynford became President and Fred Grice Deputy-President. Wynford was a champion of the Welsh landscape and of the Welsh language, which he spoke.

4 Henry Kingsley (1830-76), published 1872.

5 Hope End is located on the west side of the Malverns, facing Herefordshire.

6 Disserth Church is located 2-3 miles south-west of Llandrindod Wells.

7 In fact, Frederick Grice's book on Kilvert was entitled *Francis Kilvert and his World*. Horsham, Sussex: Caliban Books, 1982.

Chapter 6: 1976

The Great Gale
2 January 1976
This was the night of the Great Gale, one of the worst gales of the century, and certainly one of the worst for thirty years. Many trees fell during the night. One big tree near Hilda's was snapped off half way up, and fell across the road. The great chestnut at the bottom of our garden, damaged already by one storm, lost more of its branches. An old elm tree near Hallow Church was completely uprooted. The children were scrambling over it, peeling off the dead bark and looking at the insects that had eaten the bark off the tree. The church had lost many of its slates plus a large finial from the east gable that fell on a tomb and knocked the headstone crooked. But the centre of the city came off worst. When Colin and Gillian went back to Sidbury so many slates were flying that they hardly dared to stand on the pavement long enough to open the door. Slates came off everywhere in showers, and the northeast pinnacle on the central tower of the cathedral snapped off and fell onto and partly through the roof of one of the north transepts. It must have shattered the vaulting because the authorities have sealed off the transept. The rubble has not yet been cleared away. They say it will cost at least a quarter of a million pounds to repair the damage.

Trees have come down everywhere. All last night and today the air has been full of noise and power saws, and every ladder in the land seems to be in commission. Everywhere men are cementing loose tiles, putting back coping stones, mending shattered guttering, straightening bent TV aerials. We have been lucky, with no trees down and only a few tiles loosened.

What my grandchildren argue about
7 January 1976
These are things that Veronica and Aidan argue about:
I won more games of Beetle than you.
You were frightened to touch that lamb that was caught in the bushes, weren't you?
Well, you yelled blue murder that night Mum went out to a party.
It's my game of Monopoly, so I should say who plays it.

Veronica was frightened to jump over a little stream.
I should have a box with a key as well as Aidan.

Veronica insisted on making a speech at her birthday tea. In fact, she made two, being unsatisfied with the first one. She thought it over and decided she would like to have a second try.

Aidan carried his chemistry set around with him, but he says he doesn't want to do any experiments till he gets home.

The Gale

This gale swept over us like an avenging angel,
that did not know the godly from the ungodly.
Collapsing chimneys and TV aerials
sent slates and tiles in showers on path and pavement.
Church roofs were flayed, pinnacles brought down
and headstones levelled.
The dead must have thought they felt the thump of doomsday;
and trees, whose only sin was they had stood too long—
old hollow oaks, pear trees and apple trees
in long-neglected orchards,
moribund peeled elms, were felled by the score.

This morning every ladder's in commission.
Tilers spring up where shattered slates were strewn.
The day is filled with the vicious snarl
of mechanical saws;
and the world is littered with windfalls of winter firewood.

19 January 1976

Lecturing at Folkestone
20 January 1976
I was very nervous about this lecture to a group of Kent teachers. I slept badly the night before I set off, and slept just as badly at Folkestone. But the lecture went off fairly well after all. The most interesting things happened to me after I had left Folkestone. I went to see the Spanish Art at the Royal Academy, the Treasures from Thrace and the Turners at the British Museum.

The journey home was quite memorable in an unexpected way. The compartment filled surprisingly quickly. A lady with fair hair—probably bleached but not disagreeably so—sat diagonally opposite me. She had a pleasant face but looked tired and kept popping sweets (or were they pills?) into her mouth rather furtively. As soon as she had sat down an old gentleman with a bowler and a thin document case took his place opposite me. Then a second lady in a headscarf and a tweedy suit came in and shook out her Evening Standard. She was followed by a third lady who sat down beside me and took out a sheaf of papers. I glanced sideways and saw the title on the first sheet—work done by the students of...

She was obviously intending to spend the journey marking; but no sooner had she begun than the old man opposite me took out his pipe and lit it, and the second lady started on a cheroot. 'Pooh,' said the lady in tweeds, 'Let's have a window open, for heaven's sake.' And without permission she pulled open the sliding door. The old man said nothing. It was a smoking compartment and he was entitled to smoke if he wished. He went on doing so and the lady stuck to her cheroot.

Then just before the train moved off another man entered—a big man with a kindly face. 'Is this seat taken?' he asked looking down at the space taken up by the old man's document case.

'I don't think so,' I answered. 'Please, take it.'

The old man grudgingly removed his document case and the latest comer sat down. He opened his briefcase with the air of a man who is used to working on trains and began to make notes in pencil. So three of us were academics. I had no marking to do but I meant to try and read a book of German short stories I had brought with me.

No one spoke until the train pulled up just beyond Reading.

'Didcot, I suppose,' said the old man looking up from his notes.

'Yes.'

'I often wonder who lives in Didcot. I once—a long time ago—had to spend two hours here, so I went down to a pub. It was the most miserable pub I've ever been in. It depressed me just to be there.'

'You remind me of a visit I once made to the Black Bull at Haworth—where Branwell Brontë went to drown his sorrows. There were three or four men there, playing dominoes, in complete silence. They didn't even speak to the barmaid. When they wanted more drink one of them knocked on the table and held up his fingers to show her how many glasses they wanted.'

'That must have been gloomy, but Yorkshire people do have a sense of humour, you know. I was once walking in the summer somewhere in Yorkshire—I forget exactly where it was. We came to a place with a swimming bath, and my brother said, 'Can I swim in there?' The man looked at him and said, 'Well, tha's better jump in and try, hadn' tha?'

He began talking about lonely out-of-the-way places like Tow Law where he had taken an extramural class long ago. 'I was in Durham then. At the university. I used to get to Tow Law by bus. I think it was the highest and coldest spot I've ever taken a class in. But I don't suppose you know Tow Law.'

'But I do. And I must have known some of your colleagues. Bertie Colgrave, for one.'

'Oh yes, I knew him. The Bede man, wasn't he? The authority on the Venerable Bede. An Anglo-Saxon man, wasn't he?"

'That's right. What's your speciality?'

'Oriental Studies. The Ottoman Empire—especially the last years. Most of my archives are in Istanbul. Have you ever been there?'

'No, I'm sorry to say.'

'Well, if ever you go, don't fly. Go to Genoa and take the Turkish line from there. Very good. All one class but very good. The best way to go to Istanbul. They never go up the Bosphorus by night—the currents are tricky. So you always arrive in the morning. A wonderful experience.'

All this while the old man opposite me said nothing. If he had heard the conversation it had apparently meant nothing to him. He went steadily and methodically through his *Telegraph*, while the lady in the tweed suit laboured over her simple crossword. But I felt that I had been privileged to listen to something very rare, and to be in the presence of a happy and enviable man.

29 January 1976

I have started work on my 'Who's Who in Kilvert's Diary,' and have sent off two stories to OUP—one about the boy who finds a flying machine and the other about the General Strike.

23 February 1976

Today I went out to Much Marcle to see again the church and to have a look at Homme House where Andrew Pope's wife, Miss Money Kyrle lived. I was very impressed by the house and the grounds. No one lives there now, but the house still seems in good condition. There is a lake, an old stone tower-gateway, older than the main building, and a beautiful drive across the park to the church. I saw the steps on which the famous wedding photograph was taken; and Pope's grave.

The pages of my notebook are filled at this point with an abortive novel about Pope and Kilvert.

6 March 1976

OUP have accepted *Nine Days' Wonder*.[1] I can hardly believe my good fortune. And I brought my class on Victorian Literature to a triumphant climax with a wonderfully successful visit to Wightwick Manor.[2] Lady Mander went out of her way to make us welcome and to speak to us about the history of the house. It's a lovely house, and the chief room, a pseudo-mediaeval hall, which could have been disastrous, is a complete triumph.

11 March 1976

One more happy event. Today I found in the book box belonging to my extra-mural class the precious ring that I lost three months ago. 'Rejoice with me, for that which was lost is found.' I treasured this ring because Gwen gave it to me and Marilynn made it.

Men on the Road

A cold day at the end of March,
a scurf of snow on the grit piled up on the verge,
and air as thick as felt.
I overtake two men before I pull up,
then they overtake me,
turning to take a surly look—just one—
wellingtons, trousers, bottoms of their coats
caked in mud,
as if they had pulled themselves out of a swamp.
They could be brothers—same clothes, same figures,
same hangdog faces, resentful, defeated.
One dogs the other, but without persistence.
If there is enmity, the first doesn't flee,

nor the second pursue.
Apart, but still together, they shamble away,
infecting the day with their dumb enmity
or equally dumb half-wish to be reconciled.

25 March 1976

Out of Touch—Newland

Almshouses, doorways with pointed arches,
mullioned windows, barley-stick chimneys
and church with effeminate Tennysonian heads
of saints and kings for capitals,
and a sanctus bell on the chancel steps –
all the gift of a pious, long-dead,
well-heeled, magnanimous woman.

To dawdle here, admiring the creation
of a Victorian Lady Bountiful,
herself (in the age of Stephenson) in love
with gothic ritual, passé building styles,
is to be not once, but twice, removed from life.

The rest of the world speeds past,
tyres squealing at corners,
their faces behind windscreens pale and blurred.

A strange fulfilment
3 April 1976
Today I saw a beautiful photograph of an Arabian city—Sana'a. And I recognised it as a prototype of that Golden City of which I dream so constantly.

My neighbour
5 April 1976
'Tell you what, Fred, I reckon that for a couple of amateurs we haven' made a bad job

of that. We could have got a couple of men in, they would have charged us ten quid, and they wouldn' have made as good a job as that. My son-in-law gave me that stuff. And I bet you could go all over Worcester and not find stuff like that. That's what I call a finish. You wouldn' get any of them brickies round here to give you a finish like that.'

In point of fact the wall he was referring to was as crooked as a dog's leg, and within a few days the stone began to work loose.

'I had a letter from an old friend of mine that lives now in the Isle of Man. He reminded me that I was the best man at his wedding. That was 55 years ago. That takes you back, doesn' it? And I'll tell you another thing that will shake you rigid, Fred. He has to pay 13p for a small white loaf.'

13 April 1976

Today I went to London to see the great exhibition of Islamic Art at the Hayward Gallery; and a second exhibition in the Museum of Mankind on Sana'a, that fabulous Yemen city of which I saw the photograph recently. We had a lovely day—perfect—and Gwen bought a Liberty scarf which she has coveted for years, and a new dress in Marks and Spencer.

One of the revelations of the Hayward Exhibition was the display of fabulously illuminated manuscripts, as fine as anything done in the Christian world. Did the inspiration for the *Book of Kells* come basically from the East?

When we were on the way home, a girl from Malvern, who was sitting in the corner of our compartment, overheard me talking about the attractions of Islam. Just before we got out, she handed me a little booklet, saying, 'I think this will interest you after what you have been saying about Islam.' It was a cheap little religious tract called *The Way of Salvation.*

But this Easter my head has been more full of Islam than of Christianity, I'm afraid. Islamic Art has the most extraordinary soothing and calming effect on me—a sense of harmony and order.

Islam

The Caliph sits at the window,
his white burnous enfolds him like a cloud.
He listens to the quiet voices of the sages,
under white arches, ringed round by pale students,
and the noise of the women
calling to one another across the housetops.

The light creeps over the words of the prophet
spelt out in tiles above the horseshoe arch.
The gold of the day reddens the crimson, damask porphyry.
The musicians have withdrawn,
and the calling of the women dies down.
Caliph, musicians, sages, women wait
the call of the muezzin
to the last prayer of the day.

25 April 1976

A surprising hoard
26 April 1976
Tonight Miss Millest, Headmistress of the Alice Ottley School, showed us a surprising folder of letters collected in the nineteenth-century by Miss Alice Ottley, the first headmistress of the school—from Disraeli, Gladstone, Lewis Carroll, Henry Morley, Burne-Jones—even a signature by W. Wordsworth. I don't think they were written to her. I think they were given to her by Lewis Carroll, whom she knew, for her collection of letters from famous people. As far as I know they have never been properly studied.

2 May 1976
Suffering from dyspepsia. My digestive system plays all sorts of odd tricks on me. I take endless medicine and eat like a sparrow—all to no effect. I tend to wake early and have done next to no writing in the last few weeks. I wish I could eat or drink as others seem able to do. It is a simple thing to desire. But many in our family are plagued with faulty digestions. My mother has been dyspeptic all her life, is now nearly ninety, and her energy shows no signs of failing.

Mrs Lea of Hallow
6 May 1976
These reminiscences were told to me with many a nudge and wink and are probably unreliable:

'Of course she was always in the papers at that time. Cos she was a good giver, you know. Five thousand here and five thousand there. Oh yes she was a great churchwoman. Made the Bishop her executor—Biggs it was then. Fifty thousand for that little job. Not bad, eh? Mind, he didn't stay long in

Worcester after that—no, he went off to Coventry. But her husband—he had pots of money, but he was a sporty kind of feller. I don' think they saw eye to eye, them two. He liked dogs—greyhounds and his ambition was to win the Waterloo Cup. But he never done it. A lot of them rich chaps liked sport—yes, cockfighting. They had cockfighting at Witley Court. On the carpet in the drawing room—yes! On the best carpet. But that wasn't up her street.'

'Dyson Perrins was a different sort of chap, very modest. He saved the Porcelain Works. Mind he liked to know where his money was goin'. Oh, yes.'

20 May 1976
We have just returned from a short holiday in Austria. England looks cold and drab and dirty after those lovely days in Vienna and St Wolfgang.

Vandalism

Who kicked in the panes of the telephone kiosk
and ripped the receiver from the hook?
Who smashed the slats on the riverside seats,
threw the lifebelts in the water
and stoned the swans to death?
Who scrawls obscenities on the lavatory walls
and defecates in the cathedral?

Did we return from a war infected
by the evil we gave our young years to destroy?
Was the next generation mysteriously begotten
by those we thought we had vanquished?
Did we purge a continent to transmit to our own children
the virus of the swastika?

25 May 1976

25 May 1976
Reading *The Three Clerks* by Trollope, *Something of Myself* by Kipling, *The Master of Ballantrae* by Stevenson; and have been writing two or three short stories which I show to no one and never try to publish. I shall lose my copies if I am not careful.

1917

A boy sits at his desk.
He winces as the slate pencil
of a girl behind him
scringes on her slate.
It is almost the end of the week.
The teacher folds back the hymn sheet behind his desk,
stopping when he comes to the hymn
'The day thou gavest, Lord is ended.'
But the pencil scringes again on the slate.
The noise is the noise of the bullets
cutting the air as his father climbs the parapet
and runs into No Man's Land.

31 May 1976

3 June 1976
Went to Hereford to hear Charles Causley reading his own poetry. An amiable personality and a good poet. We were greatly taken by the poems about Hospital Visitors—poems that came from his own visits to his poor handicapped mother who had to go into hospital in the end.

He is a lightly-built youngish-looking man, although I have no doubt he is at least sixty. He is a good unaffected reader and a genuine poet, at his best when he is writing about schools, schoolchildren and the experience of nursing his mother. I have heard him twice and taken greatly to him on both occasions.

Rousham
8 June 1976
Went to Rousham to see Kent's garden, which begins with a large flat lawn, like a college lawn, from the far end of which one can command a view. There are two white summerhouses at each end of the lawn and a baroque statue of a lion attacking a deer. From here a wandering path leads down to two cascades, before one a circular pool with immense goldfish, water lilies and countless dragonflies. Alas in this dreadful drought the cascades are dry, but a spring feeds the pool. By more paths one comes to a kind of temple and more statuary,

and you discover that under the lip of the great lawn, so to speak, is a colonnade in stone, arcaded, with urns and what must surely still be Kent's original seats in the alcoves. It is not easy to find a satisfactory progress through the garden.

From Rousham I drove into Oxford, and had to travel so far out of it to find a parking place that I had to get a bus back into the town centre.

I bought a book on Royal Persian MSS for £4.50, a copy of *Kim*, and Eliot's selection of Kipling's verse for 80p (in Evesham).

16 June 1976

Have just returned from listening to a superb speech in the college SCR by Hugh Ford—as good as anything Thurber ever wrote. Hugh, who is on exchange here from Trenton, is a very distinguished scholar—an expert on Parisian publishers of English and American writers of the twenties and thirties, and on Nancy Cunard.

If you walk round Severn Stoke at night you will see all the Bentleys and Jensen Interceptors and Rover 3000s parked in the roadways. This is not because the owners have no garages, but because these superbly equipped garages, carpeted and heated are where the rich commuters of the village keep their pampered dogs. If rebirth is a fact, may I be reincarnated as a Severn Stoke dog, and live all my life in a state of unparalleled comfort, even luxury, being dutifully fed and groomed and exercised and put to bed each night in a first-class heated garage.

The Great Drought of 1976

29 June 1976

For the last few days we have been suffering under the worst heatwave I have ever known in this country, with temperatures well over 90 degrees Fahrenheit in most of England and Wales, and rumours of over 100 at Wimbledon. Tar is melting on the roads; tyres bursting; radiators boiling; cattle standing up to their knees in whatever they can find; lawns turning to straw; weeds flourishing; heath-fires raging; and the air full of blackfly and greenfly... Out of all this arises one incredible sound—the music of a master songster of a thrush that, morning and night, takes time off from its labours to sing in the most piercing and musical notes I have ever heard bird deliver. A Caruso—or a Janet Baker—of song thrushes; a most accomplished singer who has chosen this appalling heatwave in which to make his debut.

29 June 1976

Last week Joyce Prosser, wife of my friend Oswin, died of a heart attack. Her funeral took place on the eve of a Kilvert Commemoration Service at Builth, and Oswin insisted on carrying on with the service. After tea, when we had taken our places on the platform and I was paying my tribute to Joyce (for whom I had a sincere fondness) I was alarmed to hear Oswin getting up from his chair, which was slightly behind mine, and leaving the platform. At first I was afraid that I had tactlessly said something that had upset him. Not at all—he was simply going into the kitchen behind the platform to tell the women not to make such a clatter with the washing up!

Later on the phone, when I was telling him what a success I thought the day had been, he said, 'Yes, but you know—some folks—you never know what they are going to do. You heard me tell them, didn't you, that we would move off at half past six, and if they wanted they could go down and look at the river for a few minutes and cool off. Bless my soul, when I came back to that coach at twenty past to put something in, there they all were, sweltering away. The whole lot of them!'

So twice he forgot his dead wife, once to tick off the washing-up women for being too noisy, and once to muse on the folly of people in the mass, especially the Kilvert Society, whom he could never get to do the right thing for more than a few minutes at a time.

A talkative woman

30 June 1976

'I've just had my sister down with us for a few weeks—you know, the one that still lives in Sunderland, the one that lost her husband two years back—you know her, of course you do, you met her when we were living in St John's. That's a few years back, but you'll remember her. She's not like me, more like my dad was. I was glad to see the back of her. She never stopped talking all the time she was with us—from the minute she came to the minute I put her on the train she talked non-stop all the three weeks she was here. I couldn't get a word in edgeways. I said to Norman, I said, when she got on that train, mind I'm glad to see the back of her. Talk—she'd talk the hind leg off a donkey.'

A short holiday
14 July 1976
Eastwood, to see the D. H. Lawrence country—especially his birthplace, then Hardwick Hall and Thoresby Hall. At Eastwood we heard that Helen Corke was expected that very day to give a talk on her memories of Lawrence (she worked with him at Croydon). She is now 94, and is making the journey from Croydon to Nottingham by train and on her own. She has declined the offer of a car, saying she would rather come by train so that she can use her Senior Citizen Railcard. She is to address a large meeting—probably over 200—of the D. H. Lawrence Society. I wish I could stay and listen to her but we are due at Matlock.

Back in the North
22 July 1976
After Chatsworth, Thorsby and Hardwick, all uplifting experiences—uplifting and exalting—I find myself in this world where all that seems to matter is who has died suddenly, who has what diseases, who has been promoted and who demoted, who has bought a new washing machine or a new car, who has run away with what funds, who has an incurable disease...

It is a strange experience to be back in the North. Nobody seems to read anything but the newspapers. Nobody visits great houses, art galleries, theatres. The world of the arts as we know it is as remote as Katmandu. But they are all wonderfully free uninhibited talkers—and the common ground is more than enough for them. They ask for nothing more.

A fragment of conversation
You're looking a lot older than I thowt you would. I'm seventy now, you know. Living on borrowed time now... But I's a lot better than I was a bit back. Lad, I couldn' eat a spoonful without having to bring it all up... Ye knaa, there's a feller round here tekken to pushing his daughter's bairns around in a pram. Man, he's a scream. All the fellers on the seat take the mickey out of him. 'Has tha' gone back to hand-puttin', Geordie?' That's what they all shout. And there was a woman in the Post Office that other day wi' a postal order for £2.50. She thowt it was for £250 and she didn' half create. One feller asked her to tone it down a bit and she didn't half turn on him. 'Thoo needn' say owt,' she said. 'Thoo's got that much money in thy pockets that tha cannna stand up strite.'

23 July 1976

Hugh Ford tells me that Nancy Cunard, with whom he stayed at her home in Souillac when he was writing his book about her, was the original of Myra Viveash in *Antic Hay*. It was on her too that the dog fell that was flung from an aeroplane. She was an alcoholic—used to drink rum for breakfast; and one of her eccentricities was to wave every night to the Paris Express as it went by. Hugh's last view of her was waving a white handkerchief (or was it a tablecloth?) as he and his wife left on that same Paris Express.

The drought continues. My heathers are going one by one. Most of the bedding plants have been killed by the sun. A big cotoneaster at the end of the garden is dead. Today I saw a fisherman at Bewdley who had carried his chair out into the middle of the river and was sitting on it. Two abnormally dry summers have turned the country almost into a desert. At times the Malverns look as if they are all going up in smoke.

29 July 1976

A day out with the Archaeological Society—almost a geriatric outing now. There is one old dear who breaks wind constantly, even in church. Miss Matley Moore tells her endless and unintelligible stories; and there is an old boy with scarlet-rimmed eyes who cannot manage steps and sees only the ground floor of any place he visits.

Houses and churches were interesting, especially those at Upton Cressett. But the human element appals me. I ought not to say so, because I was aware of my own human failings—all day!

August 1976

I am knocking out some passages from a story about the cathedral. I don't suppose they will come to anything. But cathedrals are mysterious places. Worcester Cathedral Library is a very secret and intriguing place.

Gillian and Colin are in Frankfurt. Veronica and Aidan are in Worcester—staying half with us and half with the Clarkes. Nick and Erica have been staying with us for some time now. They have sold their Worcester house and are waiting for the new house at Ross to be finished. I take the children to the baths, to Lower Wick, to the city, to Tewkesbury to leave Gwen free for the afternoon. But the strain of looking after so large a family—and the endless stream of visitors who descend on us—is telling on Gwen.

We are reading *The Way We Live Now*—which I consider one of Trollope's major achievements.

The Great Drought continues
25 August 1976
It is not yet the end of August, but Autumn has already begun. Leaves browning and shrivelling and falling from the trees in showers—the trees are not merely protecting themselves by shedding leaves, but dying. A row of young cypresses on the other side of the road is giving up—a big brown stain is spreading day by day from the top downwards. Rivers are lower than we have ever known. Fish and river birds are dying from strange diseases. There is no fresh feed for cattle and sheep. The fields are turning not merely brown, but white in the heat. The earth beneath the houses is drying out and contracting, and many buildings are beginning to lean and crack. The fruit is small, and the birds are pecking at the apples, pears and plums in the search for moisture. Strangely enough, for the first time, they are not stripping the rowans. Weeds flourish where grass cannot grow. Lawns are in a desperate state, with burnt and dry patches appearing everywhere. Bedding plants have shrivelled in the heat and heathers have died in scores. Many bushes have limp undernourished leaves. Forest fires are raging everywhere. Firemen are at their wits' end to contain the thousands of outbreaks. The whole of Southern England is as dry as tinder. This is the worst drought for 250 years. And no one can see the end of it yet.

Roses are suffering from mildew. Market gardeners are going out of business. Some factories have been put on a three-day week. I have been wearing light canvas shoes for months. Most men have not worn a jacket for just as long. Parts of Sherwood Forest and the New Forest have been closed to the public—the fire risk is too great. One parson has gone up like Elijah to the top of the highest hill in his parish and pleaded with God to send rain. The temperature in Bristol on this late August day is 20 degrees Fahrheit higher than the temperature in Madrid! There is not an earthworm to be seen. Voles, hedgehogs and shrews are dying of starvation. Our bird life is threatened—their habitats destroyed by fire. The government has appointed a Minister for Drought!

August Bank Holiday
At last we have had rain—persistent and heavy. Many accidents to motorists

have been reported. The dry summer has left the roads polished and slippery.

Am writing, in fits and starts, a story about the cathedral. Marilynn and Peter have returned, a little disillusioned, from a long exhausting tent-trek in Iran. To be frank Marilynn hated it. But their account was confused and confusing.

Colonel Awdry on Kilvert characters
9 September 1976

Colonel Awdry told me today that of Squire Ashe's three daughters, Thersie was a true-blue Tory, but Lucy was a Liberal who favoured yellow rosettes at election time (it was Lucy who went to London to work in the East End and is still remembered as the Lady with the Satchel).

Herbert Prodgers, who made himself a rug out of cat skins, shot the vicar's cat to get the last skin. He was a mixture of meanness and philanthropy—would put a farthing in the church plate but give hundreds towards a new heating system. Mrs Prodgers would stay up playing the harp to him when he could not sleep for gout. Meredith Brown (was it Ettie's father?) was called Pollocky because he knew more about London scandal than even this famous sleuth.

Lady Alda Hoare
13 September 1976

Roger and I have been working at Stourhead on the friendship between Hardy and Lady Alda Hoare. What a great privilege to be allowed to work in the beautiful eighteenth-century library, and to have access to Lady Alda's correspondence and books. A very interesting story is emerging of a woman with literary aspirations, who was captivated by Hardy's fiction at an early age, and then assiduously sought his friendship. She was one of the earliest Hardy fans, and was friendly with both his wives, but especially with Florence. We hope to write a monograph of this friendship.

I am in a dreadfully nervous state about our coming holiday in Spain. I may as well confess it and get it off my chest. My digestion is in a dreadful state. If I cannot cope with the simple meals I have at home, how on earth will I be able to deal with foreign cooking? To be candid I am in a blue funk and could go on describing the symptoms of my neuroses at vast length.

Last Possessions

This is the jacket that last he wore.
When he took to his bed, I put it aside.
What were the things he kept in his pockets
before he died?

You might easily guess. There was nothing but
the little things he valued in life.
No money, no keys, but a piece of string
and a pocket knife.

And something else—a token of
the best endeavours of all his years—
a scrap of paper bearing the words
of an uncompleted verse.

15 September 1976

[*Editors*: This poem is inspired by a reference to Thomas Hardy's last possessions in a letter from Florence Hardy to Lady Hoare.]

4 October 1976

In the last fortnight I have been to Madrid, Toledo, Segovia, La Granja, Ávila and Cuenca; I have given a lecture at Stratford and another at Worcester; spoken at a prize-giving in the Art Gallery; and addressed a gathering of the Kilvert Society at Kington St Michael. What a programme! But in spite of all my misgivings I have come through it all successfully.

Erica and Nick are still with us. This is the eleventh week of their stay—but it has done Erica a great deal of good.

Next week I have to go and give a talk at Sheffield. So I work up to another foolish crisis.

Ever since Mr Howell was made Minister for Drought it has rained incessantly. There never was a minister who had such an instantaneous and complete success.

Damp Autumn

A cold limp day,
the sky like blotting paper.
The trees give up. They don't mind if they're in rags.
They let leaves slip through their fingers
to stick like stamps on the pavements,
and litter the ground with split conker husks
like crusts thrown under the table.
The spinster sun with sickly face
draws back behind dingy shades.

The true story of giving a lecture at Sheffield
16 October 1976

I brooded about this for days, hating the whole prospect with a distinct loathing. The train from Worcester was late and I missed my connection at Birmingham, but I still got to Sheffield in good time. I found my hotel room insufferably hot, escaped from it as soon as I could, went into the city centre to see what was on at The Crucible, and discovered that the play for the night was incredibly *French without Tears*, which I cannot bear to watch.

However, I went largely to see the inside of the theatre, but left at the interval. I got a bus back to the hotel, read a little, went to bed ridiculously early, woke at midnight in a fearful sweat, wondering how on earth I could endure the long night before me, ate a few biscuits, put in ear-plugs—then, to my surprise slept, although fitfully, till morning, breakfasted and settled down as patiently as I could to wait for my lecture to begin.

I was plagued for a while with a dreadful thirst, but in the end got through the talk not without success. But there was one more contretemps to come. While I was waiting for the train, I remembered that I had left my tape-recorder in Bernard Harrison's car; after much ludicrous coming and going I recovered it.

But what a way to live! I hated the hotel, though I suppose it was comfortable enough, hated the loneliness, hated the business of facing an unknown audience—and have made my mind up that, when the rest of my commitments are over, I shall never again accept this kind of invitation. All very stupid and very neurotic, but it is no good hiding the purgatorial nature of experiences such as these.

A curious thing
16 October 1976
There is something that rarely fails to have a soothing effect on me—the contemplation of Islamic Art—even (or, I might almost say, especially) Mudejar Art. I have felt this very strongly in Santa María la Blanca and El Tránsito in Toledo, in the Alcázar in Seville, in the great mosque at Cordoba and of course in the Alhambra. I think the best of Islamic Art is meant to have this effect. I remember these obscure Toledo churches when the Cathedrals of Ávila and Segovia have faded out of my mind.

19 October 1976
Today I made a dreadful blunder when invigilating for the Open University. A candidate who ought to have been at Hereford turned up at our centre—and I very stupidly sent him off to Hereford instead of allowing him to take the examination here. I am ashamed of myself for having made such a bad mistake, and only hope that the candidate will not suffer too badly from my incompetence. I seem to have been hard pressed this summer—ever since that arduous visit to Folkestone. Too many public lectures!

I grow very anxious at times about my health. I have perhaps been subject to too many pressures this summer—lectures at Folkestone, Nuneaton, Stratford, culminating in that arduous trip to Sheffield and the dreadful Open University blunder. How I wish I could be as well as Gwen is. I fear that my journal is degenerating into a chronicle of ailments—the diary of a valetudinarian. To make things worse the new slide projector I bought has broken down on me, the woodwork on the kitchen door is rotting, and moss is invading the bare patches on the lawn.

A strange happening
6 November 1976
When I received my copy of the *Transactions of the Worcestershire Archaeological Society* I was a little displeased. Mr S's article was badly printed, with some passages more deeply inked than others, as if a special emphasis had to be put on them. I feared he might have some caustic comments to make; at the least I feared that I would have to insert an apology in every copy.[3] I wrote to him offering to do so. Then I had an unexpected phone call from his wife to say that they had both been involved in a car crash, and although she had escaped

lightly, he had broken a leg and some ribs and was not likely to recover. So the man whose criticisms I was bracing myself to face is dying. I am ashamed of the relief that I feel.

A few days later he died.

Erica and Nick are putting their new house at Ross in order. We have been through twice to give them a hand. Erica is taking everything in her stride. She has found a remarkable reserve of strength from somewhere.

25 November 1976

Erica has gone into hospital at Hereford to have her baby. My *Nine Days' Wonder* is in print. Tomorrow I go into hospital myself for a gastroscopy.

26 November 1976

Erica was delivered of a daughter late this afternoon. She weighed just over six pounds and the name is to be Laura Kate. So our third grandchild comes into the world.

27 November 1976

The gastroscopy, which I was dreading, is over; and when I came round I had the unexpected sensation of having passed through a happy experience. Mr Dyer says there is no trace of an ulcer and has put me on to a diet of roughage—the very diet I have been avoiding for years.

Laura Kate is a sweet little girl, with reddish-golden hair, delicate hands and beautiful fingers, a nice mouth and shortish upper lip—a fine normal little girl with a placid disposition.

If she had been more aware she must have wondered what kind of a world she had been born into. We have had the severest weather for many years, bitterly cold nights with harsh frosts, a momentary thaw in the afternoon, then one more night of intense cold.

A Winter Child

Yours was a cold nativity, my dear,
and a colder infancy.
One would have thought the world meant to disown you
—snow, hail, sleet, ice and freezing fog,
sub-zero temperatures, impassable roads,

a bitter November, a Siberian December.
And a bleak January;
and the new year as churlish as the old had been.

It all meant nothing to you.
You slept, when you felt like sleeping, in a warm cot,
and took your fill of milk,
disliked being bathed, rejoiced in a clean nappy.
It was not rage at the weather that made you cry,
but simply hunger.
The wind that troubled you was inside, not out.
The blizzards blew but you learnt to kick and smile.

When you sit up, it will be Spring.
The weather will mend its ways,
and ape the beauty
no frost or snow can ever rob you of.

[*Editors*: Written when Laura was a few weeks old.]

Over the last months I have read to Gwen:

Wilkie Collins, *The Moonstone*—an absorbing plot which sinks in your mind without trace once you have completed the book.

Mrs Gaskell, *Ruth*—an excellent and courageous novel (but not as good as *North and South*)

The Torrents of Spring—Turgenev makes first-class family reading.

At the moment Gwen is away looking after Erica at Ross and I am at home working on the final draft of my story about the boy who finds the old flying machine. The setting is a mixture of Stanford Hall and Hanbury Hall. I am also engaged on a story about a cathedral, but I have little faith in it.

Landscape and literature

All my adult life I have been possessed by two apparently irreconcilable passions—the love of the open air, and a delight in great literature; and fortunately I have found a way of satisfying both these passions by spending half of my time in study (I was fortunate enough to be able to make my living lecturing on literature) and the other half by exploring those places and scenes where my admired writers had found inspiration.

This process began early. When I was still young, I was able, by the kindness of an uncle, to spend part of my holidays in the Lake District, which was in those day unspoilt by tourism and still close to the Lakeland that Wordsworth had known. My first literary pilgrimages were to Grasmere and to Long Meg and her Daughters, the stone circle just outside Keswick which had found its way into 'Hyperion', 'like a dismal cirque of Druid stones, upon a forlorn moor, when the chill rain begins at shut of eve.'[4]

When I came to Worcester, the scope of my wanderings was enlarged. Without going too far I could walk on those hills just south of Birmingham where Thomson had composed part of 'The Seasons', and look across into the west, as Housman did, and see the westering sun illuminating Shropshire, his own Tyr nan Og. I walked the Malverns, trying to identify that particular place where, as Masefield claimed, the purest air in England blew, and (with more success) the school where W.H. Auden taught for a year or two. Langland was too shady a figure for me to get close to, but it was easy to be near in spirit to Elizabeth Barrett Browning as she strode over the hills from Hope End to commune with that blind tutor who lived in Ruby Cottage and forget the tittle tattle, the silly ritual visits, the futile and boring tea parties to which her family wished to condemn her. Easier still to sense the presence of Robert Frost, Edward Thomas, Lascelles Abercrombie, Wilfrid Gibson and Rupert Brooke, who all came together in a corner of Gloucestershire—Dymock—in the last year before 1914. Gibson has recorded their coming together in his poem 'The Golden Room'.[5]

'Do you remember that still summer evening
When, in the cosy cream-washed living-room
Of The Old Nailshop, we all talked and laughed –
Our neighbours from The Gallows, Catherine
And Lascelles Abercrombie; Rupert Brooke;
Eleanor and Robert Frost, living a while
At Little Iddens, who'd brought over with them
Helen and Edward Thomas? In the lamplight
We talked and laughed; but, for the most part, listened
While Robert Frost kept on and on and on,
In his slow New England fashion, for our delight,
Holding us with shrewd turns and racy quips

And the rare twinkle of his grave blue eyes?...
'Twas in July
Of nineteen-fourteen that we sat and talked:
Then August brought the war, and scattered us.'

When I went in search of The Gallows, I found that it had been demolished, but The Old Nail Shop was as it had looked in 1914; and a generous old lady, who lived there, allowed me to see the inside of the room where the poets had gathered. Little Iddens too was still standing. When I was looking at the house and talking to the young couple who had come to live there and could make little of its odd name, an old man came up out of the valley and through the gate that led into the garden. He had been gathering bunches of those lovely little wild daffodils which grow so profusely in this part of the world, and was taking them to Ledbury to sell them.

'God, I be thirsty,' he said. 'Will ye let me have a glass of water, ma'am?' I felt that this was the kind of meeting, a near Wordsworthian encounter, that Frost and his friends were in search of when they came there so long ago.

Another writer to whom I have been able to draw very close is Francis Kilvert, author of the now-famous Diary. The other day, after a service in which those of us who had offered to do duty in Worcester Cathedral were presented to the Dean, we were invited to meet him less formally. He no longer lives in the official Deanery which he found too large and too expensive for his needs, but in a smaller house in the opposite corner of College Green, the very house, in fact, in which Maria Kilvert lived; and when I entered the drawing room, I realised that I was in that room where, a century ago, Kilvert sat with his father and mother discussing the eccentric Miss Kilvert, and the high-handed behaviour of her servants; and in coming to this room from the cathedral we had done in reverse the journey undertaken by Miss Kilvert to her last resting place in the Cloister Garth. For many years before this I had been studying Kilvert, and had written at some length on him. I had followed in his footsteps in Radnorshire, Herefordshire and Wiltshire; and had spent one happy afternoon finding that Poet's Stone near Tenbury where Wordsworth had rested and to which Kilvert, a true Wordsworthian, had made a pilgrimage. I had become reconciled to one of the greatest disappointments of my life, my failure to trace the missing third notebook which Kilvert's niece, Mrs Essex Hope, had carelessly given away.[6]

A troubled vicar—an incident at Hoarwithy
7 December 1976

Even though the view of the church, perched on its high terrace above the river, was obscured and degraded by bungalows, sheds and outhouses, it still looked like something miraculously transported from Italy or Spain—with a campanile, an arcade with Romanesque arches, a rounded apse—all giving the promise of rare things inside.

I climbed the steps from the roadway—half steps, half ramp—and entered the arcade. The winds that swept in from Wales had already begun to thin away the light rounded pillars, and one keystone was perilously loose. The arcade ended in a porch, open on two sides, south and west, floored with a mosaic pavement, and flanked by columns carved with such imagination and delicacy that only the subjects (a centaur for instance) betrayed that they were not mediaeval. I was more anxious than ever to see the interior, but all the doors to the church were firmly locked.

The chances of getting in did not seem good. The village was empty except for one old woman a hundred yards or so ahead of me, but before I could catch up with her she had turned into the pub. However, as I was giving up hope, I saw an old man in a yard, and he told me that the likeliest fellow to let me in would be the parson, and he just lived up there. He pointed to a grim-looking stone house that I had thought of inquiring at, but the dirty windows and the unwashed curtains hanging loosely behind them had given me the impression that the house was empty. It looked more like a disused school than a vicarage.

I knocked, and eventually the door was opened by the vicar (I do not know his correct title—'vicar' will have to do)—a melancholy man, with a face that would have been handsome, but was now marred by poverty, anxiety and a mistrust that was not natural to him but had been forced upon him by events beyond his experience and control. His skin was white, his eyes watery, and his voice tremulous.

When I asked him if I could have the key to see inside the church, he looked distressed.

'Well, I've promised the Chief Constable, you see... We have had thieves... two burglaries... and I'm expecting a visitor just now. This Christmas Fair that we run, you see, it costs... well you have no idea what it costs... forty pounds and I'll never get it back.'

He stood with his hand on the door, as if he would like to close it but could not bring himself to be so inhospitable. Beyond the door was a cold hall, with a flight of uncarpeted steps, at the foot of which stood an old stove, giving off a smell of paraffin.

'Everything's upside down,' he said, 'and I haven't had time for anything to eat yet.'

He dropped his eyes as he was speaking, and looking down I saw a robin moving about very close to my feet.

'I feed them, you see... That's why it comes so close... Well, I shouldn't do this, but I'll get the keys and let you... I'll come with you.'

He put on his hat and coat as if he was preparing for a long walk.

'You see, the vicar who built it last century had money. And he brought workmen over from Italy to have it just so. But see what happens nowadays? I got a man in the village who knows all about locks to put this special one on. But see what they do? They saw through the hasp. You go in, and I'll leave you here. There are lights behind the hymn board but please remember to put them out, will you?'

He left me in the vestibule connecting the two porches, the doors of which I had tried, and I went into the body of the church. It had a plain nave, with a row of small round-headed windows on the south side, no aisles, a stone floor rising by a step to a polished platform on which the altar stood, faced with white marble and lapis lazuli, guarded by four marble columns, blue and green and pink, surmounted with elaborate Byzantine capitals, and enriched with a fine dome in gold and white mosaic. The beauty and completeness of the design was very impressive, even without the delicately carved choir stalls.

I would like to have asked the vicar more about the affluent incumbent who dared to commission so superb a church, and the architect who designed it, but he had gone. Perhaps he was snatching a quick lunch. It would not be polite to disturb him again. I went down the church path and drove away, thinking how alike the church and the incumbent were—both suffering from age and neglect, poverty and a brutality that neither were fitted to comprehend nor withstand.

Notes

1. *Nine Days' Wonder*. 1976.
2. Wightwick Manor (National Trust since 1937) is located in Wolverhampton, the legacy of a family's passion for Victorian art and design, including the building itself.
3. Fred was the editor of the *Transactions*.
4. John Keats, Hyperion in *The Poetic Works of John Keats*. London: Macmillan, 1884, lines 34-6.
5. Wilfrid Gibson, *The Golden Room and Other Poems*. Macmillan: London, 1928, poem of 1925 cited on p. 172.
6. It turned out that the missing third notebook was in the hands of Mr Charles E. Harvey, and was eventually published in 1989 as *The Diary of Francis Kilvert; June—July 1870*, edited by Dafydd Ifans.

Chapter 7: 1977-8

1977

9 January 1977
I have spent a few days with Peter Hammond, his designer, a young man called Chris, and Veronica Openshaw Taylor, talking about the coming TV programmes on Kilvert and showing them 'Kilvert Country.' Mr Powell Jones, in funny knee breeches, looking as if he was about to go beagling, let us see round Cae Mawr, some parts of which he has redecorated with reasonable skill. The sinister Mr Knott or Nott, declined to let us see the principal rooms of Clyro Court; but I glimpsed enough to be captivated by the elegant Victorian hall and staircase and the fine drawing room. (Why does Kilvert not enthuse more about these houses which compare very favourably with his cramped lodgings?)

At Maesyronnen the dear old lady, who had lived all her life in the cottage attached to the chapel, was leaving her home. Her daughter and son had arrived and were taking her to Talgarth. She let us inspect the cottage—a big kitchen with a vast range, a stone floor, a crooked stairway leading to small windowed attic bedrooms—a neglected garden with unwanted rubbish burning sulkily on a fire; and next door, that primitive but moving old chapel with its uncouth furnishings, rough pulpit and pews, outmoded lamps. In this crooked house 17 children had been brought up; but at last it was to be abandoned. On the road over the Gospel Pass the wind was enough to cut you in two; but by the time we got back to Moccas the sun was shining.

20 January 1977
I have now read the proposed scripts for the Kilvert series and find them deplorable. I am afraid I shall not be able to cooperate as fully as I would like if they stick to these inaccurate and misleading scenarios.

The Crane
(after watching the Worcester electricity station being pulled down)

Saw a crane
pick up a steel cabin
and the steel struts it stood on,

pick it up, like Gulliver in Lilliput,
and dump it on a scrap heap.

Great!

Maybe it will come back one dark night
and pick up all the dirty houses,
broken old warehouses,
abandoned cars,
scrap-merchants' litter,
and clear them all away.

We could all do with that crane.

23 January 1977

An anecdote
23 January 1977
Once, when she was working in the cathedral, Elsie Matley Moore felt someone pulling at her ears. It was a man who said to her, seriously, 'No, you'll never commit a murder, not with ears like yours.'

Late January
I am writing fragments of my Elmley Castle story but I fear I shall never finish it. It is too far beyond the range of my experience, and I cannot identify with the girls as easily as I could with that boy in *Johnny-Head-in-Air*.

March 1977
Gwen and I have had a short holiday in London, looking at the Science Museum, the Albert Memorial, Harrods, the Daily Express Offices, the Temple Church, St Bride's, the National Portrait Gallery, the *Liber Veritas* of Claude Lorrain, and new furniture in Heal's.

The Brothers Karamazov
March 1977
What an incredible buffoon that old Fyodor Pavlovich is! I do not know anyone like him in fiction. Once you have met him you never forget him. Tough going, reading this aloud. The trial scenes entail a great deal of repetition which I tend to skip when I am reading to Gwen.

Hard Times

They have finished talking about the price of petrol,
the charges for plumbing repairs,
the rise in the rates,
what can be kept and what must be given up.
These are important things.
We must talk about them.

The car doors slam.
I hear the door key being turned in the lock,
the taps running in the bathroom.
I turn to my desk,
where the light gathers in a circle
around the sheet of paper spread before me.
I feel a gathering happiness
like the focusing of the light.
I look for words that will not sully
the purity of the page under my hand.

February-March 1977

12 March 1977
Laura is a nice-natured little girl. She charms us all with her smiles. Erica is very fond of her—and rightly so, because she is very loveable. A little more than three months and she makes a variety of sounds, and Nick says that when she wakens in the morning she will lie and talk for a while in her own remarkable language. But I don't think she will learn to speak as quickly as Gillian and Erica did.

13 March 1977
At Leominster I saw an old woman sitting on a bench in the sun, who called out, 'Tablets! Injections! Medicine! Fetch the bedpan!' What dreadful events was she reliving?

15 March 1977
A visit to Whitbourne Hall. Old Mr Evans and his wife have given up trying to keep the house in order and have retired to one small room with an electric

fire and two television sets (one on top of the other).[1] They were kind and hospitable, but what has happened to that enterprise that made the Evans fortune and drove that bearded patriarch to search the Middle East for ruins, then return to create this imposing house and beautiful grounds? The Hall is now a gaunt, sparsely-furnished vault of a place, with some fine rooms, but in the main an air of neglect and poverty. And Mr Evans seemed a vague ineffectual man who knew next to nothing about the house in which he had lived all his life.

A valetudinarian
26 March 1977
Yesterday I was twice troubled by an unexpected blurring of my vision in my right eye—momentary but very disconcerting. And my digestion is a little better. What a valetudinarian I am becoming in my old age. I keep giving up smoking, but never completely.

8 May 1977
Last night we went to a remarkable party at David Lockwood's in Hanley Swan. It was a very distinguished gathering—Sir Berwick and Lady Lechmere, Lord and Lady Hampton, Canon and Mrs Leatherbarrow and the Matley Moores, and many more whom I did not know and did not get to know. During the course of the evening Eric Twinberrow told me that some letters written by Francis Kilvert were in the possession of a Mrs White of Ombersley. An astonishing piece of news, for I know of only one Kilvert letter to survive. I am all agog to see what they contain, and hope to get permission to make photostatic copies. What a discovery—and on my very doorstep. I ought to tell the Kilvert Society about the find, and maybe the editor of the TLS will be interested.

At the party I met a rather pedantic Mr Barnes who knows a great deal about Victorian stained glass and Victorian Malvern. He was accompanied by an extraordinarily feeble old dear who sat by the fire for most of the evening (although the room was very hot) and snored through the music that followed the sumptuous meal David and Willy had put on.

Gwen wore a new long party dress for the occasion and looked very elegant. All the other women looked rather dowdy in comparison. I thought she was the most attractive woman in the room.

Reading

We are reading together *First Love* by Turgenev, a rather beautiful, evocative and poetic novella; and Trollope's *Is he Popenjoy?*—more enjoyable than the comical title suggests. A predictable story but a good family read.

I have published a note on the Kilvert letters in the Kilvert Society Newsletter (q.v.).[2]

The spring is cold and wet and very unpropitious for the BBC team who are filming in the Clyro region.

Maria Kilvert's house
15 May 1977

This is now the new Deanery, and Mr Baker lives there. It is a beautiful house with a fine well-proportioned drawing room with large windows overlooking the Cathedral meadows, a sunny balcony with a walled garden on a lower level. In the published parts of the diary Kilvert says little about it. But he was there in the winter and in any case he does not, in general, spend much time describing the interior of houses. Both Langley House and Clyro Court are more interesting than you would think from his mention of them. Perhaps Kilvert disliked Georgian architecture. He was very much a man of his time, and seems to have preferred Victorian pseudo-gothic.

The handkerchief tree
19 May 1977

This remarkable tree which stands, unregarded by most passers-by, in the Priory Gardens at Malvern, is at its best now. Its twin white leaves are more like the petals of flowers than leaves, and they enclose a beautiful little purple bobble. This tree stirs my imagination.

A day in Bristol with Hugh Dearlove
21 May 1977

To Keynsham to see Dr Fox's establishment for mental patients where Kilvert's aunt was detained; the *Great Britain* which Kilvert first saw in Liverpool; St Mary Redcliffe; the Clergy Daughters' School in Bristol where one of the Vaughan daughters attended; the house in Sion Place where Kilvert went to meet Kathleen Heanley, and where Emily, his sister, lived for a while; and lastly an unexpected but delightful bonus—Nash's Blaise Hamlet, which I loved—an enchanting little place that gave me great pleasure.[3] And all this in superb weather.

28 May 1977

Laura Kate, now six months, is a healthy, almost athletic little girl—pretty, with a fine complexion and, as far as we can judge, keen senses. She is very placid and greets everyone with a wide toothless smile. She is now almost able to sit up—which is just right and proper for her age. A good-natured and very loveable child.

After many cold weeks, a sudden burst of almost tropical heat. Lovely holiday weather, and the trees at their most sumptuous. The shops crowded with people buying deckchairs, patio furniture, summer dresses, sun loungers. We bought two new chairs for our terrace. After all the rain in the spring the flowers have done well, and the gardens are in full colour.

A day in Kilvert's Wiltshire

3 June 1977

Starting at Mrs Payne's home, The Old Brewery, we walked towards the edge of Chippenham, then through the paths and walks of Bird's Marsh, by Jackson's Lane and another lane up to the Ridge to see the house, the view, the Poet's Gate and the wall of the Mausoleum, then back to the church and tea on the lawn with Mr and Mrs Payne. We ended the day with a visit to the house from which Keren Wood was married, and Langley Lodge, once the home of the Hockins and the Dallins.

And on this day I was informed that I had won THE OTHER AWARD—whatever that may be. The citation says 'for literary excellence and enlightened social views.' Hm.

An incident at the Archaeological Society outing

17 June 1977

At Castle Frome we waited for a long time for Elsie Matley Moore who was to give a talk on the Herefordshire School of Sculptors—and in particular the Castle Frome font; but she failed to turn up, although we had seen her waiting at a crossroads only a few miles back. Matley, her brother, fell into a rare state of panic. He was convinced that she had had an accident and that we would find her bloodstained body lying on the road. I have never seen him so unsettled. He could hardly control his limbs and was totally persuaded that a great calamity had taken place.

In point of fact she had merely become separated from the convoy and lost her way, although she had been over this ground only a few days before. She apologized at tea, but characteristically maintained that it was not her fault. 'If only people would learn how to drive in a convoy and have the sense to keep the following car in sight, this would never have happened.'

It did not take Matley long to be once more his old caustic self.

20 June 1977

A Kilvert service at the beautiful church at Madley. The church as always very impressive, but it was cold and the service long and platitudinous. I read the first lesson—I am always nervous on these occasions. Wynford, on the other hand, has no nerves at all. After tea I spoke on the three Kilvert letters I have unearthed, but was troubled with a feeling that what I said about Mrs White and her incomprehensible reluctance to let us publish them was perhaps indiscreet. Oswin was looking old and yellow and I have a feeling that he will not live long. There were two sparrows at large in the church. They flew down towards the congregation and then off again as if they too could not find much to interest them in the sermon.

An arduous week

On 29 June we drove to Castle Howard in brilliant weather. What a magnificent palace—fit for one of the great kings of Europe. As I approached the house I had that feeling of exaltation that came over me when I first saw La Granja near Segovia (not that La Granja is on anything like the same scale). The grounds, the trees, the walks, the park ornaments are superb. But I must confess that I was a little disappointed with the interior. Was it because so many of the state rooms had been destroyed in the 1940 fire? Whatever the reason, the interior is far inferior to Chatsworth or Wilton. After Castle Howard we discovered by chance the fascinating Rievaulx Terrace with its classical temples and lovely views over the ruins of the Abbey. This part of the East Riding is really very beautiful.

After all these pleasures, a series of small disasters. I had great difficulty in starting the car, and when eventually I managed to get to Langley Moor and leave it with my brother-in-law Albert and walk into Durham to catch the train for Newcastle, the engine broke down about a hundred yards out of the station![4] When I got home Albert told me that I needed a new distributor cap. I spent the whole of the next morning trying to find one. I do not think I would have been successful if it had not been for Tommy Watson who, in situations such as these, has far more patience and resourcefulness than I have.[5]

9 July 1977

As soon as I got home I had to begin thinking of my trip to London for my award. I dreaded the prospect. The weather turned insufferably hot, and there were so many people queuing for the Fabergé Exhibition I gave up and went instead to see the lovely pictures at Somerset House which I had long wanted to see. The Other Award was announced at a strange informal gathering of teachers, editors, critics, etc. in The Plough in Museum Street. I gave my little talk and listened to complimentary comments from the Award people. Then the next day, to celebrate the passing of this much-dreaded occasion, I took myself off to Brighton to see—at last—the Royal Pavilion.

The day after I got home I took a National Trust party around Kilvert Country and *incredibile dictu*—the bus broke down on the way home, just as it did on our last National Trust visit to Clyro.

The day after the visit to Clyro I went to Stourhead with Roger to continue the work on Thomas Hardy and Lady Alda Hoare—a lovely day spent in the beautiful Stourhead Library looking over the notes made by Lady Alda on the course of her friendship with the Hardys. Can there be a happier way of spending one's life? We are writing for the Trust an account of Hardy's connections with Stourhead which I think will add a little to Hardy biographical studies.

17 July 1977

Today, at last, we have seen Sezincote. First, the house is more beautifully sited than I expected, tucked away under a little hill, as Roman Chedworth was, with a lovely view; and more beautifully proportioned than I thought it would be—very faithful to the spirit of Moghul Islamic architecture. There is about it that special serenity that characterises the best of Islamic Art—unity, clarity, harmony. Clearly the work of a man who had fallen in love with the India that had provided him with his wealth, and was determined to recreate, at home in England, the exotic oriental landscape he had come to admire. The stone of the main building is a rich orange—is it true that it was stained to acquire this hue?—but that of the auxiliary buildings is lighter in colour. Some of the small pavilions and the elegant curved orangery are as pearly grey as Painswick.

The gardens are romantic and delightful. Repton landscaped the grounds and made good use of the little stream that runs down from the hill above the house. It pours around a shrine that once contained a Hindu statue (of Coade stone?) into a clear pool, then tumbles away under an Indian bridge decorated with four small cast-iron bulls, over stones and falls past neat lawns down to the lake at the bottom of the estate. The gardens are full of rare and common flowers, and the trees smothered in fragrant climbing roses.

I liked everything about the house—its setting, the copper onion-dome, the miniature minarets (are they chimneys?), the cast-iron verandahs, the scalloped window frames, the fountain of intertwined serpents. To be able to visit it I look upon as one of the privileges of my life.

Miss Nash Peake, who drives a beautiful green Rolls Royce, wears extraordinarily an eye-shade, like those worn by Suzanne Lenglen or the news-office men of the early movies.[6]

A Kilvert memento
19 August 1977
Mrs Earle, the granddaughter of Dora Pitcairn, one of Kilvert's sisters, has a rare Kilvert memento. It is the travelling clock that Mr Venables gave Kilvert on one of his birthdays on behalf of someone we cannot precisely identify—A. J. C. Venables. Mrs Earle and her sister—a rather wayward daughter of Dora's who married a Frenchman, and lives now in a condition of rather resentful dependence on her more affluent sister—have allowed us to transcribe and publish their grandmother's 'honeymoon journal.'

Gwen and I have just been to see Arbury Hall near Nuneaton, which I found very interesting and at its best, beautiful. It is the setting for George Eliot's *Mr Gilfil's Love Story*—one of the least exciting love stories I have ever read.

Last days of Oswin Prosser
Oswin is beginning to fail and has to go into hospital tomorrow. He bore up very well after the death of his wife Joyce, and for almost a year gave the impression that he did not mean to be broken by her death; but it became clear that he was missing her. He began to look shabby and uncared-for. He grew

forgetful—forgot to answer letters, mislaid correspondence, failed to keep promises. Now his legs are swelling and water is forming in his body. I spoke to him last night on the phone but it was a sad conversation. He fears the worst.

Later

Deeply concerned about Oswin. When I saw him in hospital I knew that I was looking at a very sick man. He begged me to do certain things—to confirm the service at Condover and to see his proposed publication through the press. Towards the end of the visit he grew more cheerful, but he died quietly in his sleep a few days later on 7 September. What will become of the Kilvert Society now?

At the funeral I made hurried arrangements for an emergency committee meeting; and Mrs Turner and I set to work to go through all the papers that Oswin had left behind him—a melancholy task which I have never had to do before.

Cirencester
8 September 1977

Today young Mr Merry, the curate of Cirencester, told us the fascinating story of the rehabilitation of the church by an Oxford Movement incumbent in the late nineteenth century—how he cleared away the galleries, stripped the fine pulpit of its wooden casing, removed the box pews, revealed the ancient glories of the side chapels—and gave us the church as it is today. A fascinating story of an ecclesiastical rescue operation. Then he led us up stairs into what I had always taken to be the abbey gatehouse, but it turned out to be a kind of council chamber, with stone steps leading to a third-storey room which I never knew existed.

We fell in love with Cirencester all over again. I think it is my favourite small country town.

A tribute from a wife
18 September 1977

David Lockwood told me that he had seen at Canon Leatherbarrow's a birthday card with this message printed or more probably written on it.

'To the best, dearest, most thoughtful and considerate of husbands.'

And on the inside of the card there was a message in Mrs Leatherbarrow's hand—'From the management!'

A spate of activity
October 1977
I have had to deal with a lot of Kilvert Society business; I have been to Venice; judged a competition in Evesham; and tidied the garden. I have to go to Llyswen for a Kilvert Society service tomorrow, and on Monday Gwen goes to Liverpool to stay with Gillian. I begin my Open University work on Tuesday, have a Kilvert Society Committee meeting on Wednesday, go to Liverpool on Thursday and drive back home on Friday.

25 October 1977
Met a man today who never eats meat, cheese or eggs, but who prefers bread and butter and baked beans, maybe with a spread of tomato sauce on his bread. Yet he looks strong and fit, never ails and does an onerous job.

14 November 1977
I have been reading *Castle Rackrent* (c. 1800 by Maria Edgeworth) and *Lothair*, a much later novel by Disraeli. *Lothair* is a brilliant but uneven book—one cannot get too fond of this immature little man or too worked up about his vacillations between Anglicanism and Catholicism. On the whole I think *Castle Rackrent*, though far less ambitious, is the better novel.

Lecturing on Kilvert
23 November 1977
I had a rather disturbing experience at Weston-super-Mare. A wild, dirty, stormy journey (I have hurt my left arm and it makes driving a little difficult). Mr Challenger's house is very cold. And the lecture itself was a series of mishaps. First of all my projector, which had to be cocked at an impossible angle, jammed; then the old man who volunteered to put my slides through the replacement projector dropped them all on the floor, and I simply had not the time to rearrange them. I read badly, and ended the visit to Weston wondering if I would ever be able to go on with my next lecture which is at Leamington.

In point of fact this turned out to be just as enjoyable as the visit to Weston had been unsettling. Everything went sweetly and without a hitch.

4 December 1977
Three days in London, during the course of which we saw Kensington Palace

and Gardens, the V&A (Gwen's Wendy Ramshaw jewellery has appreciated enormously since that day when I bought the first set of rings), the National Gallery, the Wallace Collection, the Royal Pavilion at Brighton, the Banqueting House and the Houses of Parliament. In addition we saw *Filumena* which is a very good play and *Once a Catholic* which is, in my opinion, not so good. Coming home we turned up for the 5.15 pm train that didn't go till 6.15; but that didn't trouble us too much. Hilda met us at the station shortly after 8.20 pm.

1978

Dead Elms

These are the dead that will not take their leave.
These are the skeletons that keep upright.
Haunting the stricken landscape they disfigure
by day and night.

These are the fossils that no earth conceals.
No foliage their limbs will ever dress.
Dead from the bole they keep their spectral stance
of nakedness.

May 1978

Misgivings

When the wind comes the great trees swell
as a man will fill his lungs and brace himself
and the high boughs rise and fall
like the arms of tragic heroines on a stage.
It seems they are grieving for trivial disasters—
that bird hit by a car, plastered to the road
by following wheels—
that elm dead on its feet, as white as a bone.
The year is passing without cataclysm.
The fields are full of cubes of fragrant hay.

Nothing disturbs the placid grazing cattle.
The corn is turning gold.
An armada of clouds sails over the pacific sky.

But it is the trees I listen to.
The sound that speaks to me is the voice of their misgivings.

July 1978

Encounters
Gloucester Cathedral
25 September 1978

As I passed around the space behind the high altar I saw a young woman kneeling before a mediaeval tomb; and peering over her shoulder I read what I ought to have known—that it was the tomb of Edward II who was murdered in Berkeley Castle. It was a fine tomb with an ornate and elaborate canopy, and the figure of the murdered king was lifelike. It seemed strange that such a young girl should be paying her respects to a king who died so long ago. Her fingernails were coated in a red lacquer so dark that they looked almost black, and her fashionable and expensive shoes had preposterously high heels. Her dress was simple but she wore her hair long and frizzed, and combed and brushed straight out so that it spread over her back like a black shawl.

'I think you must have come a long way to see this,' I said.

'Yes, I'm from Idaho. Do you know where that is?'

'Yes—on the map. I can find it on a map.'

'I did my research on Edward II, and I think it's really thrilling to come over here and see his genuine tomb.'

'Have you been to Berkeley?'

'No, I don't think I dare. In any case I don't think I'll get there. I'm with a group and I had to bribe them to stop off here for me.'

'Edward's is a sad story. I saw Marlowe's play in Edinburgh some time ago.'

'You saw McKellen in person? Live?'

'Yes.'

'That must have been beautiful.'

Her dark rather swarthy face lit up with enthusiasm. She reminded me of a pilgrimage I once made to Autun to see the sculptures of Giselbertus—how, when at last I found myself in the cathedral there, I sat minute after minute in a trance of fulfilment. But passion such as that is almost beyond me now.

Highnam Church

I was lucky. An old woman whom I met outside the school told me that the church would not be open, and that I'd have to go to the Rectory to get the key; but I thought I'd try the door myself, and as I approached the church by the long winding path, I heard the sound of someone working in the churchyard, and a brown and white spaniel sprang out to meet me. It belonged to the rector, and it was he who was clearing brambles in the graveyard. He had a key and very kindly offered to show me the church. We went in through the vestry.

Inside I felt once more the pathos of the great Victorian dream. It was Thomas Gambier Parry, who lay in the churchyard in his elaborate almost Episcopal tomb, who had commissioned the church, chosen the eccentric and flamboyant Woodyer for his architect, and decorated the walls himself with those still-glowing frescoes. A dreamer, the creator of a dream church bound to crumble in a less affluent age, and doomed to become, in a few generations, as ruinous as Rievaulx or Tintern.

The dream was already turning into a nightmare. 'I can't keep the roof in decent order,' said the rector. 'Every wind that blows brings down dozens of tiles. You can't replace tiles like these nowadays. And there's subsidence. The sanctuary floor is beginning to sink, and as you can see I'll never be able to do anything to the frescoes. It will be all we can do—we're a small parish church—to look after the main fabric.'

Men such as the visionary Parry did not foresee the penury of succeeding ages. Who will care in the future for his shining candelabra, his intricately cut capitals, the paintings on the altar wall? Most of our churches are doomed. In a few more generations they will be one with the ruins that the Dissolution brought in its train.

A remarkable man

28 September 1978

On the train to Oxford Deb Burrows told me about her father-in-law, Ted's father—a man of remarkable strength of mind, intelligence and independence. His parents were illiterate, but they produced brilliant children. One was the last Governor of Bengal. Old Mr Burrows lost his wife fifty years ago, when Ted was only seven. Once his children had left him he had lived alone, cooking, cleaning and gardening for himself but, alas, losing both his sight and hearing as he grew older. However at 78 he taught himself Old Testament Greek so that he could check for himself the versions given in the New English Bible, and he preached two sermons every Sunday up to his mid-90s. He could have written a book to equal *Lark Rise*, but he disliked biography and autobiography, and thought the genre beneath him.

At 95 he got up one day at 6 am, cut the lawn, did his washing and his ironing, laid it out to air, put his head on the table and did not waken. A remarkable story of a remarkable old man.

Autumn
October 1978

Not the golden autumn of Keats's ode, but a cooler greyer season, when the sky is almost covered with thin grey clouds that part from time to time to reveal a tempting patch of blue; when the light wind stirs with a sighing sound and rustles the dry leaves of the taller trees; when starlings rise and wheel in fluid rings, elastic clouds that stretch and close, close and stretch in fascinating changing patterns; when fallen leaves skid across dry roads, stained with the pulp of fallen crabs and damsons; when, between the embrowning trees, the far hills are a deep violet; when birds gathering on telegraph wires look like a page of musical notes; when the restlessness of growth and increase is over and all the birds have fallen silent.

This year the country is glutted with apples. Record crops everywhere. We have had scores of pounds from our few trees. Only the Cox's Orange has refused to join in the jamboree.

Reading
24 October 1978

Over the last few months Gwen and I have read biographies of Louis XIV, Frederick the Great (neither as exciting as they might have been)—and George IV, who is for both of us the most surprising of our monarchs; and the second volume of Robert Gittings's work on Thomas Hardy—*The Older Hardy*. It is a very critical portrait of the writer, a sobering exposure of Hardy's indifference to the real women in his life as opposed to the great tenderness he felt for the women of his fiction. Some aspects of his behaviour towards Emma and Florence are inexcusable. He was apparently capable of incredible meanness, miserliness, and self-absorption. In addition we have read an essay on Maria Theresa, a general study of the Habsburgs (Gwen has re-read Trevor-Roper's *Princes and Artists*) and Girouard's book *Life in the English Country House.* I have also read out to her a brief account of the life of Rousseau (Le Douanier).

A walk to Durham
3 November 1978
In October I went to see my mother and stayed with my sister Mary at Langley Moor. I meant to drive to Durham, but since the weather was so fine I left the car at Mary's and walked. I took the road—the old road—to Stone Bridge, and met there a well-dressed man who got out of an expensive car to ask me the way to the betting shop in Langley Moor. An unlikely query addressed to an unlikely quarter! The walk down from Lower Barns was delightful, the trees in their autumn colours and the pathways covered with fallen yellow and orange leaves. The little road that turns off to the Gulbenkian Museum always gives me great pleasure, and today it seems as it was sixty years ago when my father first took me this way.[7] The Gulbenkian was, as always, full of lovely things, lovingly arranged. What caught my eye this time was a collection of Chinese ivories, rare works of superb art. I love this museum, which, in spite of my aversion to the excesses of Indian Art, always wins me over.

Then followed what is one of my favourite walks—over Prebends Bridge, through the arch and along the Bailey. No change here either. The tranquil street is as it was more than half a century ago. I went into the Cathedral Close and into the cloisters, and found that the authorities had constructed a new treasury near the restaurant, and it is there that the famous Cuthbert relics are now housed. So, on across the Palace Green down Saddler Street, past the house in which I first met Gwen, through the city, now free of traffic, and along the banks past the Old Fulling Mill which is now a Museum of Archaeology.

Two things reminded me poignantly of the past. As I passed opposite my old school, now demolished and replaced by luxury flats, I heard the cathedral bell begin to go ding-dong, ding-dong, as it always did at a quarter to three, and thought of those monotonous history lessons in which the sing-song of the cathedral bell seemed to mock the dull voice of the History teacher rehearsing the dreary dates of battles and treaties. Then I heard the splash of oars and saw a four gliding under Prebends, and thought of the days when my friend John Danby was Captain of Boats at Hatfield, and I coxed the B crew that never got beyond the quarter finals.[8] Durham is a superb city which will always be close to my heart.

I had good experiences of this little holiday which took me first to see my daughter in Liverpool and then to Durham. In Liverpool I saw for the first time the new cathedrals—the Anglican building rather bare and characterless, the Catholic Cathedral swarming with devout and slightly disorderly people (there was being held a special service for the disabled of all kinds); St George's Hall, a sumptuous Victorian building with which I was greatly impressed; and the fine display of Victorian paintings in the Walker Art Gallery.

My second good experience was walking round Barnard Castle. This charming town was almost empty and, parking the car near the museum, I walked along an attractive little street to the castle. Golden sandstone, dark cobbles, fallen leaves, russet, yellow and golden, and brilliant sunshine—and the memory of how John Danby and I once cycled here and stopped for a while on our way to High Force. This place seemed to me to be all that was desirable—romantic, unvisited, but a treasure-house of lovely things. After I had walked all around the castle I went back to the Bowes Museum which seemed an epitome of the whole experience—its rooms almost empty but full of rare and beautiful things, especially the El Greco and the vast number of Canalettos.

In the Gulbenkian Museum at Durham there are a hand and foot carved in jade which had been placed in a coffin as a substitute for those limbs that had been amputated as a punishment for criminality:

> Because he broke the law we sentenced him
> to lose a limb.
> The executioner cut off his foot.
>
> His partner's crime was of a different hue,
> but he had to suffer too.
> This time the axeman severed his right hand.
>
> Now they are dead, with them in earth are laid
> this hand, this foot of jade.
> We must not go on punishing the dead.

Somewhere must be an end to retribution
and a start to forgiving.

4 November 1978

The state of the country
6 November 1978
While I am making my modest personal notes the country is in a dreadful state of turmoil—Ford and Leyland workers on strike or threatening to strike; the bakers out and people queuing hours for bread; the railwaymen giving notice they will come out at Christmas; the miners preparing huge wage claims. We seem to be a country dominated by greed, irresponsibility, violence and criminality. What is to become of us? A moral revolution is called for, but I see little signs of it appearing.

The suicidal umbrella
20 November 1978
Our little brown umbrella seemed fated to part company with us. While we were waiting in the taxi queue Gwen realised she had left it in the train. She went back for it, and I was afraid that as soon as she entered the train it might move off to the sidings or even farther away. But with the help of a porter, she recovered it, and returned before I had reached the head of the queue. The umbrella stayed near us during our few days in London, but as I was getting back into the Worcester train it jumped off my arm and fell through the gap between carriage and platform. Impossible to rescue it. We had to leave it there. Clearly it had an affinity with trains, and was fated to rest near them.

During our three days in London we saw three exhibitions at the V&A (of which the best was the designs for Ludwig's dream palaces; Chiswick House (which I admired greatly); Goldsmiths' Hall ; St Vedast-alias-Foster, St Mary-le-Bow and St Stephen Walbrook; the Houses of Parliament; Lancaster House; the Ritz; the Jewel Tower; St James's Piccadilly; Fortnum and Mason; the Design Centre; Heal's; Apsley House.

After breakfast on Friday we walked through Green Park and peeped into those mysterious courts and squares that are all that seem to be left of the Palace of St James—tudor brick buildings with mysterious plaques (Lord Chamberlain's Office etc.) fixed to them. A very distinguished gentleman got into a 'cab' that had come out of the Royal Stables and went clip-clopping off in the direction of the Palace. A marvellous atmosphere of privacy, secrecy and privilege. The next time I am in London on a Sunday I must go to a service in the chapel. Is it true that it has a Holbein ceiling?[9]

On Saturday afternoon we were fortunate enough to get into Lancaster House. We had the house almost entirely to ourselves. The door was kept by an unhelpful young man, but the attendants inside were very kind and attentive. I found the rooms superb, with a Regency opulence and glitter. A magnificent hall, a superb staircase, a beautiful Long Gallery and a Music Room in which (we were told) Queen Victoria listened to Chopin. The house is kept in immaculate condition and is used constantly for State receptions. I found it impressive, opulent, palatial.

The guides at the Houses of Parliament are a vulgar crowd. I find their patter offensive ('Napoleon wasn't at the Battle of Waterloo. He had haemorrhoids at the time and couldn't sit on his horse.'). Mercifully I seem to have put out my mind most of their vulgarisms.

In St Stephen Walbrook and St Mary-le-Bow a score of men from shops and offices all round were peacefully listening to lunch-hour concerts. They sit mainly with closed eyes listening to the music, as if they found the strains infinitely consolatory. And so I suppose they are—to men who spend their lives at this accursed trade of buying and selling. What refreshment these moments of heavenly music must bring to them.

We went to see *Vieux Carré* by Tennessee Williams—an imperfect play; and *Beyond the Rainbow* a charming light musical imported from Italy.

Surges of emotion
24 November 1978
From time to time I am troubled with strange and inexplicable surges of emotion that flood my eyes with tears. At funerals I am disgracefully tearful, and cannot help being overwhelmed time and time again with foolish and excessive weeping. The sight of a bereaved person, though he or she may mean next to nothing to me, unmans me. No good trying to prepare for it. My incomprehensible tearfulness always gets the better of me. I must have a weird subconscious.

4 December 1978
One more old friend has died—Harry Sill from lung cancer. He never smoked a cigarette in his life.

At a poetry reading in Malvern
16 December 1978
The guest readers were three poets from Liverpool. The first had rather a cool reception although his poems were not without interest, and there was one about a parrot that belonged to two aunts and lived on long after they had died, saying 'How do you do?' in the pseudo-posh voice of the one, and 'Would ye like a cup o' tea?' in the homely voice of the other. It was like listening to the voices of the two ghosts. The aunts lived on in its mimicry. The second young man who read some disagreeable poems about the cruelty of animals had the dark pointed beard and long melancholy face of a Spanish grandee. The third was an ass. First of all he made a lot of fuss about a height-measuring device that happened to be in the room, a loose board under his feet, and four jokers which for some never divulged reason he had laid face upward.

22 December 1978
Went to Oxford to see, among other things, Worcester College Chapel, an intriguing Victorian creation, largely the work of that wayward architect, William Burges, the creator of Castell Coch. On the bench ends are carved numerous wild beasts—not the mediaeval kind, half mythical, out of some bestiary, but a kind of roll call of the fauna of the British Empire—alligators, gnus, camels etc.. An extraordinary footnote to Victorian taste.

It was a cold foggy day, with the trains delayed and crowded, but I enjoyed my little outing. I went to the Ashmolean and saw some good Thornhill designs for Stoke Edith (what is the history of this place?), read a great deal of *The Middle Passage* by Naipaul, and wasted ten minutes in that barren place, the Museum of Modern Art. One more boring and repetitive display.

Later this month we went to attend the funeral of poor Mary Smith who never recovered from having to leave her beloved Worcester.[10] Her husband condemned her to living death when he took her to that lonely cottage on the edge of the Peak District. He behaved in his customary enigmatic way. 'A Merry Christmas to you,' he said, standing on the step of the coach in which we had travelled to Rainow. 'I hope you've all had a nice Christmas because I've had a lovely one.' This—on the day of his wife's funeral!

Notes

1 Mr Evans was owner of Hill, Evans and Co., Vinegar Works, Worcester.
2 See also the Appendix to Frederick Grice's book on Kilvert—*Francis Kilvert and his World* (1982)—which contains a summary of the three letters that Kilvert wrote to Marian Vaughan between 1873 and 1876 (pp 246-8).
3 Blaise Hamlet, a collection of nine cottages around a green, has been owned by the National Trust since 1943.
4 Albert Swithenbank, Fred's brother-in-law.
5 Tommy Watson and his wife Lila from Ferryhill were lifelong friends of Fred and Gwen.
6 Miss Nash Peake was a member of the owner's family; and Suzanne Lenglen was a famous French tennis player.
7 Now known as the Oriental Museum, Durham University.
8 John Danby was a Durham Johnston School contemporary and close friend of Fred's, who took first degrees at both Durham University and Cambridge, and became Professor of English at the University of Bangor in North Wales.
9 The ceiling of the Chapel Royal in St James's Palace is attributed to Holbein.
10 Mary, who was sociable to the very core, was the wife of Bill Smith, one of the original lecturers at the Training College.

Chapter 8: 1979

An incident at Harrods

1 January 1979

A young assistant allowed a titled lady to take away a valuable coat which was to be entered in her account, but was so overawed by her customer that she forgot to take her name and address. The floor manager, reckoning there were at least twelve ladies who answered to the assistant's description, decided to send a bill to all twelve. Six paid without raising a single objection. Surely this is an apocryphal story.

Siberian weather

5 January 1979

Ever since New Year's Eve, we have had bitterly cold weather with piercing east winds. Most of Europe seems in the grip of arctic weather. I think this is the coldest spell I have ever known. Yet I have been able to walk regularly. On one walk I met a man with a golden retriever. It was carrying his hat in its mouth. He took the hat from it and put it on, but the dog turned to him, asking as clearly as it could for the cap to be returned to it. The man bent down and the dog cleverly lifted off the cap from his head and walked on with it. Being a game dog, I suppose it was happier to be carrying something in its mouth.

12 February 1979

More snow—one exasperating fall after another. And almost the whole of the country on some kind of strike or go-slow. We have been reading a life of Jane Austen with some remarkable revelations about her handicapped brother who was farmed out when he was young and never lived with the family; and the affair of her aunt who was arrested for suspected shoplifting and narrowly escaped transportation; and the fate of the first husband of her cousin and sister-in-law, the Comte de Feuillide, who was guillotined. And *Brideshead Revisited*—a flawed novel. David Lockwood came to see us yesterday and read us the lesson for the anniversary of the martyrdom of modern—a very moving passage. And with all this—more snow. This is a memorably severe winter.

A butterfly in church
18 February 1979
Today during Communion I saw a purple emperor painfully crawling across the aisle carpet, climbing the step up to the floor of the pews and looking as if it meant to explore the skirt of an elderly lady sitting there. I was afraid it might alarm her, but she did not see it, and it crawled away from her out of sight. When the service was over and I had done my duty reckoning up the collection and entering it, I mentioned it to the vicar who picked it up and set it down on a big chrysanthemum that was part of the decorations left over presumably from a wedding.

Another fine day in Oxford
28 February 1979
Saw a fine exhibition in the Museum of Modern Art (for once) of the work of the Russian Alexander Rodchenko—and the superb Codrington Library at All Souls. This and the chapel are worth seeing.

Hope End
4 March 1979
Yesterday we had a beautiful ride over the Malverns to Hope End where Elizabeth Barrett Browning lived as a child—rather, as a young girl. We saw all that is left of the neo-turkish house that her father built there—a range of stable buildings, a kind of clock tower with a Moorish cupola and one minaret-like tower, very thin and topped with an Islamic crescent—all in a glorious setting, in woodland filled with thousands of snowdrops and aconites. A young man and his wife have modernised the block and turned it into a small hotel, Lantern Grove. The Hope End landscape is very beautiful.

Things seen on a visit to London: The Gold of Eldorado Exhibition; Osterley Park (which I found very beautiful); the Inigo Jones house in Lincoln's Inn; the Sir John Soane Museum (which Gwen enjoyed far more than I thought she would); an excellent exhibition of jewellery at the British Museum; 'Vienna in the Age of Schubert'; the Design Centre; 'The Voyages of Captain Cook'; and two plays, one on the Empress Eugenie and the other *Whose Life is it Anyway?*

16 March 1979
Margaret Rawlings's one-woman show on the Empress Eugenie was not quite good enough, but it spurred us on to read more about her, Louis Napoleon, the

fall of the Second Empire, the Franco-Prussian War, that terrible episode, the Commune of 1870, and the last years of the century—La Belle Epoque.

A surprise
16 March 1979
Mother, who has never saved a penny in her life, has in the last few years accumulated no less than £500, and has decided to give it all away— £100 to each of her children. I must say that my father and mother have displayed in their lives an almost saintly disdain for money.

Another
Today I heard from Sid Rapperport who was with me in the Western Desert in 1942-43.

A third
4 April 1979
Dr Graham, who works with me in the Cathedral Library, came to tea the other day and showed us some of the slides of her recent holiday. And where do you think this elderly and arthritic lady had been—to Tassili in the the Sahara! What an enterprising woman. Next time she is going to show some slides of her holiday in the Yemen—to see the fabled city of Sana'a!

A cold busy winter
April 1979
I have made few notes this winter. I have been busy writing a book which I would like to call 'Children of the House' but that's a title already used by P. Pearce. It is based on the memories of Helen Davies and her sister. I am not sure that the book will be accepted but I hope it is because it is in many ways far better than my recent work. I ought to make a note on Helen but perhaps the book itself will explain her career. In addition it has been a bitterly cold winter, with endless falls of snow and endless troublesome thaws. But at least it seems over.

12 April 1979
On Sunday we celebrated our Ruby Wedding anniversary. Erica made the main course and Gillian brought a mousse all the way from Liverpool. After lunch we looked at a few old slides which I projected on the dining area wall—of

Aidan and Veronica when they were young, Gillian and Erica before they were married, Colin at Malham, Gwen on holiday in France, Florence, Portugal, Spain, Austria. The great success of the day was Laura who got up on the steps and treated us to a series of nursery rhymes, culminating in 'I'm a little teapot,' with appropriate actions. The happiness of the day helped me to forget a very unsatisfactory Kilvert Society AGM the previous Friday.

Strange visitors
13 April 1979
Last night we had a visit from two people who are virtual strangers to me but not to Gwen—Brian and Doreen—the richest couple I have ever known. Last year he paid over £70,000 in tax! But they are not happy. They have few friends, have their own physical and emotional problems, and are searching anxiously for some kind of tax haven. They are contemplating living in Spain although neither knows the country and neither can speak a word of Spanish. I have advised them against it, and am trying to persuade him not to think of winding up his business till he has built for himself an alternative career to fall back on. A strange experience for me to meet people of this calibre. I liked them, but did not feel very envious.

Mid-April 1979
I have been reading *Palaces of Europe* (good illustrations—poor text); Alistair Horne's *The Terrible Year*, an interesting study of the Paris Commune of 1870; V.S. Pritchett's *Balzac* (very clear and informative and as strange as fiction); *La Belle Epoque*, a very good history book about the end of the nineteenth century in France.

I have sent off my Elmley story to OUP, and am now in a kind of writing vacuum—the kind of phase that all writers detest. And I am receiving a stream of letters from my old friend Sid Rapperport—now Sid Rapperport Harris. He sends me intriguing photographs of himself in the company of Brigitte Bardot and her sister Monique (and Sacha Distel). How on earth did he get to know these people?

The mysterious parson
22 April 1979
More often than not he comes to Holy Communion on Sundays at 8 am—a stiff, unbending, slightly built man, dressed in a tightly-buttoned suit of

clerical black of an old fashioned cut, too short in the sleeves. He has a cold unsmiling face. I never see him talking to anyone, or exchanging the simplest form of courtesy. He walks with his head tilted slightly on one side, in a kind of Malvolio-like dream of self-love, lost in a dream of his own consequence. One cold day he appeared in a red college scarf, as incongruous and showy as Malvolio's yellow stockings. He is an intriguing person.

Gwen has gone away on a short holiday with Hilda to Weston-super-Mare. I hope conditions are not too cold and wet for them.

25 April 1979

Gwen has returned and enjoyed her stay at Weston. The weather was far better than I feared. She took with her some Town Trail booklets that I got for her and used them religiously. She is now quite an expert on Weston.

29 April 1979

Yesterday we had the Matley Moores to tea and heard more scandalous gossip about Sir George Vernon of Hanbury Park and his mistresses (Matley calls them 'whores' in that rather gross manner he occasionally exhibits). He is very dependent on his sister but in general has a low opinion of women.

'We've tried this business of not having a coach for our Archaeological meetings and just using private cars. Doesn't work you know. You say you'll give lifts and you find yourself saddled with some old hag for the rest of the day... I used to write to people and ask them if they would let us have a look at their house. Sometimes I'd get a letter saying they'd be honoured to have such a learned society visit them. Learned society my foot! Just a bunch of old hags wanting a day out!'

He tells me that the Hon. Percy Allsopp's wife was a Miss Cheshire from Essex. It was the Hon. Percy who was the Romantic of the family. Matley possesses two of the urns from his garden.[1]

Helen Davies has a cup that was presented to her by the Empress Eugenie—for consistent progress at school![2]

1 May 1979

One of the coldest May Days ever known. The following day it snowed again. We have had a great deal of snow this winter.

East Anglia
7 May 1979
Today we set off for five days in East Anglia—ten friends in the familiar minibus driven by Hugh. I'll give first a catalogue of the things we saw—Weston Underwood where Cowper stayed for a while—his house and his alcove; Olney, museum, church, garden, garden house; Beck Hall where we all stayed for five days; Claydon where Father Ignatius had his first curacy; a museum at Ipswich with some Constable pictures; Flatford Mill; East Bergholt (nice church and pub); Dedham, a supremely beautiful village with fine houses and a fine church; Nayland with its Constable psalter painting; and Ickworth, a superb country house; Gainsborough's house at Sudbury; Lavenham, one of the loveliest churches in the country; and a memorable tour of Cobbold's village, Wortham;[3] late night visit to see Mrs Parker at Woolpit; Fressingfield, Framlingham which we liked greatly, and Heveningham, which we found cold and uninviting and unvisited; Huntingfield with its rare painted ceiling; Ely, Cottisford (Fordlow), Juniper Hill (Lark Rise) and Fringford (Candleford); celebration dinner at The Quiet Woman near Chipping Norton.[3] (Cost of whole expedition—£50 each—a great bargain.)

Of all our experiences the most memorable were these: reading Cowper's 'The Colubriad' just outside the shed (the adder house?) where the incident took place; looking at Cowper's little summer house; the glories of Ickworth, which I love; the village of Dedham as fine close at hand as it is in Constable's views; the secret charms of Cobbold's village scenery; the discovery of Edith Thomas's notebook on Radnor folklore at the home of Mrs Parker; Lavenham Church with its two parcloses; Framlingham Church and Castle and close with its delightful bookshop; Ely with its beautiful Prior's door and Comper window—I liked everything I saw at Ely; Flora Thompson's incredibly humble cottage at Juniper Hill, Queenie's house nearby, and the charming village of Cottisford with its humble church, run-down rectory and charming manor house.

Another note on Juniper Hill and Fordlow
Juniper Hill is still much as Flora Thompson described it—an out-of-the-way, impoverished hamlet in the middle of a featureless plain, scattered and formless. The cottage in which she lived as a child is approached by a rutted and muddy lane that wanders around the perimeter of the hamlet. It is small and unpretentious, and is defaced with an ugly outshed in the yard. Lark Rise is

painted in crude lettering on the gate. Yet this plainness and bareness is an integral part of the scene. It is possible still to see the hamlet as it was at the beginning of the century; and Queenie's house is virtually unaltered.

Fordlow (Cottisford) is a different story. The Rectory looks neglected, but the church is well cared-for, and the Manor House has clearly found a loving owner. What Brancepeth was to Brandon, Cottisford, with its neat stone cottages, white-doored and white-windowed manor house, church and tall trees, is to Juniper Hill. I noticed the name of Flora's brother Edmund (E. Timms) on the memorial tablet in the church. On this holiday came Hugh and Guy Dearlove, David and Willy Lockwood, Mervyn and Lilian West, Kate Goodwin, Godfrey Davies, Gwen and I.

A troubling visit
May 20 or so 1979

When they had put their bags in the bedroom they came downstairs—there are five or six stairs from the upper part of our living room to the lower—and sat down on the long sofa.

'Would you like something to drink—tea or coffee?' asked Gwen.

'I'd rather have a whisky,' said Helena.

'And for me,' said Gertrude.

Gwen was a little taken aback. We had never before had visitors asking for whisky at teatime, but she brought the tray and they helped themselves fairly liberally. Gertrude had dry ginger, but Helena chose water and ice.

They drank off their whisky and then to my surprise Helena reached for the bottle and poured herself another glass, if anything a larger measure than before, as if to indicate to Gwen that this was the size of drink she preferred.

'My, I think your hand's slipped, hasn't it?' said Gertrude, but Helena took no notice.

'She likes her noggin',' said Gertrude with her habitual note of complacency. 'She has to have her tipple,' and settled down to help herself to another drink.

The next day, by accident rather than design, the bottle was left in the kitchen, and the drinks brought separately. Neither wanted anything as feeble as sherry for their aperitif. It had to be whisky. When Helena had finished hers, I was surprised to see her get up and make for the kitchen. When she reappeared it was with a full glass of whisky, diluted, it seemed to me, with nothing but a single cube of ice.

5 June 1979

A weekend in Cardiff, which I found a most interesting and in some respects beautiful city. We went early on Friday to have time to see Castell Coch and Cardiff Castle—and the weather was fine and sunny. We took a bus to Castell Coch (we had come by train) and with the help of a kind bus conductor and a friendly woman who, seeing us hesitate in the village came out of her house to put us in the right way for the castle. The whole pilgrimage, the steepish walk through the woods, the coming upon the tall cylindrical towers, the smell of the flowers—all put us in mind of the approach to Neuschwanstein. Castell Coch is not Neuschwanstein of course, but it is arresting in its own way—and colourful and dramatic.

A purist would say that Burges was as decadent as Ludwig when it came to decoration; but there is much to admire at Castell Coch and Cardiff Castle—especially the statuary (the work of a man called Nicholls) which is generally very good. Of course the decoration is overdone and often vulgar but, in a shrinking age, when everything rare and unique becomes less and less accessible, such extravagance, such boldness of bravura ornament become more and more attractive. (I have many a detailed account of Burges's fabulous rooms in my notebook.)

I got something out of everything we saw—Tredegar House with its beautiful neglected Restoration rooms; all of St Fagans, especially the little castle itself with its wonderful collection of Tudor furniture, its Regency library, and its Victorian bedrooms and fine kitchen; Penhow Castle, dark, crumbling, uncouth, a more honest reminder of the primitive culture of mediaeval life than many a better-kept castle; the phoney, but beautiful St Donats near Llantwit Major (an interesting countryside here); the marvellous pearly Civic Centre (who planned and built this?); and the charming mediaeval Church of St John the Baptist tucked away behind busy shopping streets. In an almost inexplicable way I enjoyed Cardiff as much as Vienna and Edinburgh and Amsterdam.

We went by train through Hereford and Abergavenny and stayed at the Royal Hotel, a very pleasant place, sporting in the Hall a framed poem by Wynford Vaughan-Thomas.

A week of varying experience—Oxford and the discovery of the plaque to Cuthbert Shields on the outside wall of Corpus Christi chapel; the lovely John Piper exhibition; a visit to Hagley Hall—a beautiful house redecorated, not too successfully, by Lady Cobham; vexation at the stingy behaviour of M who is staying with us; intense annoyance at her failure to be interested in anything except the effect the new budget proposals are to have on her income; a day out in the country, including a visit to the marvellous cathedral in Hereford, Madley, and Moccas Court, more remarkable for its lovely setting and grounds than its architectural interest—an excursion not fully appreciated by our prosaic and mercenary guest; finally a lecture to the Malvern Architectural Association, followed the next day by an afternoon in the grounds of Croome. I was pleasantly surprised by the condition of many of the rooms in Croome Court—especially the early William Kent-like drawing room, the hall, and the later long room. I feel that I am the rightful heir to the landscape of Croome for no one seems to care for it as I do. I had fifty or so in my party and we enjoyed uninterrupted sunshine.

Farewell to my oldest friend, John Danby
6 June 1979
As we said goodbye I saw something in his eyes and his face that I had never seen before. I had never been in any doubt about his feelings for me. To him, I was a kind friend but an inferior spirit. I could support him and second him but never lead him into any region that he had not already himself visited and known. I could never provide him with new insights, could never resolve any of his academic problems, could never contribute anything to that deeper understanding that he sought.

Yet as we said goodbye I felt—and the sensation was as incredible as it was unexpected—that a certain affection for me had suddenly possessed him—a kind of regret for all the indifference and neglect I had had to put up with, even a love for me, the friend whom he might never see again.

I never did see him again—alive or dead.

His wife did not invite me to see him in his coffin. I learnt later that she had allowed no one to see him in the later stages of his illness—not even his own brother. Why? Was his end so dreadful that his face in death was not to be looked upon?

When I asked her, injudiciously, 'Was he long in hospital?' she answered, 'Do you mind if I don't say anything about it?'

Was this because the memory was too painful to be revived? Or the truth so horrible that it had better be concealed?

[*Editors*: Fred's recollections of their last meeting, probably in Stratford-upon-Avon, in the early 1970s.]

18 June 1979
This morning I met in town a Mr Baker, ex-primary school headmaster, who was on his way to do duty in the WVS shop at Powick Mental Hospital. 'A sobering experience,' he said. 'My father used to go there, and one day a patient stepped out of line and said to him, "Have you remembered, sir, to thank God for your reason this morning?"' I wish M had been there to hear him.

20 June 1979
My booklet on the Worcester Misericords is in proof stage, but it is very badly designed, with a set of appalling line drawings on the front page. I wish I had been consulted and had been able to call in Erica to help with the layout.

21 June 1979
My birthday. Brian and his wife took Gwen, Hilda and me to dinner at The Elms—an uncomfortably posh place where the evening cost him (probably) about £70. He is fantastically well-off but even the expense makes me uneasy. He drives a superb automatic Daimler, the most comfortable car I have ever ridden in in my life. Brian is a riddle. I must write more about him later.

22 June 1979
A little party at the Deanery to say goodbye to Geoffrey Pick and the Jellymans (sounds like a pop group). Another opportunity to look at the interior of Maria Kilvert's home. The house seems partially supported on a stretch of city or cathedral wall, and is difficult to photograph from the garden. The rooms are spacious and elegantly proportioned. I have found that after Maria K's death the house was sold to the Dean and Chapter for £750.

Petrol is now (at the minimum) £1.10p a gallon.

I have been reading a great deal about the Victorian architect William Burges. I have heard that Disraeli's *Lothair* is based on B's patron, the mediaevalist and millionaire Marquis of Bute. There was an excellent Burges exhibition in Castell Coch when we were there. I would like to see his church at Studley Royal and even more his house at Melbury Street, Kensington. He was an intriguing designer.

24 June 1979
More rain!

A Kilvert Memorial Service at Langley Burrell
4 July 1979
On the occasion of the presentation of a Kilvert letter to the Society by Mrs Hurlbutt of Hawaii.[4]

Mrs Hurlbutt had told me that she would like to say a few words, and as I moved away from the lectern to give way to her I saw the rows of faces in the congregation turned towards us, attentive and affectionate. Although both doors were open the air inside the church was still, and through the clear windows I could see the trees crowding around the church like a second congregation. The sunlight fell through the south door in a warm bright bar on the cool floor, and on the tombstones beyond it, doubly dappled with yellow and brown rosettes of lichen and the shadows of the leaves. It was a moment that Kilvert himself might have savoured, the whole pacific summer scene caught in a trance of light and warmth. Then, just as when Kilvert was reading the burial service over Alice Grimshaw and looked up to see the figure of the Squire moving across the churchyard, I caught the heads and shoulders of visitors whom our little gathering apparently did not concern, going from grave to grave looking at the inscriptions.

But by now Mrs Hurlbutt had begun to speak and I turned to listen to her. The extra height she gained from the lectern stand must have given her the sensation of being once more on a stage. She began to speak, fluently and eloquently, of her grandmother, the friend of the diarist, who when she was still young, had left Brobury and emigrated with her father and mother to the States. 'And I am sorry to say,' she went on, 'that although she left the shores of England a good Anglican, she fell in love with and married a Baptist, and was eventually received into the Baptist Church. Imagine what Kilvert would have thought of that!'

We smiled, sharing her sense of the incongruity of her grandmother deserting the church in whose tabernacles she was now speaking. Then her mood began slowly to change. 'I loved my grandmother,' she said, 'and loved to talk with her about her life in England. A few days ago my husband and I made a pilgrimage to Brobury and saw there the graves of her and my ancestors. And now I have come to fulfil the pledge which I gave to my dear father. Last year when he knew that he had not much longer to live he asked me to return to England and give this letter and this little booklet—mementoes of Mr Kilvert which my grandmother had taken with her to America and preserved till the day of her death, to the Kilvert Society to keep in honour of her and her friend the Rector of Brobury. And I here, in enactment of his wish, solemnly hand over to Mr Grice the letter and the book...'

Her voice had begun to tremble and tears began to fill her eyes. I looked from her through the window, and saw the visitors to the churchyard, unaware of that moment of pathos. The congregation fell silent, and the only noise around us was the cheeping of the sparrows on the sunny paths beyond the open doors.

At Blenheim
4 July 1979
An enormous crowd had gathered on the steps leading up to the main entrance—so large that I began to think that it would be more than half an hour before we would be admitted; but after only a short interval the door opened and a hundred and maybe more of us were allowed in. We were told to group ourselves in the Hall, and there we were addressed by a man with one of the loudest voices I have ever heard. His voice could have filled a cathedral. But he was efficient and very courteous, and with great skill marshalled us on through the Churchill rooms, after which we were conducted in smaller parties through a sequence of rooms—the Porcelain Corridor, the Green Drawing Room, the Red Drawing Room, the Saloon, the three State Rooms and the Library; and so out into a yard from which we visited the Chapel—less a place of worship than an elaborate tribute to the Marlboroughs.

The rooms at Blenheim are not as fine as those at Chatsworth or Wilton. They lack magnificence, but the Hawksmoor ceilings, the Blenheim tapestries, the Marlborough mementos are of great interest. So is the symbolism of the exterior—the lion of England savaging the cock of France, Pallas and the bound captives, the cannon balls seemingly embedded in the gatepiers, the bust of Louis XIV on a pediment, the flaming grenades, the trophies etc.; and the park and gardens are superb. Blenheim is now the focal point of an enormous industry. Tourists pass through it like cars on an assembly line. But I enjoyed visiting it.

After lunch we saw the private apartments of the present Duke and Duchess, the best room of which (for me) was the Regency bedroom with the campaign furniture. Two house martins had got into the rooms and the guide had to make an emergency call for someone to come and expel them.

A rather tortuous cross country drive took us to Claydon House, near

Aylesbury, and a series of surprises culminating in that incredible caprice—the Chinese Room. Who was this extraordinary man Luke Lightfoot, the half-inspired half-demented Romantic who created these remarkable fantasies in wood? Much of the decoration, which outraged the Palladians of the day, teeters on the brink of absurdity. It reminds me of the work of Ludwig of Bavaria and his architects, and the excesses of Burges in a later century. The Chinese Room is almost too much to take. But Claydon is not all Lightfoot, and it possesses what is surely one of the finest staircases in England.

10 July 1979

I have just finished reading to Gwen *The Europeans* by Henry James—an early novel and presumably a lightweight, but a literary pleasure after the inept *Cakes and Ale*—Somerset Maugham—which neither of us cared for.

News has come that Jeremy Sandford has put his Kilvert notebook up for sale. Sotheby's are expecting it to make £6-8000! We cannot hope to rise to that figure. All we can hope for is that it falls into the hands of a sympathetic buyer—preferably a library which will allow us to have access to it. I am planning to go to the sale.

Conversation with a young man on the train

17 July 1979

'What have you been doing in Leominster?'

'Getting a job.'

'What sort of job?'

'I'm a welder.'

'And where are you off to now?'

'Back to Doncaster.'

'You'll find Leominster a bit of a change after Doncaster.'

'I don't mind. I can settle down anywhere. And my girlfriend lives in Leominster. I used to live there myself. I went to school in Leominster.'

'The Modern School?'

'It was Comprehensive then.'

'Did you know a Mr W, in charge of English there?'

'Yes, I did. I liked him. I didn't like him at first, but when you got on to A level and stuff, he was good. Mind you, he was a rotten teacher.'

'He was a good student. He was one of my best students.'

'But he committed suicide. Did you know that?'

'No.'

'Yes. I saw him the day before and he seemed alright. The next day he did hisself in.'

The shock was so great that for a few minutes I could not go on with the conversation. Fortunately just at that moment the train ran into the long tunnel just out of Ledbury, and I had time to collect myself. That a young man so personable and talented should take his own life seemed incredible.

24 July 1979

Today I went to London to attend a sale at Sotheby's. One of Kilvert's notebooks, the one Essex Hope gave to Jeremy Sandford, was up for sale, and I had an opportunity to inspect it before it came up.[5] In most respects it was like the Plomer notebook—the same size, the same cover, to all appearances a fair copy, with few alterations or erasures.[6] It was labelled No. 2 in Kilvert's own hand—a clear proof that he did not begin his diary before 1870. It was sold for £11,500 to Bernard Quaritch (Antiquarian Bookseller), who were buying for the National Library of Wales, Aberystwyth.

I am probably the only person alive to have inspected both the existing Kilvert notebooks.

What a claim to fame!

25 July 1979

A beautiful scented day, with the smell of meadowsweet, cottage roses and baled hay carried on the wind, till it shifted and brought to my nostrils the odious stink of some chemical fertiliser that a man on a tractor was spreading.

A deflating comment

14 August 1979

When I was walking from Hallow village down to the Camp Hotel I came upon two children who were playing outside a house. The older of the two was about six or seven, the girl much younger.

'We seen you before, en' we?' said the boy.

'I should think so,' I replied.

'You out for a walk then?'

'That's right, taking a stroll.'

Then, to my surprise and chagrin, he peered at me more closely and said. 'You're looking poorly, 'en you?'

I was taken aback because I had already walked a few miles and was thinking how well, for an elderly man, I was going. Besides, in the last few weeks many had told me how fit and well I looked.

'I don't think I'm poorly,' I said. 'Why did you say that?'

'You're looking poorly here,' he said, rubbing under his eyes.

'Oh no, I'm perfectly well,' I said and hurried on.

I hurried on because I was a little nettled at being caught out by a seven-year-old boy who, with nothing to go on but my appearance, had seen more than all my complimentary acquaintance. It was true that in spite of my rosy cheeks and outward show of fitness I was not a fully healthy person, unable to eat a square meal and distressed by anything but the simplest of diets. How did that boy know? When I came home I scrutinized myself in the looking glass and saw only too clearly the telltale pallor under my eyes.

An ironical story
19 August 1979
A woman who had delusions of grandeur—or rather a great longing to belong to the aristocracy (she actually called herself Lady—) was found dead in the grounds of Windsor Castle, presumably from an overdose of sleeping pills. Under an ancient law, the inquest had to be held on court premises. So she had, in the end, the satisfaction of having an inquest held over her dead body in the Court of St James. The kind of story Hardy would have delighted in.

Kilvert Service at Wootton-by-Woodstock
19 August 1979
Wootton is a charming village with a very attractive church which was decorated with flowers for our visit. Perhaps it is more correct to say that our visit coincided with a flower festival. I noticed a glowing reredos, two fine candlesticks of an elaborate design, polished tiles on the chancel floor, and a dove made out of white petals. It was here that Kilvert was married exactly a hundred years ago. The bride's family lived in a spacious Victorian house about a mile from the village, built of grey stone and dated 1862, far larger than any house Kilvert lived in till he came to Bredwardine.

The service was not without its odd moments. Mr Jelfs read the lesson well, but he ended with a revivalist flourish that was somewhat out of place. 'And may the Lord,' he declaimed, 'bless this day the reading of his Holy Word.' I performed the act of giving to the church our present of a cheque to buy hymn books, but did it very gauchely, saying nothing and clearly puzzling the person who expected me to say a few words.

But the real joy was Mrs Clutterbuck's house—Wootton Place, the old Rectory, a beautiful Cotswold stone house with lovely wooden-floored and wooden-panelled rooms, Morris wallpapers and curtains in excellent condition, French windows opening on to level lawns with fine trees. They say that Capability Brown designed the garden. True or not, it reminded me of the lovely garden at St John's College in Oxford—the same spaciousness, the same level sward backed by noble trees.

David Lockwood devoted his sermon to a rather sentimental and fanciful picture of what might have happened if Kilvert had recovered and lived on to have a family. This involved setting up a fictional biography, and then of course having to demolish it—which I did not find wholly satisfactory.

I forgot to mention that we spent the morning looking round the gardens of Blenheim. Gwen wanted to see the sphinx with the face of that vain mistress of Blenheim who ruined her looks by having wax inserted into her nose to make it look Grecian.

29-31 August 1979

The night before the Archaeological Summer Meeting at Moccas (for which I am responsible) I did not sleep well. I suffered from indigestion and palpitations. All through the night I was trying, in a kind of nightmare, to solve a giant crossword puzzle made out of an incomprehensible map of Herefordshire. I felt sure that after so many fine days we were certain to have rain for our visit. All my responsibilities—which in all conscience are not too heavy—worry me inordinately nowadays.

The Archaeological visit to Madley and Moccas was a success after all. Mr Paterson of Madley charmed everyone with his good nature, humour, geniality and knowledge of his church. Both Moccas Court and Moccas Church were highly admired and we managed to get to Bredwardine and Eardisley as well. After it all I slept the sleep of the relieved.

Matley Moore did not attend, but he came to tea a few days later, and I thought he was at his worst—a sneering ugly old man, pontificating about marriage, although he never married himself, and in all probability never found a woman who would accept him. 'You should never get married for love,' he said. 'All that comes to an end very quickly. Pick yourself a partner you can get on with, not somebody you go gaga over for a few months. Darling this and dearest that. That's not good.' He flipped through the typescript of the latest findings about mediaeval Worcester (not mine), and dismissed it with, 'No good. Nobody wants to be bored with stuff like this.'

Kilvert Celebrations
24 September 1979
We have just come to the end of the celebration of the anniversary of Kilvert's death—a weekend of intense activity, beginning with the anniversary address from Sir Victor Pritchett in the Town Hall, Hereford, going on to a walk around Bredwardine and a ploughman's lunch, a morning service (Holy Communion) in Bredwardine church on Sunday morning, another service in Clyro in the afternoon, and a series of readings with commentary from Timothy Davies and Colin Davis in the Bishop's Hall, Hereford in the evening. Not everything was successful. Sir Victor was genial, affable, delightful to meet and talk to, but woefully unprepared, and wildly inaccurate *(Plate 7)*. He talked at immense length, and I had to cut out the time we were to give to questions and discussion—probably a godsend, because I do not know how he would have coped with any searching questions. Lady Pritchett was a very unassuming, handsome and companionable person.

The Bredwardine walk was enjoyed by everyone (the weather was superb), and the congregation at Bredwardine and Clyro were just what we expected and could cope with. The Vicar of Bredwardine gave Willie Price to understand that he (Willie) was to preach, but coolly informed him at the beginning of the service that he would not be wanted; and the Right Revd Charles Edwards, one-time Bishop of Worcester, was not treated as courteously as he might have been (the tea arrangements at Clyro are always bad). But the evening recital was superb. When Timothy Davies, made up as Kilvert, entered there was a gasp of incredulous delight.

In addition to these events we had earlier in the year held a service at Langley Burrell, and another at Wootton-by-Woodstock; there was a good Kilvert Exhibition in the Public Library at Hereford; and I went on to give a lecture in Birmingham at the Midland Institute, and to read a paper to the Worcester Archaeological Society on 'The Good Fortune of Francis Kilvert'.

I was deeply disappointed by the response to my Worcester lecture. I took

Plate 7: Sir Victor Pritchett talking to Miss M. Kilvert in the Town Hall, Hereford after giving the Kilvert Address.

great pains over it and made it scholarly but entertaining and new—it certainly contained a great deal of original research. But there were only two questions, and both stupid. What did I think of the television Kilvert programme, and did I know how it was that Hay-on-Wye came to acquire the biggest second-hand bookshop in the world?

Wives and Daughters
21 October 1979
I have just finished reading this fine novel to Gwen, who has enjoyed it very much. And so have I. A first-class novel with an impressive array of characters—Lord Cumnor, generous, talkative, henpecked; Lady Cumnor, imperious, arrogant and overbearing (perhaps out of reaction to her feeble husband); Lady Harriet, her good-natured, unassuming but forthright daughter; the manly and admirable Dr Gibson; his silly, vain and hypocritical second wife; Cynthia, daughter of Mrs Gibson by her first husband, the victim of her stunning good looks and natural attractiveness; Hamley of Hamley, the pitiable old man whose first son

Osborne is so great a disappointment to him, proud, dignified but lost after the death of his wife; Roger, a kind of youthful Darwin, scholar and explorer. A marvellous canvas. A pity the story was never finished, but Mrs Gaskell brought us close enough to the end not to feel too dissatisfied.

Now we are reading Laurie Lee's *Cider with Rosie*, enjoyable enough, but not in the same league as Mrs Gaskell's novel. I enjoy it, am impressed at times by the beauty of the prose, and do not wholly believe it.

I shall go from this to read Gwen Mrs Gaskell's little known *Lois the Witch*, a novella which is a remarkable anticipation of Miller's *The Crucible*.

A disappointment—OUP have rejected my Elmley story.

Three days in London
Late November 1979
Saw the play *Night and Day* by Tom Stoppard which meant nothing to us; and the film *The Europeans* which we greatly admired.

A surprise
3 December 1979
Walking with Gwen down Bridge Street in Hereford, I pointed out to her the ill-proportioned front of the Roman Catholic church of St Francis Xavier, and decided on the spur of the moment to look inside. The interior was vast and reasonably well-proportioned, but cluttered with rather mean pews and elaborate sculptured representations of the Stations of the Cross. The priest was in the church and looking for a purse that one of his congregation thought she might have lost there and, seeing that Gwen was reading a kind of placard that bore a sepia photograph of something that I could not recognise, he asked us if we would like to see the famous hand of Saint John Kemble.

By this time Gwen had read something of the saint's story on the placard and she said, yes, she would very much like to see the relic. We were both intrigued by this time with the story, for the saint had been martyred as late as 1679, long after the hunt for Jesuits had died down in this country. So the priest took us up the altar steps, helping Gwen very politely, and unlocked and opened a door that led into a little passage to the right of the altar where, through a big glass frame, we saw the ornate glass and gilt reliquary in which on a purplish cloth lay the preserved hand of the saint—blackened as if with pitch, but with surprisingly long and delicate fingers.

John Kemble, the priest told us, had been found guilty of complicity with the Titus Oates plot, and was hanged on Widemarsh Common, Hereford in August 1679. After the hanging the executioner, it is said, struck off the dead man's head, and with it, his hand. The hand was picked up by a Catholic lady who kept it in the family, and in 1806 it was given to Father Anderton, the Rector of Hereford. Some time later a benefactor gave the reliquary and money for the making of the display case in St Xavier's Church. John Kemble was canonised in 1970 and the priest told us he had been invited to Rome to witness the ceremony.

He went out of his way to show us all that was interesting in his church, including a reproduction of a portrait of Sarah Siddons, and a copy of another drawing that intrigued him.[7] 'Look at this now! Here's a picture of the saint just before his execution. They told him, as they always do, you know, that he could have anything he liked before he went to the scaffold. And do you know what he asked for? A pipe of tobacco and a mug of ale! Now there's a funny thing, isn't it? So now in Hereford if they have a last smoke before they part, they call it a Kemble pipe. Take care now as you go. God bless you. It's been a pleasure to meet you and show you round.'

Of the church belonging to this kindly old man, Pevsner says, 'It would have driven Pugin frantic if he could have seen it.'

Christmas Day
A cold raw foggy morning. A man at morning Communion whose asthma and bronchitis was so bad that he sounded like a stiff old pump—the ugh-ugh of his breathing was like a machine badly in need of maintenance. Few presents—books for me, and a clock and jewellery case for Gwen. We do not spend lavishly on presents.

Notes

1 The Convent in Battenhall, Worcester.
2 Wife of the French Emperor Napoleon III, resident in Britain and a close friend of Queen Victoria.
3 Similar to *Kilvert's Diary* is Ronald Fletcher (ed) *The Biography of a Victorian Village: Richard Cobbold's account of Wortham, Suffolk*, 1860, 1977.

4 An Honorary Life Member of the Kilvert Society.
5 Later published in 1982 as *The Diary of Francis Kilvert, April – June, 1870*, edited by Kathleen Hughes and Dafydd Ifans.
6 The Plomer notebook was originally bequeathed by him to Durham University Library along with his other literary papers. In 1989 it was published as *Kilvert's Cornish Diary from 19 July to August 6 1870*, edited by Richard Maber and Angela Tregoning.
7 Born in Brecon, Radnorshire, Sarah Siddons was one of the most celebrated Shakespearian actors of the eighteenth century.

Chapter 9: 1980

Winter Scene

Three sharp reports somewhere beyond the wood.
Muted and muffled in the still winter air.
But one has found its mark.
The sun is hit. Bleeding like a shot pheasant,
it slopes down to the rim of the horizon,
its blood spatters and stains the western clouds.

4 January 1980

The charnel house

12 February 1980

I had often been told that there was a charnel house under the house in College Yard that was once the home of Canon Braley and is now occupied by Canon Fenwick. I never believed the story but yesterday, when I was having tea there after a meeting, Canon Fenwick took me to see it. We went out of the drawing room into a kind of half-kitchen where the family washing was hanging out to dry, then down into a cellar where bottles of home-made wine and apples were being stored, then down farther still into a garden room with forks, spades, nets, polythene sheeting; and in this room there was a well or small pit with one side covered by a sliding door. When you lift the door out there is the charnel house—or rather a kind of charnel cupboard, filled with thigh bones, arm and leg bones and skulls, brown as if varnished, and giving off a faint but disagreeable odour. An incredible sight. I would never have believed it but there it is—no legend but a true charnel house.

18 February 1980

I have been working steadily in the Cathedral Library, gathering notes on the Revd Frederick Goodman, the extraordinary Archdeacon of Arctic Alaska; checking the text of our Worcestershire anthology; reading in haste a book on Charles II and an obscure but not entirely worthless eighteenth-century novel *Emmeline*;[1] reading Brian Wilkes on the Brontës; working away at my Kilvert; entertaining the Matley Moores; planning a visit to Barnsley Park in August with the Archaeological Society; discussing the new *Transactions*.[2] I will not say anything about Frederick Goodman. There is a copy of my article on him in my diary—the Archdeacon of Arctic Alaska. It appeared in *Berrows Worcester Journal* on 17 April 1980.

Jacqueline Twinberrow's story
4 March 1980

Jacqueline lived in Occupied France. Her uncle, who lived near the Swiss border, offered to look after her, so she went with her father from Paris to Lyons by train. The journey took three days. In those days it was so difficult to get a place on a train that people would sleep for nights at the station. When the train came in people would cling to the outside like bees swarming—or like the tram-travellers I used to see in Cairo. When she got to Lyons her father, afraid that she might be picked up by the SS, left her in a convent for safety. There she lived the life of a privileged pupil, called 'mamselle' by the sisters and sleeping alone in a big dormitory, but hating the isolation her privileged position condemned her to, and envying the coarse grey clothes the other girls wore.

How did it all end? I can hardly say. Jacqueline still speaks a wild English and gabbles in her excitement—so that we cannot catch all she says. I hope she will write it down some day.[3]

A case of despair
14 March 1980

As I was driving to town I passed three women holding a fourth, an old woman, pale and gaunt, in a long grey dress, and trying to persuade her to walk with them down the road. I stopped, thinking that they might have some distance to go and I could perhaps give some of them a lift. As I crossed the road the old woman flung her arms towards me and cried, 'Help me! Help me! I am not a patient in this home. I am not a patient in this hospital!' One of the women assured me there was nothing I could do. They were taking her back to the Old Folks Home across the road—presumably she had tried to escape from it. The old woman kept calling out to me, but it was clearly not my place to interfere. Since I could be of no help, I drove off. But what sad story lies behind this little episode?

An important event

On March 21, Friday, around teatime, Luke Oliver Johnson was born in Hereford Hospital. Both Erica and her baby are well.

A visit to the Bishop

23 March 1980

Yesterday I went with David Lockwood to hand over to the Bishop the specially bound volume of *Blue Remembered Hills* which is to be presented to the Queen today (Maundy Thursday).[4] I was greatly impressed by the wonderful collection of watercolours he possesses. He sketches—not especially skilfully—but his collection would grace any museum.

Today, while Gwen was watching the Queen distributing her Maundy money in the cathedral, I was attending the funeral of my dear old colleague, Reg Westgate. George Lovatt delivered the funeral tribute. 'He was a man of great talent and academic distinction. As Head of the Education Department in the College of Higher Education at Henwick Grove, he was responsible for the placing of more than a thousand students in schools scattered all over the county—and beyond.' I did my best not to become too involved in the service. I become tearful far too easily on occasions such as these.

Gwen meanwhile had a good view of the Queen and Prince Philip, both of whom seemed to be tired and dispirited. They had bad colds.

Another death

21 April 1980

On Tuesday last I met Mrs Peirson in Pump Street and she told me that if I hurried I might catch Mr Peirson as he was walking past the Guildhall.[5] I ran after him and caught him at the Guildhall gates. I thought he looked very well, sunburnt as if he had just returned from a holiday, energetic and cheerful. We spoke together for a few minutes and I came away with the impression that, for a man who was supposed to be sick, he looked very well and fit... But during the early hours of Wednesday he had a haemorrhage of some sort and died before a doctor could get to him.

I was never close to him, but I always admired his devotion to his job, and believe that the College owes almost everything to him.

Within the last few months—or at least the last year—many whom I worked closely with have died—Mary Smith, Bill Smith, Muriel Stone, Michael Hickling, Reg Westgate and now Mr Peirson. The grim reaper!

The decline of an old man

30 April 1980

For a long time now I have seen him sitting on a seat near the centre of the city—roughly shaven, a stubbly moustache failing to hide his harelip, his clothes shabby, his shoes scuffed. Sometimes I have seen him sleeping on this bench—where did he spend the night that he can sleep so long on a hard bench? Lately he has begun to look more unkempt. The seams under the pockets of his trousers are pulling apart. His old cardigan is frayed. And I noticed yesterday that he has begun to talk to himself. He was walking up Bridge Street noticing no one, but holding a conversation with himself or some invisible auditor, gesturing but seeing no one. I wonder how long he will stay alive and how many more times I will see him walking the streets, sleeping with his back to a warm sunny wall, keeping up his unintelligible monologue.

A memorial service

2 May 1980

A memorial service for Mr Peirson was held yesterday. Attended by old students, old and present members of staff, friends and well-wishers from the city. But a strangely cold occasion. Tom Finnigan spoke feelingly but George Lovatt (another funeral oration for him) was flatly factual. It seemed to me a cold almost phlegmatic farewell to a man who was himself perhaps without feeling. I had a great admiration for him, but we were not congenial spirits.

12-16 May 1980

A week in the North, largely in Yorkshire, during the course of which we saw the Gladstone Pottery Museum, Saltaire (no more than a glimpse), Halifax, Huddersfield, Glossop, Chapel-en-le-Frith, Kirkstall Abbey, Haworth, Harewood, Bolton Abbey, Richmond Castle and Georgian Theatre (and a glimpse of the Culloden Tower and the now converted railway station), much dale scenery, Fountains Abbey, and on the way home Cowan Bridge, Tunstall Church, Churches Mansion, Nantwich Church and St Chad's in Shrewsbury. But alas I was stricken on the very first day (at Haworth) with some kind of strange viral infection from which I have still (3 weeks later) not completely recovered.

6 June 1980

Gael, my GP, tells me that the cardiogram reveals that at some time or other—maybe in Yorkshire, maybe before that—something has inflicted some damage on the muscles of my heart. So I have to take it quietly for a while. I need not be unduly concerned, but I have had a little warning. And now that I do think back I can remember two very brief blackouts that I suffered some time ago—momentary, but perhaps a warning symptom. I have been suffering for some time now—since Haworth—from a distressing breathlessness. But I feel that I am recovering.

Last week while I was working through some routine correspondence in the Cathedral Library I came across a letter from Cardinal Newman from the Oratory, Birmingham. I wonder if the Oratory people know of the existence of this letter. Maybe I ought at least to tell Canon Fenwick about it.

My breathlessness was so bad that I had to call off our projected holiday in Durham and the Borders. So I missed seeing Newby Hall and Cragside and all the other places I was looking forward to. And I missed my mother's birthday. Gwen's friend, Lila, was very disappointed at our not getting to Ferryhill. But I think I was right not to go. Have I reached a critical stage in my life? I feel that after a while I shall carry on as I have always carried on. As soon as I am able to walk a few miles I shall do so.

Birds in Winter

A flock of lapwings rises,
hangs trembling in the clear air,
like drops thrown up by a fountain,
caught between rising and falling.

Starlings, alighted on a telegraph line,
drop off, one by one,
like flakes of soot.

A magpie drags its way
from tree to tree
as if someone had tied
an invisible thread to its tail.

Rooks stalk and swagger
across the green fields
like self-important fellows
in glossy waistcoats.

A series of visits
June 1980
With the Archaeological Society to the Cotswolds. We went first to Cornwell Manor, the attractive home of one of the Ward family (George Ward used to be the MP for Worcester)—a beautiful eighteenth-century front with fine terraced gardens (designed by Clough Williams Ellis) and good outbuildings.[6] I thought the hall was charming, but the dining room with its strange panels was dull and depressing, the pink salon was rather vulgar and the ballroom (restored by Williams Ellis in 1939) was deplorable with its hideous antelope heads, stretched big game skins etc... Pevsner calls the village 'stagey', but I found it rather charming.

From Cornwell we went on to see Combe House, the home of the Revd Francis Willis-Bund, Chaplain of All Souls, and a descendant of our local historian. I hoped that he would tell us something about his house, but he did not say a word—not even about the Strawberry Hill Gothic additions—and left us to go from room to room without a word of explanation. His second wife said she could not understand why we had come, because in her opinion this was a dreadful house to live in. I made several blunders during the course of the day. I was taking a photograph of the exterior of Cornwell when Miss Matley Moore said in a sharp voice, 'Have you permission?' Then later when Homery was talking to me about his lecture I must have seemed very inattentive, for he said, just as sharply, 'Are you listening? Or has the architecture more attraction for you?'

The second visit was with the Kilvert Society to Wiltshire, a trip that could have been calamitous. The weather was atrocious and the bus three quarters of an hour late. We stood in the gateway of the Town Hall in pouring rain. Gwen was suffering from an aching back, and I from my persistent breathlessness; but the day was not without its pleasures. We saw the inside of Nonsuch, a house I like very much; learnt a great deal about Malmesbury; and saw Bowood at last. There is not a great deal to see of the great house at Bowood, but Westmacott's famous *Distressed Mother* is in the sculpture gallery; there are fine pictures, and fine exhibitions and an interesting chapel. Unfortunately, I saw neither the mausoleum nor the cascade. At all three places I was able to read from Kilvert—on his visit to Malmesbury, his visit to Nonsuch and the description of Ettie, and finally his walk around Bowood. On this outing I met Tom Hewitt, who was at school with me. Characteristically I failed to recognise him.

The third visit was with the National Trust party to Sezincote—another appallingly wet day. Mrs Peake showed us the house—so at least I got inside what is for me one of the most exotic houses in the country. Before we started someone had a bright idea. She suggested that since it was in a sense a Moslem house, we might take off our shoes. Then what a display of gnarled, twisty, elephantine, varicosed feet was on display! But shoeless, we were allowed upstairs, up the supremely beautiful staircase, a Regency masterpiece, and saw a succession of rooms, in general rather fussily (occasionally disastrously) decorated. Some of the furniture, notably the ivory inlaid chairs, and some of the pictures were unattractive. The garden on the other hand, which we were not able to see properly because of the rain, is a masterpiece, and I would love to go over it more carefully.

A holiday in East Anglia
July 1980
It began with a long damp journey from Worcester to Pershore, Flyford Flavell, Inkberrow, Rugby to Wisbech where the rain we had been fleeing from finally caught up with us after pursuing us across the dispiriting landscape of Fenland. Wisbech looked sodden and depressing and we had a picnic lunch in the least prepossessing of milieus—a side street by a car park. But after King's Lynn the country grew more varied—picturesque, well wooded, even hilly, with full hedges, saltings and dunes in the distance, and unexpectedly charming villages with cottages built of gamboge carrstone, flints and large beach pebbles.

Holkham is set in a large park as well wooded as Warwickshire. Its brick exterior is disappointing, especially the back of the house where one enters; but who can ever forget that magnificent hall with its ambitious basilican shape and design and the columns of coloured Derbyshire alabaster that adorn it—or the superb series of state rooms that encircle that hall—Kent and Coke and Burlington at their superb best—the North Dining Room with its busts of Aphrodite and Venus, the sculpture gallery, the drawing room with its marvellous canvasses (Claude, Pietro de Pietri, Maratti) the majestic saloon with its cunning ceiling (the shape of its detail changing subtly as they move from centre to edge)?

After breakfast we were taken to Norwich and then conducted round the city—from the plain undistinguished new Town Hall (with its two clocks giving different times), past the Assembly House, across the market place to a paved area around London Street by the Colman's Mustard House to the twin halls of St Andrew's and Blackfriars, through the Crypt Restaurant to

Elm Hill, with its cobbles, art shops and the house where Father Ignatius first tried to set up his monastic establishment—and on to the Cathedral which a certain Dr Fielding had kept in such marvellous condition during his period of office as Cathedral architect—its open triforium and its wealth of superb bosses. (Has anyone made a full study of these masterpieces?)

After a scrappy lunch and a lot of time wasted trying to find a bus we managed to get to the University Campus and find the new Sainsbury Centre for the Visual Arts. Another great aesthetic experience—far superior to our visit to Peggy Guggenheim's home in Venice, and recalling in excitement our first view of the Musée D'Art Moderne in Paris. There was work by Henry Moore, Giacometti, Segonzac, Francis Bacon (whose work I detest), Seurat, Morisot, ungainly Bauhaus furniture and very elegant art nouveau glass, writing desk, chairs etc., Cycladic and primitive African sculpture of rare quality, and excellent prints. A brilliant exhibition in a building that looks from the outside like a hangar, but inside is flexible, serene, almost classical in its beauty. Much of the untreated concrete of the campus buildings is now looking shabby but this, clad in aluminium, still shines. How long will it keep its good looks?

On Sunday we went to Blickling Hall. The famous pink brick was a bit subdued in the wet weather but what a romantic and harmonious facade! The great hall was a little gloomy—hardly any light was getting in—and it was a little difficult to decipher details of inscriptions, but we made out Queen Elizabeth I and Anne Boleyn and the enigmatic figures on the newel posts. From the hall we went by a devious way to a drawing room with a Canaletto and a view of Blackfriars Bridge, the south drawing room with a large plain lighter-coloured overmantel, fine paintings and ornate ceiling pendants, the stunning Great Library (the Long Gallery) with its emblematic and symbolic ceiling, and the state bedroom, once the chapel.

The church, which stands apart from the house, is not outstandingly beautiful, but contains a wealth of fine brasses and a spectacular, overdone effigy of the 8th Marquis of Lothian (whose wheelchair we had seen in the house) who died of a mysterious disease contracted in India. *The Effigy* was by G. D. Watts—a recumbent figure being supported by two large and undeniably Pre-Raphaelite angels.

We saw little of the grounds. The weather—and time—were against us.

From Blickling we went on to Felbrigg—a Jekyll and Hyde of a house, with a Jacobean beginning (Victorianised—not badly) and a 'Grand Tour' extension—a series of State rooms, some too dark and too overloaded with pictures for my liking, an Octagon, designed specially to exhibit pictures bought on the Tour, a series of dull bedrooms, and then Paine's Gothick Library—surely a curiosity. Felbrigg does not come high on my list of great houses, but I was intrigued by the story of the mad heir who was infatuated with trains and ended his days driving one at a guinea a week. I would very much like to read Ketton-Cremer's book, *Felbrigg: the Story of a House.*

On this holiday I seem to have specialised in rescuing elderly ladies from bathrooms. On my first evening I was waiting in Gwen's room (keeping an eye on her valuables while she went for her bath) when I heard a distant banging on a door. I hardly knew what to make of it but something told me it was Gwen in trouble; and when I went along the corridor I found that she had locked herself in the bathroom and could not get out. I could see that she was failing to turn the catch fully and persuaded her to rest, and try again, this time giving the catch a very firm turn. It worked and a hot and relieved Gwen was free.

Some time later I heard a similar sound and found that this time it was poor Mrs Allely who was trapped. I called out to her the instructions I had given to Gwen and eventually she too freed herself. But, looking back, I wonder if this scare did not contribute in some measure to her collapse.

On the way home from Felbrigg we were almost held up by an extraordinary cloudburst that flooded the fields, made the topsoil run in coloured rivers over the surface of the road and brought cars to a dead stop. Huge raindrops hit the road and spirted upwards like bullets exploding.

During the night I dreamt that I met John Danby and his family on a railway platform. They were on their way to Tewkesbury where they had bought a cottage. I was surprised—and a little offended—that they had decided to live so close to me without telling me.

Sunday

Poor Mrs Allely never saw Wimpole Hall. She tried to look round the house but felt ill and tried to get back into the coach; but before she could get in she collapsed and died. We heard of her death as we were having tea. Poor Edward Tebbutt, who had come with her, was deeply affected. He seemed stunned and was incapable of any decision for hours afterwards. Both his first and second wives had died of similar attacks, and now his friend, who was a very forceful woman and had brought many new interests into his life, had died in the same way.

It seems callous to enthuse now about a visit that was so sadly clouded, but I fell for Wimpole Hall in a big way. Surely few families can have had the services of so many distinguished architects—Sanderson Miller, Flitcroft, Sir John Soane, Sir James Thornhill, Gibbs, Kendall et al… The result could have been a series of disastrous compromises, but in fact the total effect was stunning—Kendall's fine Hall, with its golden pillars and tiled floor, Thornhill's painted chapel, Soane's yellow Reception room, Gibbs's classical Library, the Book Room—all delightful. Wimpole Hall is a great house—and how ironical that it, like Felbrigg, should have been almost bedevilled by one extravagant heir. The estate was almost beggared in the last years of the nineteenth century by a Champagne Charlie of a man, a great friend of the Prince of Wales. Fortunately it was bought by Kipling's daughter, Elsie, the wife of Captain Bambridge, and she and her husband restored it to its former glory before handing it to the National Trust.

24 July 1980
Gwen's birthday. We went to Malvern, and at Warwick House she bought two woollen jackets (about £80 in all!) and picked up a little vase in an antique shop for 75p. Gillian failed to send a card on time, but redeemed herself with a telegram and flowers from Interflora.

Sunday 27 July
A visit to Ditchley Park, surely one of the most handsome great houses in the Cotswolds—an exterior of golden stone, Palladian with two wings connected to the main house by quadrants; a most impressive Kentian Hall, with fine doors and stucco ornaments; a series of good state rooms culminating in a fine Stucco Room, poetic, almost baroque (perhaps rococo rather); and a series of upstairs bedrooms unusual enough to titillate the kind of Great House voyeurs of which our Archaeological Society is largely made up. In the grounds (largely lawns) a semicircular pool, a Tuscan temple (used as a garden room) and farther off, across the Capability Brown lake, a round temple which I did not get close to. A lovely house which we explored in detail.

Ditchley Park stands in the middle of a lovely district which repays exploration. I have somewhere a Trail Guide published from the Oxfordshire Museum at Woodstock.

A friendly curate
29 August 1980
I went back to Cheltenham, this time by train and went first to Christ Church. In the church I found a young man who clearly had some kind of office there.

'Are you the incumbent?' I asked.

'No. Actually I'm the curate. I've just come. I've only been here a few days.'

'Then you have come to a fine church. I admire it greatly.'

'Do you? That's nice to hear. Of course this bit (indicating the altar rail) is very new. Very recent.'

'But it's good. I think you've managed to make changes without destroying the character of the church.'

'Do you think so? You make me very pleased. Look, can I give you a lift?'

And so this kindly affectionate curate, who reminded me strongly of my own Francis Kilvert, took me to Montpellier and left me with kind wishes.

What a city Cheltenham must have been in the early nineteenth century! Even now it is beautiful—even in some of the Victorian suburbs—or quarters. I went by train yesterday and got out at the city's only surviving station, a shabby affair, and had a longish but interesting walk from the centre. I saw the King Edward statue and the William IV statue, the Rotunda (now Lloyd's Bank), Christ Church, Lansdowne Crescent, the College, Thirlestaine House and most of the main buildings, such as Suffolk Place. It was a very wet day for a change and a long walk back to the station, but neither the weather nor the distance discomposed me seriously.

When I walked into the Town Hall to take a close look at the Central Hall, I saw a man walking purposefully toward me, and was afraid that he was going to ask me what I was doing there. Instead he said to me, 'I bought a hat like that one of yours. Nice, aren't they?'

In the North again
8 September 1980
Lila Watson, Gwen's friend, with whom we stayed at Ferryhill, is suffering badly from arthritis. Her hands are twisted, her knees stiff and her eyes affected. And she was one of the great athletes of her school! Tommy, her husband, seems to have had a mild stroke and has lost his confidence in himself as a driver. They told us the sad story of Bet L and her husband. They have a phone but he will not let her use it except for emergencies. He spends his days

polishing and cleaning the house. He expects her to be at home at stated times and meets her off the bus at the time he has chosen. In company he can be quite charming and articulate, but in the privacy of his home he is impossibly demanding. Once I thought highly of Bet, and considered her an articulate and gifted young woman. What an unhappy fate!

At Sedgefield the church was open. A communion service was in progress and we joined it. After the service we met Canon Edmondson who is the incumbent and a friend of Tommy's. In fact he officiated at the wedding of Lila and Tommy's daughter Margery with Mike Lees. He told us that he has to keep the church firmly locked now. The local Comprehensive School children bring their fish and chips in and smoke there, and then do endless damage. And this is one of the most beautiful parish churches in the county!

At Bishop Auckland I found the gateway to the Bishop's Park utterly charming. How was it that I never knew it was the work of James Wyatt? I was disappointed to find Escomb whitewashed on the inside, but it is a wonderful thing that after centuries of neglect this humble building should once again be a parish church.[7] You can get into neither church nor public lavatories here without calling at No. 38 for the key!

Manderston is a surprise—an Edwardian house but so well built and so elegantly designed you can hardly tell that it is not eighteenth century. Some of the rooms are ornate, but the best—the entrance hall for instance—are almost as good as Adam. The stables and domestic arrangements are lavish and sophisticated. The stalls are of mahogany; and the tiled kitchen has an island range, separate rooms for ice, cold meats, fish, game—and a lever for a servant to operate by remote control to open the top half of the tradesman's door.

Manderston is very popular but at Mellerstain we were virtually alone. We walked around this lovely house in peace and comfort, and had virtually the freedom of it. Room after room was an Adam triumph. The House was a procession of superbly decorated rooms. I thought I would find Mellerstain with its rather forbidding exterior a dull house. In fact it was the highlight of our holiday. I loved it—the gardens, the superb view over the lake towards the Cheviots, even the gift shop where Gwen bought a mohair scarf and from which, months later, came a mohair cardigan. What curiosities in this house—a spider table, a signed book of poems by the Earl of Haddington—and what charming and courteous assistants. Mellerstain is a place to visit again.

Lady S
24 September 1980
Lady S who showed us round her house today was a strange languid woman whose zest and energy seemed to be visibly leaking from her. She was wearing cheap ill-fitting shoes with incongruous wedge heels and cloth uppers, and a stained pale blue skirt. Beneath her make-up her skin had a faint bluish tinge, like the skin of some alcoholics. She spoke of everything in the house in a vague offhand manner, as if she had lost all interest in her possessions, hardly bothering to make herself audible, lighting cigarette after cigarette and reaching over to knock the ash into some tray or saucer. Yet for all her vagueness and apathy it became obvious that, in spite of her apparent indifference, she had a great knowledge of and affection for the treasures in her house—the Islamic armour in the Hall, the great Oriental carpet that had been smuggled out with the Elgin Marbles, the Moroccan saddlecloth, the Dutch landscapes. There was a strange feeling of absent-mindedness in this house. There was a bewildering vagueness even about the alterations that Nash had made to it in the late eighteenth or early nineteenth century—those odd parodies of Norman pillars, the flight of steps to the chapel that was no chapel, the Adam ceiling that had lost its colours, the pram standing in the hall, the creased anoraks piled under the Kneller portrait, the Grinling Gibbons carvings strung ponderously across a bare patch of wall.

The memory of two disasters seemed to cling to Lady S, the cataclysmic flood of 1959 that filled the drawing room with five feet of water, damaged furniture and carpets, and left an indelible stain on the walls; and the death of her husband four years ago. For all her vagueness she was not inconsiderate, and allowed us, with a lack of suspiciousness that was rather touching, the freedom of her beautiful rambling house. On that disastrous night of 1959 eight inches of rain fell in a few hours, the stream was blocked by rubble and fallen trees and water poured down the slopes into the hollow in which the house is built. When the water had receded the floors had to be taken up, the carpets cleaned, the books dried out in the sun and the broken furniture repaired. The damage was serious and the whole experience clearly traumatic.

As she spoke of these disasters the glorious September sunshine filled the valley, and the splendour of the autumnal light gave the landscape an idyllic and paradisal appearance.

15 October 1980
Yesterday I got into conversation on the train with an elderly woman who told me she was from Durban, but was here on holiday seeing her friends and relatives. She was travelling on a Round Britain rail ticket which had cost her £75, but was proving invaluable. She was related to the Crofts of Croft Castle—I think she said her maiden name was Croft Mowbray—and I fell into conversation with her because she was reading a booklet on Tennyson's Lincolnshire. She had just been exploring the countryside around Somersby. The train was like a Turkish bath, but she had one coat over her knees and another, even thicker, ready to pull over the first.

I was so interested in her conversation—and at the same time so anxious to get out of that overheated compartment once she had got out (at Ledbury) that I left behind me, when I moved, my pochette containing my driving licence, Barclaycard, Senior Citizen Railcard and £30 in notes. But, although the realisation of what I had lost troubled me during the Kilvert Society Committee meeting, which I had to chair, all was well in the end for the missing pochette was waiting for me in the Left Luggage Department at Hereford Station. I was grateful for this stroke of good luck.

Family disasters
15 October 1980
In the last few days Bill, the husband of Pat, my neighbour's daughter, has gone off to set up home with his boyfriend. He has been gay for 20 years but no one has admitted it. And the wife of a man near Jennie, whose husband is having an affair with her best friend, tried last night, for the second time, to take her own life.

A weekend in London
20 October 1980
We caught the train at Foregate Street just after eight but had to endure the inevitable delays. For some reason we stopped for nearly 20 minutes just beyond Oxford and were late into Paddington. But we had not to wait long for a taxi. We left our luggage at The Washington, and began in earnest, booking tickets for theatres and taking the tube to Covent Garden. A charming scene—stalls manned by artistic young women, pleasant little shops, a musician playing good classical music and that remarkable Inigo Jones church flanking one

end of the market. Incredibly there was a man lying in the damp churchyard, apparently fast asleep.

At last I saw the Queen's Chapel in St James's Palace—plain, very austere for a Roman Catholic Chapel, with little decoration other than the Royal Balcony, its fireplace and the beautiful Venetian window.[8] I looked upon it as a great privilege to be shown this historic chapel.

Tea at the Royal Academy and a long inspection of the Stanley Spencer exhibition which left me curiously disappointed and in a kind of suspended state of mind. Was he really a great painter? He seemed to me to be at best a visionary, at worst almost a cartoonist. His work appears to me to be in danger of losing vitality—a kind of dullness, in spite of all his humour and quirkiness, seems to be creeping over his paintings. I can hardly explain the mixed feelings this exhibition left me with (though I did enjoy the Burghclere Chapel paintings).

We did not greatly enjoy *Born in the Gardens* by Peter Nichols.

The next day we got to the V&A early to make sure of being first in the queue for the great exhibition there. And what a revelation! 'Princely Magnificence' was one of the most brilliant and beautiful exhibitions I have ever seen—a mixed display of Renaissance portraits and jewellery—in some cases one could examine the portraits and then turn to the actual jewellery, miraculously preserved. It was all brilliantly staged, brilliantly displayed, and laid out with art and clarity. This was one of the highlights of my year—a great aesthetic experience.

While we were waiting to go in we talked with an elderly lady who loved churches and cathedrals and had spent all the summer visiting them—but she was not enthusiastic about Durham where the people in the cathedral shop had been unexpectedly offhand with her. A group of foreign students were singing on the steps, but the only tune I could recognise was *Frère Jacques*.

Butterfield's All Saints, Margaret Place is a fine Victorian Church; I liked All Souls, Langham Place, but we were vexed to find St Mary Aldermary locked with no indication where the key might be found; and there was a service in St Paul's. Finally we found that our favourite restaurant was closed and we had to make do with an extraordinary improvised meal at Macdonald's. What a strange set up! You queue downstairs for your burger and chips, sweet and coffee, then carry them upstairs and eat them with your fingers. But the end of the day was worthwhile. We very much enjoyed *The Dresser*, a clever study of an old actor-manager struggling to keep his company going in wartime and collapsing under the strain.

Mr Peirson
8 November 1980
I ought to make a note on the sad end of Mr Peirson. He was an enigmatic man who came to life when he was performing some public duty. In committee he was tireless, a master of his facts, and so dedicated that he soon exhausted most of his fellow-members. In the chair at public dinners he was thorough and exhaustive, thanking at inordinate length all who had to be thanked, omitting no one however unimportant—but in the end wearying everyone with his prolixity. He could be witty and even eloquent, although as he grew more and more experienced and confident he grew repetitive and emptily rhetorical ('I have been told there is a rift in this college between staff and students. What is the evidence of this rift? In my opinion there is no rift).

On his feet in public he was confident and persuasive; but when he ceased to be a public figure he tended to slump, to grow uncommunicative, difficult to talk to, empty and almost morose. He was for many years an energetic leader, but immediately after his retirement began to ail. He had been suffering for some time from a kind of leukaemia, but had never given me the impression of a sick man. He had been robbed by retirement of his role in life, and did not survive the deprivation.

In a way the same thing happened to Mary Smith. When her husband Bill retired, they went to live in Cheshire. She had to give up her job, the work that was her joy and main reason for living. She suffered two heart attacks and died. Ironically her husband survived her by only a year when he too succumbed to a heart attack.

All who financed *Blue Remembered Hills* have been repaid. Both Gwen and I have received back the £100 we advanced.

My Desert Island Discs
To Music—Schubert
The Mahler theme used in *Death in Venice*[9]
The Mozart theme used in *Elvira Madigan*[10]
Northumbrian Pipe Music
A passage from Kilvert [11]
November by Kurt Weill
From Vivaldi's Seasons
Mingulay Boat Song (Robin Hall and Jimmy McGregor)

Vignettes of a day around Malvern
11 November 1980
Rain falling vertically on Newland Avenue. The dark mysterious jewelled interior of the church; the brilliance of the flash of my camera on the sedilia.

The vault-like cold of Eastnor Church. The marble effigy of some dead lord glimpsed through the dark red curtain. Children coming noisily out of school. The exotic beauty of the altar. A golden glow stealing upwards on the shoulders of the hills.

A still autumn day in a cemetery.
Purring limousines reversing towards the chapel.
Keepers sweeping up fallen leaves. A man and a woman
discussing a headstone that had fallen.
White marble crosses against black yews. City of the dead.

A day in Cardiff—on a citizen railcard £1 anywhere ticket
13 November 1980
The train was late at Worcester so I walked up and down the platform—looking at the workmen most of whom were doing nothing; the damage done to the station by vandals; the ill-kept houses on the hill beyond. When the train did arrive I had a compartment to myself. I meant to read but I enjoyed looking at the grey outline of the Malverns, Bredon with its landslip clearly visible, the pheasants in the field, the flocks of gulls rising and taking off as our noise disturbed them, a little Gothick cottage in a wood, the Gothick tower of that Cheltenham church I once inspected.

A delay at Cheltenham, a bewildering change of direction and then that uncomfortable Bristol Parkway junction. My second train was also late, but we got off at Cardiff only ten minutes or so behind schedule. I jumped quickly from the train and caught a bus immediately to Llandaff, reaching the cathedral at last. It is not the greatest of cathedrals, but I liked the unpretentious Close, the absence of tourists, the Epstein Christ (which I had long wanted to see), the unusual reredos with its Mary flowers, and the new pulpit, the touching sanctuary.

I could not stay long because I had to join the 2 pm tour of the Castle. Right at the beginning of this tour however, I did a silly thing. I climbed the 101 steps up to the Summer Smoking Room and put too big a strain on my weak heart muscles, and the discomfort prevented me from taking in fully the extraordinary series of Burges rooms we were shown. Besides, on this occasion, we had a kindly but not too helpful guide who did not seem to know much about Burges, and he had a strangely uninterested way of speaking that I did not wholly like.

As soon as we had finished I went to the National Museum in the Civic Centre to see the Monets, a small but distinguished collection of which I liked best the railway and Thames studies (far better than the Venice pictures), two surprising views of Norwegian landscapes, and Verteuil in fog (a tour de force). The Museum building is handsome—so is the Town Hall, especially the Upper Concourse (if I can call it that); I saw some Thomas china of which we have two sets, and took the liberty of speaking to Emrys Hughes, the actor, whom I met looking at the Monets.

After that there was only time to look at a few shops, and catch the 5:10 pm for Hereford. I travelled from Newport with a woman and her daughter laden with pillows and duvets; and at Hereford met a Welsh boy going to Malvern whose English was so bad he was almost unintelligible. When I got home I found that I had to go to Droitwich for a BBC interview on Kilvert. At Llandaff I gave thanks that at my age I could still face such a day as this—but after that climb in Cardiff I still feel some strain.

17 November 1980
Today Gwen reminded me of that story about Bill Gwilliam and Matley. On one of their excursions they went somewhere for tea. No one came to serve them and Matley, growing more and more impatient, pulled a whistle out of his pocket and gave a long blast on it; when the manager hurried over to see what was the matter, he said, 'Tea. We've been waiting here too long. Kindly bring us tea.' It arrived.

The tactless Harry S
20 November 1980
H S: It was at this time last year that I had the pleasure of nominating Mrs L for the office of President of this Society. I would like to follow that up by proposing that she now embarks on a second year of office. It seems to me just and proper that now we have a woman as PM we should have our own Mrs Thatcher to push us along and keep us on the right tracks. I sometimes feel that I am back in my army days with the sergeant major to bawl me out now and then. Don't get me wrong, ladies and gentlemen, I like it. I'm the sort of person who likes being

ordered about and told what to do. Oh yes, it's good for us all to be told in no mean fashion just where we stand. So I have the great pleasure etc. etc..

Mrs L: Thank you very much for your confidence. But I would like to remind you that I am not a sergeant major, and I do not like ordering people about. Nor am I a Mrs Thatcher either. Let me remind you that our committee meetings are timed to end at 12.30 pm and it is my job to see that we do not exceed our time. So having disposed of that let us now go on to the next item on our agenda...

A prickly response to an undiplomatic proposal?

A last fling
November 1980
A successful visit to London to see the 'Loot' exhibition. Before we had left Goldsmiths' Hall we had gone berserk and ordered a gold ring for Gwen and a beautiful neo Art Nouveau box (about £110 in all). I love this exhibition—the setting, the building, the contact with the brilliant young artists who exhibit here. Later saw the 'Treasures from Chatsworth'. Gwen had a recorded talk to help her, and enjoyed listening to the Duke of Devonshire talking about his Rembrandt drawings, the Inigo Jones designs, the Book of Hours and the Lucien Freud portraits. But it was very hot in the Private Rooms of Burlington House and we were glad to get out into the fresh air.

Early Morning, Worcester

To see the city like this,
the roofs, the church spires, the cathedral tower
silhouetted in deepest black against a primrose sky,
the mercury lights on the bridge like a rope of pearls,
the river, a stream of molten gold reflecting
the yellow dawn—to see it like this,
you must be in a particular place,
at a particular time of the day,
at a particular time of the year,
and on foot.
Such a sight is not seen often.
So I put it down

that I saw it once,
in November, just after seven,
from the Hylton Road in nineteen hundred and eighty.

29 November 1980

A discovery
29 November 1980
Today there came through the post a most important document, a hitherto unknown photograph of the guests at the wedding of James Pitcairn and Dora Kilvert; and among the guests is Kilvert himself—a fine full front photograph showing how tall and handsome he was, and no signs of a squint or any eye defect. A great find from the Langley House archives. I understand there are more photographs there but Mrs Scott Ashe is not too enamoured of Kilvert and his Society.

12 December 1980
Today I went into the abandoned church of St Mary Magdalene in Sansome Walk. The pews have gone, the font taken out—the sump hole still visible—the flooring gone here and there, but the pulpit (without its handrail) and the reredos still in situ. A great feeling of spaciousness now that the floor is clear. What a short life for this church—little more than 100 years has seen an appeal for it, its construction, its years of life, its death. It is up for sale now and will probably be totally demolished.

I have been looking up the work of the Forsyth brothers and have come across many things. One of my best discoveries was William Forsyth's statue of Flora in the grounds of Chateau Impney, near Droitwich.

In October we heard that Meinrad Craighead and Rosemary Davies had left the monastery at Stanbrook (they call it a monastery). Just before Christmas they came to stay for two nights with us. We still cannot understand completely why they have 'jumped over the wall.'

Yesterday went with other members of the Archaeological Society to present a copy of 'Mediaeval Worcester' (our latest *Transactions*) to the Mayor. An interesting occasion.

Notes

1 Charles Turner Smith, *Emmeline: The Orphan of the Castle*, 1788.
2 Fred was still editor of the *Transactions of the Worcestershire Archaeological Society*.
3 WW2 People's War, BBC—Jacqueline's Story.
4 D. N. Lockwood and F. Grice, (Editors), *Blue Remembered Hills: An Anthology of Worcestershire Verse in Celebration of the Thirteenth Centenary of Worcester Diocese*, 1980. Many of the most recent poets, contemporaries of the editors, are represented in the collection and are mentioned by name in this journal—Roger Alma, Molly Holden, David Lockwood, Gael Turnbull and Philip Worner.
5 E. G. Peirson, Principal (1951-78) of the Training College, later University of Worcester.
6 The Hon. George Ward was Conservative MP for Worcester (1945-60); Sec. for Air (1957-60); and Lord Ward of Witley (1960). Clough Williams-Ellis was an architect.
7 Escomb is a Saxon church.
8 The Roman Catholic Chapel had been built for Queen Henrietta Maria.
9 Gustav Mahler, Symphony No 5, Movement 4—Adagietto.
10 Wolfgang Amadeus Mozart, Piano Concerto No 21.
11 *Kilvert's Diary*, recording with Timothy Davies, Saydisc CD SDL 309.

Chapter 10: 1981-2

1981

Telepathy
6 February 1981
I was hurrying to town, beginning to fear that I had set off far too late to catch my train, and thinking how unlikely it was that anyone would stop to give me a lift—I was not even looking round to give the impression that I was in need of help—when an elderly man with a foreign accent pulled up in a maroon mini and asked if I would like a ride to town.

'You must be a mind-reader,' I said. 'How did you know that I was hoping for a lift?'

'I did not know,' he replied, 'but I have been in trouble many times in my life and I like to help others when they are in trouble as well.'

I caught my train to Oxford and saw the Ashmolean exhibition by my friend Robin Tanner.

Late Poems

A Still Day

No keeping secrets on a day like this!
Every sound comes through this air like a clear prompt.
Three miles away a dog warns off some stranger.
Three fields away a magpie clears its throat.
I hear a dry leaf falling through the air
and a blackbird turning things over in the hedge bottom.
If I knew starling language I'd get every word
that flock is saying in the mile-off ash.
Better keep all my thoughts to myself this day.
Just hint a whisper and the world will know.

22 February 1981

Collection

My wife has arranged her pots
on shelves in the spare bedroom.
Who will cherish her collection
when we, who recognise their beauty
and bought them year by year,
are no longer here to care for them?

24 February 1981

Yobbos

With matted hair
and straggly beards,
in studded blousons and
faded jeans,
they gather in the new precinct,
eating chips from papers,
drinking endlessly from cans.
They colonise this place.
It is pleasant to think
they have found somewhere they like.

But later, when it is dark,
they will come back,
snap off the branches of the trees,
uproot the plants
and throw them away like chip papers.

24 February 1981

Winter Scene

Retreating snow
leaves a sea of green
with fraying floes
where the disconsolate lapwings stand
waiting for something to change.

Snow falling from trees.
Suddenly, without warning, a branch will begin
to bob up and down,
as if some invisible bird had lit on it
then taken flight again.
But it is only a pad of snow
that, melting, slips from the twig
and falls
with a soft plop
into the drift below.

24 February 1981

In the Station Buffet

First there was the voice of the station announcer—
'The next train to arrive at platform 2...'
Then, in the silence that followed,
I heard a man behind me say to a girl—
'One day I wrote her name upon the strand.'[1]
What strange impulse made him quote—
of all dead poets—
Edmund Spenser—
on a cold March afternoon in a station buffet?

4 March 1981

A great event
5-8 March 1981

Today Colin has been elected a Fellow in Geography of Jesus College, Oxford—his old college. He is taking the place of his old tutor, Mr Paget. A great triumph for him. And a fitting reward for years of hard work.

A few days later Gillian was appointed Head of German at the School of St Helen and St Katharine in Abingdon. A great triumph for her too.

A Dr Richardson wrote to me the other day (16 March), and in the course of his communication mentioned his wife Linetta de Castelvecchio Richardson, née Palamidessi. I was intrigued by the name and inquired about it. He told me that she was the daughter of the Comtesse Josephine, third daughter of Comte

Louis de Castelvecchio, natural son of Louis Bonaparte, brother of the great Napoleon and ex-king of Holland. A living link with the Napoleonic Age!

An old acquaintance
21 March 1981
Today after many years I again met G M. I was helping at a National Trust jumble sale when I saw him going from stall to stall, picking over the rubbish, collecting knives, forks, odd pieces of material, useless bric-à-brac. What a change has come over him! He is now like an old man, shabby, down at heel, like someone who has spent the night in a dosshouse. Did he have a shirt? None was visible. There was an anorak, a pullover, a scarf, but no collar, no tie.

And he gave off a disagreeable smell, so loathsome that when he sat by me in the car (he had impudently asked us to take him and his things back to Edith Lodge) I had to lean away from him and open a window. In what squalor does he now live?

A Lull

Suddenly the wind fell,
the leaves stopped falling,
and birds stopped singing,
and the spell was complete
as if the whole world had stopped spinning.
I came to a halt myself
and stood listening to the silence.
It did not last long.
At some signal that I never heard
the leaves stirred again,
the birds woke
and the road moved under my feet.

23 March 1981

Reading
26 March 1981
Greville's memoirs—Greville is a fine writer, and I think undervalued.[2] *Frankenstein*—a fine novel, far superior to all the spurious adaptations that have been made of it.

In the Design Centre, London
A thin old woman, over seventy I should think, but dressed in a scarlet sweater, scarlet corduroy trousers, and scarlet knee-high boots. She was so old that she was round shouldered, and her sharp shoulder blades stuck out through her sweater. Her hands were bony and veined and her legs almost skeletal. But she was trying to swagger like a young actress, like Diana Rigg as Viola.

In the pub
A beefy butcher, and his thinner friend, a part-time lecturer and a local councillor (Labour) who talked freely to us while we had our ploughman's lunch. They told us a great deal about Shoreditch and its traditions, its craftsmen etc.. They both shook hands very cordially with us before they left.

Contrasts
In the Royal Academy Gwen heard a conversation between a woman and her friend—the woman unable to face any kind of social commitment—even a dinner party—without flying to the bottle. In the train a family from Hereford who had come up for the day just to see and enjoy Madame Tussauds, Buckingham Palace and Kensington Palace.

Editions Graphiques
Victor Arwas from whom I bought a few lithographs a long time ago, before he had a shop, has now a magnificent collection of art nouveau stuff in his Editions Graphiques. A wonderful treasure house—I could have happily spent thousands there. Victor Arwas is now an authority on art nouveau and art deco (which I dislike intensely).

Visitors, Visitors
Brian, who came in his Rolls; our two refugee nuns who are apparently now living quite happily with Alan Knight; Erica and Nick with their family; Gillian and Colin with their family (looking without much success for a house in Oxford); Maxine and Jim Bullock, and later David and Marjorie Brazil...

While I am entering my trivial and unimportant notes what is happening in the great world? Black youths are rioting in Brixton, an IRA prisoner on hunger strike is dying, unemployment in Britain rises alarmingly, firm after firm collapses, prices soar and living standards fall, the spectre of uncontrollable inflation corrupts our life, terrorism threatens not only Uganda, Lebanon, and Iran but many of the Western European countries. An attempt has been made on the life of President Reagan. The whole world seems plagued with a wave of greed, aggressiveness, violence, envy... In the midst of it all we are preparing for the Royal Wedding in July.

The fall of my feet on the rutted car track.
The lark in the air,
the rusty pheasant call which I have never found
the proper word for,
the pouring of water down a drain,
or the scrape of a shovel over tarmac or concrete—
why should these things bring back
feelings I have not known for sixty years?

23 April 1981

A day at Lichfield
25 April 1981
Mary P treated us to rare pantomime. No sooner had the coach set off than she stood up, pulled down a bag from the rack overhead and poured herself and her friend a cup of coffee. Then she stood up again, put her many bags on the seat, found she could not sit down, removed them, sat down, only to get up again for a dingy scarf, which she wound round her woolly fez-shaped hat. No sooner had she settled than she got up again to fish out of one more bag, four plastic cups and a bottle of lemonade. This called for more manoeuvres, more standing, more rummaging in bags (of which she seemed to have a vast number)—more attacking of things on the rack and reaching down of others.

She consumed the whole of her time on the bus to Lichfield poking about in her bags, standing, blocking the gangway, arranging things on her seat and getting in everybody's way. On more than one occasion she blocked not only her own exit but that of the people behind her by parking her many belongings in front of them. Then she crowned an incredible display by taking one more swig of lemonade, forgetting the empty cup, and pouring the remains over the woman behind her when she tried to park one more bag not in her own rack but in the space belonging to the unfortunate traveller over whom she had spilt her lemonade. What a performance!

This was one of the most vicious days I have ever known—a poisonous north wind was sweeping through Lichfield. But I loved the tour of the cathedral and was interested in everything I saw—the unusual vestibule to the Chapter House itself with its rare carvings, the chantry monuments (especially the Sleeping Children), the Westmacott monument, the glorious glass in the Lady Chapel, the fascinating Victorian screen, the Epstein of Bishop Wood's father, the rather ugly pulpit—and the very fine Cathedral Close.

When we were waiting for the bus Mrs P said, 'We are all waiting like somebody on a peak in Darien. Was that Shelley?'

'No,' I said, 'Keats.'

> 'Or like stout Cortez when with eagle eyes
> He star'd at the Pacific—and all his men
> Look'd at each other with a wild surmise—
> Silent, upon a peak in Darien.'

While the guide was talking to us two foolish old ladies in the party kept on rudely with their own conversation. Gwen uttered a loud 'Sh!' in her best schoolmistress voice. I contented myself with a sour look.

The visit ended with an extraordinary freak blizzard which covered us in many inches of snow.

A visit to Forthampton Court

Mr Yorke, who owns the house, a lean old man with discoloured teeth, tanned leathery skin and bony hands half covered with brown mitts, told (greatly to his own amusement) that as Lord of the Manor he has the right of eyry—that is, to take all fledgling falcons from their nests and hawk them in the Malvern Chase. He has the responsibility too of looking after the parish whipping post and stocks (a good punishment for football hooligans, you know, make them look silly and give them frightful cramp). He also showed us a battered Greek head which he had helped his father to smuggle out of Greece a long time ago—under a bowler hat on the seat of a first-class carriage. He and his wife were as merry as crickets (How do you keep warm? Well, you just pile on the clothes you know. Learnt to do that when we were in China). When he feels pious he looks through one window to get a view of Tewkesbury Abbey; when he feels otherwise he looks through another at a birdbath decorated with grotesque faces.

Forthampton is an interesting shapeless house with a beautiful central mediaeval hall, lofty and open and covered with a very large Morris Workshop carpet, still in good condition, and furnished with some good Louis XVI chairs (or XV), and a not too handsome bookcase designed by Philip Webb. There is a good Webb staircase, at the top of which in a glass case is kept a very fine mediaeval painting of Edward the Confessor and a pilgrim; many good pictures including two small Turners and a large portrait of Queen Anne with a ring-tailed raccoon in the background; a gracious six-windowed lounge with a marble fireplace in need of a good cleaning; a library designed by Philip Webb with Morris curtains and fabrics and a valuable piece of Charles I embroidery; a mediaeval tomb in the corner of a shady garden; and a most beautiful peony with a Polish name—a mass of lovely golden flowers.

Forthampton Church has a great deal of interesting Victorian sculpture (font, pulpit, corbel heads, etc.) which could be by Forsyth; and a small row of not-too-satisfactory almshouses reputedly by Burges (but you would not recognise them as his work). The whipping post and stocks are near the church.

Later in the day we went to the Saxon church at Deerhurst, and I saw for the first time the famous Deerhurst Angel.[3] But Deerhurst is such an architectural puzzle that I came away confused. At Bradford-on-Avon and Escomb I know where I am. At Deerhurst I cannot see the wood for the trees.

The Succubus

Who or what is it that in the small hours
steals into my bedroom, lies down with me,
melts my body, finds access to the
chambers of my mind, changes my blood,
plies me with strange medicaments,
shapeless itself, accomplishing with me
a metamorphosis,
turning my courage into nameless fears,
love into hate, assurance to alarm,
pride to self-hatred, confidence to distrust,
and fixes on my face a hateful mask
that only daylight, water, razors, breakfast,
can peel away?

10 May 1981

A Dorset holiday
18 May 1981
We drove to Hanley Swan, left our car in David Lockwood's garage, and then set off with David and Willy in heavy and threatening rain through Chippenham and Frome to Stourhead, where in a very wet car park we rendezvoused with Hugh and Guy Dearlove, Mona and Reg Morgan, Mervyn and Lilian West, Kate Goodwin and Margaret Mathers in their minibus; and after a picnic lunch we all gathered in the church by the entrance to the gardens, where I gave a short talk on Lady Alda Hoare's friendship with Thomas Hardy, and where we saw the plaques commemorating first the double death of Lady Alda and her husband, and the death in a foreign hospital of war wounds of their only son.

It was a rather damp walk around the gardens, but somehow in this green and dripping weather the trees and shrubs looked more living than in brilliant sunshine. Many things were missing, especially from the Pantheon, which is being renovated, but real smoke was rising from the chimney of the woodman's cottage, and there was an estate workman there with a cheerful glowing fire going. The serious miss was the Bristol High Cross, which had also been taken down for repair.

The house was delightful and full of happy memories for me of those sunny days when Roger and I worked in the handsome library with its custom-built Chippendale library furniture on our essay on Lady Alda and Hardy. The house is superbly kept and full of treasures—and some curiosities such as the portrait of Sir Henry with his cigarette smoke shaping itself into the silhouette of his wife. The Administrator's wife, who was so considerate to us when we were working there, asked me archly if I had been kind to the memory of Lady Alda, implying that Lady Alda has less agreeable sides to her character than she had shown to Hardy and his wives.

From Stourhead we drove to Shaftesbury, where we managed to find a few moments to look at Gold Hill—how picturesque it was in that now clearer light—and Sturminster Newton; but we failed to find the house in which Hardy and Emma had lived, and drove over higher more open country through Dorchester to Winterborne Abbas. There we all made ourselves at home in the Church View Guest House, run by the talkative Mrs Ansell. Gwen and I had a reasonably sized bedroom with one double bed and one single bed, a wash-basin with a mirror so high that you had to stand on tiptoe to see in it, and a variety of plugs all in the most inconvenient places. But it was not at all uncomfortable, although I had my customary bad first night's sleep, going all night over the arrangements I had made for the following day, and wondering if they would turn out right.

Tuesday

Then after what was for me a moderate breakfast (how I envy Gwen and her ability to demolish eggs, sausages, bacon and fried bread) we left for our first visit—to Stinsford Church. It proved a devil to find for some ass had altered all the signposts, but help was at hand. We found the church—and found it fascinating—the tell-tale signs of the old gallery; the Grey memorial near the Hardy pew, with its grinning skull and the curious Christian name, Angel; the organ given by Hardy's sister; the memorial window of the Still Small Voice; the gargoyles on the outside, and the impressive row of Hardy tombs lining the church path. David read us two or three poems which relate to the church—Afternoon Service at Mellstock, and A Church Romance. And at last we felt we were very close to the man of whom we had all come in search.

I have forgotten something. Before we came to Stinsford we paused to look at the church at West Stafford—the church in which Angel and Tess were married. (Nearby, David had noticed a house with the name Talbothays and it reminded us that we were near the Vale of the Great Dairies—though the cattle are no longer red and white but black and white). The vicar had just ended his weekday Communion service and invited us into the church—he disappeared immediately, probably in search of his breakfast. It was a charming little church with a Jacobean screen and unusual pre-Raphaelitish paintings on the walls and even behind the pulpit, and a funeral monument cunningly bent at the top to fit the barrel roof. I could not help looking at the chancel steps where Angel and Tess had knelt to take their marriage vows.

Two more visits before lunch. One to see the little school that Hardy attended—the school built by the pious evangelical Mrs Martin—a charming little building with a stone porch over it and a bell-cot with a school bell and its pulley still in position. Then Kingston Maurward, which was a revelation to me. We were welcomed by the most kindly man, a Mr Bob Jones, a senior lecturer in Horticulture. His interest was mainly in the gardens (which are largely post-Hardy), but he went out of his way to show us the magnificent Hall, enormous, lofty and almost theatrical with its lavish fireplaces on either side, the elegant drawing room, with large windows overlooking the spacious estate with its lawns, lake, park buildings, islands and superb trees. The house with its Palladian grace was a far finer, more palatial building than I had imagined—opulent and aristocratic. What must the young Hardy have thought when he came from his modest Bockhampton cottage to see Mrs Martin in her great home? I do not think his biographers have yet made enough of the enormous jump he must have had to make coming from his humble cottage to this noble mansion.

Mr Jones, who was anxious that we should see everything, showed us the formal gardens, the great cedar which is his pride and joy, the lake, the temple by the lakeside and the cascade which figure so largely in *Desperate Remedies*, and finally the ghostly second mansion, the Elizabethan Maurward in which Manston lived.

I have said we made two more visits, but there was a third, because before lunch we went to see Hardy's birthplace. Since the weather was still wet Hugh drove us to the door, and was kindly allowed to park his minibus close to the gate. Mrs Winchcombe and her friend, who now live in the birthplace, could not have been kinder. She showed us everything in the house, especially the tiny room in which *Under the Greenwood Tree* and *Far From the Madding Crowd* were written, and the steep little ladder-like stairway used by the boys of the house. She very kindly signed for us copies of her little book on Hardy.

We had a scratch lunch in the King's Arms, which I find a most attractive inn. Perhaps the most spectacular thing we saw there was the big room now called the Casterbridge Lounge, prototype of the room in which the Mayoral dinner is held in the novel. How close one gets to Henchard in this place!

But the highlight of this day was our visit to Max Gate. We were given a most cordial welcome by Mrs Jesty, a slightly built and rather attractive woman, with strong white but slightly irregular teeth. She was very affable and after a few words of welcome at the door invited us to see the inside of the house. It is not actually hers. It is owned by the National Trust and she rents it from them on a repairing lease. She has been there only a few years but it seems to me that she has wrought a great change in the atmosphere of the house. Fifteen years ago we thought it dark and unwelcoming; but now the brick seems to have mellowed, and the outside lightened by the addition of a white painted sundial. The hall now seems well-proportioned, the staircase modest but not inelegant, and the two rooms on either side, the 'library' and the parlour or drawing room, light and spacious. From the drawing room a door led to a small conservatory from which one could get to the garden.

We saw two rooms on the second floor, one which Hardy first used as his writing room—I think he wrote *The Woodlanders* there—and a second, his main writing room which was specially designed for him, and is the room which is to all intents and purposes reconstructed in the Museum. But the most extraordinary room is that to which Emma retreated in her later years, a small attic-like room at the top of the house, half maid's room, half children's den. It was a curious room for her to choose—or for her to be banished to. It is airy. It has exciting views. The songs of the garden birds can be clearly heard here. But it is reached only by a steep twisting staircase, a very difficult approach for an elderly and ailing woman. Was there no more easily accessible, more comfortable room than this? Was it really her choice? What motives led her to seclude herself in this poky little refuge? And how moving it was to be standing by the very bed on which poor Emma died!

When we came downstairs Mrs Jesty showed us many of her treasures, rare and illustrated editions and photographs. I felt that she had found Robert Gittings an unsympathetic biographer and preferred Professor Millgate and Professor Purdy who are bringing out Hardy's letters.[4] She herself is knowledgeable and perceptive and could write an interesting book on this house, maybe dispelling some of the legends, such as the legend of the separate staircase, and telling the true story of the burning of papers on Hardy's death.

Before we left she took us into the garden and showed us the grave of not only Wessex but the other pets. I think we all realised what a privilege it was to be shown the house by so intelligent and affable a woman. This for me was one of the highlights of our holiday.

In the evening we all gathered in Mrs Ansell's little sitting room and enjoyed readings from some of the novels and poems.

Emma's Room at Max Gate

This is the place she made her own
In her last sad years, this plain and bare
Retreat reached only by a steep
And twisting stair.

Did she choose it because the song of the birds
Sounded more sweetly there,

And the view of the Downs from these windows was
More close, more clear?

Was it a refuge she preferred,
A den by the rafters where perhaps she could play
At being a child again and act
Her sorrows away?

Or was it a flight from the presence of one
Whose silence she could bear no more,
A place where she could turn her back
On the present, and lock the door?

Whatever it was, who can stand here
And fail to pity this childless wife
Who saw all her hopes of happiness turn
To discord, estrangement, strife?

Wednesday

We approached Dorchester this time by a different and more pleasant road which took us through Martinstown (was this the village W. H. Hudson had in mind when he wrote *A Shepherd's Life*?) and on to Wool Manor.[5] It was here that we encountered one of our rare rebuffs. We had a good view of the house—and lonely heron by the riverside, saw the bridge over which Angel and Tess drove—they spent their honeymoon in the manor house—but the lady of the house declined to show us the Durberville faces on the landing and advised us to look at the copies in the Museum. Then we failed to find the stone coffin in the grounds of Bindon Abbey. The Abbey provided me with a conundrum I put in verse.

The Abandoned House

Outside the door a car is parked,
And a dog inside it looks up at me,
But does not bark. Why does it look
At strangers so indifferently?

The porch is open, the rooms unlocked.
A handbell stands on a nearby chair.
I ring it and ring it but nobody comes.
It seems there is nobody anywhere.

I could have ransacked the place, but this
Was not my purpose. I wished to be shown
Something I'd heard of, but no one came.
I found myself all on my own.

Who was the unseen one that lived in this house,
With an unlocked limousine standing by,
A friendly dog, and a handbell that one
Might ring for ever, and get no reply?

At Bere Regis we saw the famous Durberville window in the parish church, the places where the brasses had been ripped from the wall with the rivet holes still visible, and the place outside where Tess set up her four-poster to shelter her family. In this close I feel Tess's presence, and can almost hear her voice as she stamps on the floor above the vaults and says 'Why am I on the wrong side of this floor?' One can almost identify—at the risk of being too literal—the tomb on which the abominable Alex stretched himself out. Is it curious that Hardy makes no mention of the great mediaeval roof which is one of the glories of this fine church?

At Blandford Forum we were prevented from viewing the church at leisure by a funeral which was just about to take place. We had to concentrate here on the little town, which I found as intriguing as ever—the monument to the great fire, the decorative pilasters on the house fronts, the engaging mixture of red and grey brick. We had lunch in the Crown, where Gwen and some of the others found themselves required to order a soup they disliked. David, Willy and I had our usual ploughman's lunch which I liked. Margaret Mathers to my surprise said she could see nothing to admire in the town.

Puddletown is one of my favourite churches. It is full of interest—the gallery with its steps, the royal cartouche with the date of the gallery's rebuilding, the high box pews, the even more elevated squire's pews with their two sets of buttons, one on the inside, one on the outside, the three-decker pulpit, the elaborate font with the wooden cover, the defaced tomb in the Athelhampton Chapel, the old instruments in the vestry (not seen this time), the name Nenery carved on the book rest of one of the pews...Was it in the porch of this church that the repentant Troy spent the night? Was it in this churchyard that Fanny Robin was buried? No church evokes the world of Hardy novels more poignantly than this—for me at least.

We spent the evening reading from Hardy—Gabriel Oak's proposal, the chat in the Malthouse.

Thursday

By the time we reached Cerne Abbas the skies had cleared and the village looked idyllic. I went off first to see the Tithe Barn and was fortunate enough to meet the lady of the house driving away in her mini. She freely gave me permission to look at the Barn and photograph it—so at least I saw the barn where Troy had held his disastrous party and persuaded the men into a drunken orgy. It is a fine stone barn, with gothic windows inserted now into that half that has been turned into a house (the other half looks like a garage). While I was doing this the others had found the ruins of the old Abbey Gateway. Gwen and I set off to see the intriguing and beautiful gateway which one approaches by one of the most picturesque village streets in England. I thought Cerne Abbas the most enchanting village I had seen for many years.

From there we drove to Sherborne, passing the famous giant still sprawled over his hillside, and were greeted there by two kindly church guides who helped us to see the best of the Abbey. What a beautiful church! Now the scaffolding is down one can see clearly the wonderful fan vaulting over both nave and chancel. And what an extraordinary variety of good things—the reverent mediaeval Leweston tomb, the irreverent but irresistible Digby tomb, the Forsyth reredos, the intriguing mediaeval roof bosses—and a Rex Whistler engraved altar glass which I do not admire as much as Gwen does. Probably I miss the symbolism.

After lunch we went to Montacute which we have visited before—and which I like as much as ever. After tea we all set off to see Beaminster and possibly Abbotsbury, but the unexpected events at Hawkchurch completely disturbed our plans, and set us off on a search which may prove one of the most exciting in the history of the Kilvert Society.

It all began when Reg reminded me that Kilvert had twice come to

Hawkchurch to stay with his 'Uncle Willy'—whoever he was. We set off to find the village—a hard time we had of it, seeming to wind endlessly (at one stage we passed Racedown, where Wordsworth stayed) through narrow lanes, but at last we came to a biggish church, where we found a list of vicars that told us that the mysterious Uncle Willy must have been William Pigott Cay Adams. We still did not know his exact relationship to Kilvert but this was revealed in a dramatic manner. Someone—I don't know exactly who—found a gate in the churchyard hedge and through the gate was an imposing Victorian Vicarage, beautifully sited and in good condition. I was summoned urgently to come by David and found that the party that had gone through the gate was now earnestly in conversation with the lady of the house—a Mrs Clarke-Irons who turned out, incredibly, to be a Kilvert enthusiast and remarkably well informed about him and his relations.

First she told us that Mr Adams had married Augusta Coleman, Mrs Robert Kilvert's sister, and he had had the house built in about 1862. She still had the prayer that he had composed to celebrate the laying of the foundation stone, and David very impressively read it out to us as we stood in the hall. There were further surprises for us. Mrs Clarke-Irons told us that Hicks of Dorchester (for whom Hardy worked) had had a hand in the house and there was actually a reference to it in Hardy's Architectural Notebook. Did he then help with the design? She went on to tell us that when she had been working in London University she had been given access to facsimiles of several (did she mention fifteen?) Kilvert notebooks. Astonishing information! Can these facsimiles really exist—or is the material she referred to one of the missing transcripts about which Plomer was so vague? I have written off in haste to check on this. But if Mrs Clarke-Irons is right we may find ourselves on the brink of the biggest ever breakthrough in Kilvert studies. [6]

This was the second high spot of our holiday—and though it seems silly to say so my pleasure was even further enhanced by seeing on the vicarage lawn an ailanthus—a tree of heaven, which I read about in Helen Davies' memoir but had never seen.

We had no time to stop at Beaminster but hurried back to Winterborne Abbas just in time to enjoy Mrs Ansell's fish and chips.

For Kilvert at Hawkchurch

Twelve people packed in a minibus
Margaret, Kate and Hugh and Guy,
David and Willy, Mona and Reg
Lilian and Mervyn and Gwen and I,

Set off in the steps of a man we admired,
By by-road and lane, going out of our way
To find a house where he once had stayed
On a leafy Devonshire holiday.

We found it. We found the Vicarage
Where his uncle lived, and the pathway through
To the church, the great ailanthus tree,
The lawn and the long lime avenue.

To celebrate the completion of
His house, the Vicar had written a prayer.
In remembrance, David, himself a priest,
Read it out to us all as we gathered there.
We stood in the hall and listened to
The prayer, and looked at the open gate
Where, on his way to worship had passed,
The man we had come to commemorate.

Not much to record. Just the modest end
Of an unpretentious pilgrimage,
But an unforgettable day for us,
Deserving an entry on someone's page.

So I write this verse and add our names,
Margaret, Kate and Hugh and Guy,
David and Willy, Mona and Reg
Lilian and Mervyn and Gwen and I.

Friday

The next day we tried without success to buy a copy of Hardy's Architectural Notebook. Then Gwen and I parted, she to travel in the minibus and I to go once more to Marnhull with David and Willy. A happy choice for me, for during the course of our ride north we had lunch at the Pure Drop Bar and then found Tess's cottage. Marnhull Church turned out to be very interesting, with a remarkable beaded alms purse dated 1640, but the find of the day was the cottage.

A workman helped us to locate it. When we showed him Willy's postcard of it, he said, 'Yes, it's summat like that' and told us exactly where to go. Halfway down a lane not too far from the inn we came to the cottage, a charming white-washed affair (of which Tess occupied only one half)—and one more of those affable and cooperative Dorset ladies to whom we have been so deeply indebted, anxious to invite us in, to tell us how the cottage had been identified, and to offer us her modestly priced leaflets, and show us the little window up to which Alec Durberville had reached his hand to touch Tess. A very happy discovery and one that I would not have missed for anything. I was only sorry that Gwen was not with me.

So on to Bradford-on-Avon where we joined the rest of the party and then to Lacock, where alas we found the main room a little tatty and neglected, and the only parts that really moved me were the cloisters, the lovely Gothick gateway, and the beautiful setting.

The rest of the journey was almost an anticlimax—but no serious disappointment because this was one of the most exciting and happy of our holidays—a holiday packed with astonishing discoveries.

Holiday in the North

May 1981

We stayed at the Croxdale Inn, Spennymoor of all places, and found it quite comfortable, though the landlord was rather a rough diamond. Instead of saying, 'Dinner is served,' he would say, 'She's dishing it up, if ye're arl riddy.' We went to see Mother, who is very frail but determined to visit Alice in Birmingham.

A most enjoyable day in Durham. I took my friends (Guy, Hugh, Mervyn and Lilian) again in lovely weather, along the Bailey and over Prebends, then back through Windy Gap to the University Library—there was a library here before Columbus discovered America, said Mr Burnett, who showed us the old rooms and the Kilvert notebook that Plomer gave to the University. Then we saw the Cathedral, had a snack lunch in the Cathedral restaurant, and enjoyed a wonderful tour of the Castle by the Master himself, Dr Salthouse. We saw rooms I had never suspected existed—such as the Sanderson Miller Gothick rooms. But the climax was the inexpressibly moving Norman Chapel—far more evocative even than the Chapel in The Tower. No windows here—the chapel really is a crypt, like a grotto or one of those subterranean refuges where early Christians used to meet in secret. No glory of stained glass, no wrought iron screens, no pews or carved seats, no painted altarpiece or carved reredos—nothing but these heavy pillars with a few primitive and enigmatic carvings on their capitals, their sandstone drums eroded by some strange force into whorled patterns of orange and beige, the columns spreading overhead into dark vaults. The light of the world has not yet begun to shine in this place, it is still the abode of mystery, secrecy, silence, darkness.

The Master went with us from room to room exchanging friendly remarks with the students he met. It was the morning after the end-of-term Ball, and the students were tidying up after the beano.

This was the end of the sunshine. It was cold and wet on the way to Tow Law, and there were no views as we came over Kilnpit Hill. Corbridge was grey and inhospitable, and the weather was so bad on the Roman Wall that Mervyn and Lilian did not get past the Museum. But Guy, who enjoys everything, found the weather appropriate—just as he imagined it to be on the Wall. So we crossed the Border and came to the loved land where I first holidayed with my dead friend, John—the scene of our epic ride from Durham to Edinburgh and Lakeland. We stayed in Peebles at a homely hotel, The Border, and saw both Mellerstain and Floors before we turned south. Before we got back to Croxdale, Mervyn distinguished himself by setting off two burglar alarms, one at Floors and another in Cragside.

Mother, who was determined to come back to Birmingham with us, ought not to have undertaken this long journey. She is too old and weak. 'Folk shouldn't live as long as this!' she said sadly to Mary one day. 'They shouldn't live to be a burden to their children.' It is alas Mary who has the greatest share of the responsibility of looking after her.

Ladies
4 July 1981
Gwen walking along Friar Street with X met Miss Matley Moore. When they were introduced Elsie, as she always does, gave a little bow, X bowed back.

Some time after they had parted, Gwen said, 'You did the right thing. She hates shaking hands.'

'Oh,' said X, with breathtaking conceit, 'I daresay she recognised that one lady was speaking to another.' This 'lady' is in reality rather sluttish, insensitive, consumed with self-love, ignorant and slothful. In contrast, Gwen's modesty, good-nature and vivacity shone like a beacon.

Spelsbury
23 July 1981
The Revd A.C. Sparling, the one-time Rector of Spelsbury, told us this strange story. Some years ago, the organist and his assistant were alarmed by strange noises coming from under the church, took fright and fled. The noises were not explained until some time later when workmen, clearing the wood store, uprooted a hawthorn bush, lifted a grating which they found under the bush and discovered a way into a hitherto unknown vault. There they found that coffins, piled one on the other, had begun to collapse—this was the noise that had frightened the organist. They discovered there was an iron box which seemed to contain viscera, several brass plates, a ducal crown, and at the bottom of the pile, the funeral plate of the nefarious John, Earl of Rochester, the Restoration wit and debauchee! Mrs Leatherbarrow took a photograph of the plate for me. It came out well.

We had a superb day at Heythrop, Spelsbury and Ditchley, marred only by the bad temper of the Matley Moores, who lost their way and blamed me for my mismanagement of the excursion.

The Royal Wedding
30 July 1981
It was celebrated yesterday (29 July) in perfect weather, with great pomp and circumstance. Everything went off well except that, incredibly, the bride made a blunder over her husband's name, calling him Philip Charles instead of Charles Philip; and he seems to have omitted the word *worldly* from his oath. Lady Di looked every inch a princess but—dare I mention it?—she does not seem too bright to me. Is it possible that she will turn out to be a dull person? Her academic accomplishments are not even minimal—they are non-existent (not even one O level)—and the list of her interests is brief. I am sure that she is a warm-hearted and generous woman, and truly fond of children. But has

she the intelligence to be the consort of an able and academically competent young prince? To me the Queen looked a little ill at ease during the ceremony.

A day in Shropshire
August 1981
Mawley Hall is a fine early eighteenth century house near Cleobury Mortimer, which was rescued from demolition some time ago by Mr and Mrs Galliers Pratt. It has many interesting rooms but the *pièce de résistance* is the wonderful hall which boasts some of the finest plasterwork in the country—a lovely blue and white room with, beyond the arches that divide it, an extraordinary staircase with a serpentine rail ending in a snake head devouring a ball—the sides of the treads adorned with fishing and hunting emblems. At one time it was proposed to demolish the house and create a caravan park on this site—incredible! It was a great experience to see this house, but we were hurried through the rooms—the party was too large—and I could not keep up with the guide for taking photographs. But many of these rooms were very fine with glorious woodwork.

Dudmaston was an experience of a different order—a fine hall, beautifully panelled in dark wood, with a garland decoration on the ceiling and many interesting pictures, a lovely staircase and a fine library looking out over the lake—then a fine series of galleries housing Sir George Labouchère's collections of early watercolours and contempory art. An extraordinary experience to step from a 17th century room into a gallery containing work by Barbara Hepworth, Henry Moore, Alan Davie, Ben Nicholson. Very dramatic and inspiring—though many of our members thought the pictures deplorable. 'Look at this muck,' 'Here's what the dog has just sicked up'. The Matley Moores were a little taken aback when I said I saw a great deal to admire in these rooms.

A reproof
24 August 1981
Matley: Would you like one of these scones?

Me: I'm afraid my digestion is too feeble nowadays to cope with scones.

Matley: My mother always used to say to me. 'Eating is a public business. What happens to food after it's got into you is a private affair.'

When I told him that Colin was now a Fellow of Jesus he told me how Winston Churchill had once gone to France in the uniform of Trinity House. When his host asked him what his regalia was, he said, 'I'm a brother of the Trinity.' 'Mon Dieu,' said his host, 'Quel honneur!'

Matley is weak in his legs now, very bent, and gets in and out of chairs with difficulty; but when we were talking of Tennyson he began to quote 'Ulysses' and went on for almost a score of lines till his memory failed him.

Sapperton
6 September 1981
Yesterday we went to Sapperton, the village where Ernest Gimson and the Barnsleys worked in the early part of this century, and saw first the church with the graves of these notable men. There was clearly a long tradition in Sapperton of marking graves with incised metal plates, probably of brass, and the graves of Gimson and his friends are in the same mode—a fine way of marking their affection for Cotswold traditions. An interesting church with two fine (though over-pretentious monuments), a remarkable second-floor squire's pew, and nave pews with unusual Renaissance bench ends.

At Daneway House we were shown the house by Sir Anthony Denny, who, in his gardening hat, dirty shirt and workman's trousers, looked more like a servant than a lord. We saw the screens passage, ceilinged room with a big inglenooked fireplace, then the small finely plastered rooms that were reached, one by one, by a spiral staircase. This was the 'high room'—five storeys in all including a crypt which we did not see. Off it was another room, converted by Oliver Hill, the architect, into a chapel once used for a family wedding. An interesting, beautiful rambling house that provided the Barnsleys and Gimson with a working place and storeroom.

Perhaps the greatest surprise of our visit was the discovery that Sir Anthony is the brother of Robin, the painter. There is clearly an artistic strain in the family. Sir Anthony's son and his wife (whom we did not meet) also paint.

A sad Story
28 September 1981
Today Gael came to see us in some distress. For some time he has lived apart from his wife, sleeping in a kind of flat he has in Malvern; now they have decided finally to separate; but the real cause of his distress is not this, but his being thrown over by the woman for whom he was prepared to leave his wife—a woman whom we do not know and have never met. He seems to have suffered a series of blows. He has been on a course with a number of young people with whom he hoped to collaborate, only to find that he could not keep up with them—they were far beyond him in skill and inventiveness. His book

is proving difficult to place, and he feels that his poetry is suffering. Today he struck me as the saddest man I have seen in a long time—absent, apologetic, perplexed and even incoherent. He now has to contemplate leaving the district. He has a little money to keep him afloat for a while, but his whole future is uncertain and alarming.

Burne-Jones at Wilden
2 October 1981
Today we went on a Burne-Jones day at Wilden—a day devoted to an examination of the famous series of windows in the late Victorian church built by the Baldwin who was the creator of the steel works at Wilden—another benefactor's church, built in 1880 to the designs of W. J. Hopkins. The building itself is unprepossessing but all the windows came from the Morris workshops, installed after the death of Morris and Burne-Jones but clearly based on their designs. The link with Burne-Jones is easy to explain. Lady Burne-Jones was the sister of the wife of Alfred Baldwin. A very rewarding visit—the windows and the church fittings (probably by Hardman) are excellent.

A day in Cardiff
16 October 1981
Today I went to Cardiff to see the Burges Exhibition and to pick up two pieces of pottery from Geoffrey Swindell that Gwen had ordered. The pottery is exquisite and Geoffrey an unpretentious young man who came up to Cardiff in his Dormobile to meet me. And the Burges show was first class. I enjoyed it—and having another look at that marvellous Civic Centre.

On the way home by train I met a young woman with her three-year-old son, a remarkably self-assured and clever little boy. He could read the on and off signs on the heat switch, and was capable of taking himself off to the toilet in the corridor. Mother and son seemed to have struck up a wonderful relationship—trust and confidence on both sides. He was an amusing little chap who at one stage said, 'Listen, everybody, you have to listen to this noise that I make,' and then blew down his straw into his green fizzy drink and made a bubbling sound. Not all the passengers were amused—and I was faintly distressed by the *Sons and Lovers* relationship that I could already see forming here. The young woman told me she was divorced, had spent five years on an Open University course and was now at university. She has custody for the five days she spends in Cardiff, and the father takes the boy for the weekend.

I like to sit in the front of the train. In the distance you can pick out the orange jackets of the railway workers. The driver presses a button and sounds his klaxon (making that melancholy sound that is peculiar to diesels), and the men down the line raise their hands and move off the track.

It is a lovely autumn. The leaves are all turning colour but few have fallen. We are waiting for that overnight storm that will strip them.

1 November 1981

Today I learnt officially that Puffin books want to issue as a paperback *The Courage of Andy Robson* which is being filmed by Tyne Tees TV. *The Bonny Pit Laddie* has done very well, and my reputation is rising a little.

Rhulen Church

'Mrs Griffiths told me that a few days ago a man named Evans kicked his wife to death at Rhulen.' Kilvert's Diary, vol. 1, 3 June 1881, p 351.

Whoever ventured first into this lonely place?
Who made in this lost valley their abode?
Who dared to clear the steep and stubborn slopes?
Who survived there, and built a house of God?

Whoe'er they were, their handiwork remains,
Though more like a barn than a church. Around it press
Dark pagan yews, brown and affronting hills
And, beyond them, a Celtic wilderness.

Its roughcast walls lean outwards like the stones
That, now a churchyard wall, once ringed the place.
The interior is cold and bare and plain,
The altar little but a hollowed space.

But from afar the white and leaning walls
Shine through the darkness like a hovering dove,
Bringing new light to a barbarous land,
Flying a flag of truce, amity, love.

1 November 1981

After a hair-raising ride along the narrow roads through Aberedw to Rhulen, a second church that caught my fancy was Llanbadarn-y-Garreg.

A cold December

A sudden and unexpected fall of snow, a calamitous drop in temperature, incredibly severe frosts and then more snow—all giving the worst winter weather we have known for years. The nights are bitterly cold. I have slept with a hot water bottle, a duvet, a quilt and a blanket over the foot of the bed. Gwen has been wearing thermal underwear, thick stockings and two pairs of pants. It was so cold going to the newsagent's on Sunday morning that we wondered if we would survive the journey, short though it was. Condensed water on the inside of my bedroom window froze. The Severn actually iced over—for the first time in my memory. Then the climax came with a fearful blizzard which mercifully brought in its wake a kind of thaw.

NB The Queen had to take refuge in an inn near Old Sodbury on her way to see Prince Charles.

13 December 1981

On Sunday night when the blizzard had blown itself out a little, but no thaw had yet set in we had an urgent call from Hilda. Her gas cooker, she said, was making strange noises. Could we help her? After many phone calls and exchanges of symptoms from her and fruitless advice from us we decided that, cold as it was, we ought to go and see if we could do anything for her, if only to turn off the gas at the main. (Hilda, as is her custom, had undressed at about five, had a bath and was now in her nightdress and dressing gown); but when we got there we discovered that it was not her gas but her water supply that was at fault.

Some pipe had burst, and water was pouring down the inside wall of her garage. Then the fun began. The only way of cutting off the water was to turn off a stop-tap outside the house, in the strip of land between her hedge and the road; and the cover of this tap was now under at least a foot of snow. For a long time it seemed as if we would never find it because even Hilda didn't know where to look. But at last Hilda uncovered it. I prised the cover up, inserted a tool that turned the two-feet-deep tap—and the water stopped flowing. All this operation had to be carried out on one of the dirtiest, coldest nights of the year; but Gwen is a brick in situations such as these and we had the satisfaction of knowing that we had carried out a tricky but worthwhile operation.

Queen Adelaide's Window in Worcester Cathedral
For three sick widowed years the Dowager Queen[7]
Graced with her kindly presence this western scene,
Enough for all to honour and to praise
Her bountiful and charitable ways.

When her end neared she asked that she might be
Borne to her grave with all simplicity,
With no pretence or show to vulgarise
The Christian piety of her demise.
'I die disclaiming pomps and vanities.
Let no proud rites deface my obsequies.
Let not me lie in state. I would dispense
With all superfluous and vain expense.
Let simple sailors bear me to my rest.
For me a meek obscurity is best.'

But those who felt some honour should be paid
To the kind self-effacing Adelaide,
Erected, where she sometimes came to pray,
A stained-glass window on which to portray
Her virtues, a deserved memorial of
Her many acts of charity and love.

A generation later, other men,
With less respect for this retiring Queen,
Blocked her memorial with an organ case
For which they could not find another place.
The tribute to her cannot now be seen.
Upon this modest, unassuming Queen,
Time, in league with ignorance, has conferred
The anonymity that she preferred.

1982

17 January 1982
My mother died today, aged 94. Her life was arduous, but not without its triumphs. She survived great poverty, especially in the bad twenties, the loss of three children, and two great wars, but lived to see better times, to enjoy a pleasant little bungalow, relative comfort and even prosperity, and the society of a happy and united family.

We set off for the funeral in reasonably mild and clear weather and seemed to be enjoying an unexpectedly untroubled journey until, just beyond Wetherby, we began to run into fog, a grey fog that seemed an omen of the ordeal ahead of me. I call it an ordeal, because funerals distress me, and the only method I know of restraining my over-ready tendency to weep is to anaesthetise my feelings to the point of seeming callous. Happily the fog grew no worse, and we reached Ferryhill safely.

I did not see my Mother, as I had been able to see my Father. I was to be honest relieved, but as her tiny coffin was carried into the church I was overtaken by that foolish tearfulness of which I am so ashamed. I could not join in the hymns. I looked anywhere but at the coffin. I could not bear to think of that tiny indomitable woman who had left school at eleven to look after a family of four working men and one erring sister, had borne eight children by the time she was 36, had lived through wars and depression and survived to enjoy a life of greater comfort than she ever dared to hope for. Father Stretton, the kind-hearted priest who conducted the service, delivered a brief and touching tribute that helped to calm me *(Plate 8)*.

The rest of the event is perhaps best recorded in my poem.

As we drove north, we found to my surprise
Blue skies, clear air. It seemed an irony
That after weeks of bitter winter weather
So sad a journey should turn out to be

Blest with Spring sunshine. But the day's end was
Like the conclusion of my mother's years,
And the last stages of our journey were
Darkened with fog that brought alarms and fears.

Plate 8: Mary Jane Grice (Fred's mother) being presented with flowers by Mary Wilson, and congratulated by Prime Minister Harold Wilson on her long service to the Labour Party in Durham.

Shroud-like it closed in on us, halting us
As age has halted her life's impetus.

❧

Then, driving southward, after the funeral,
The family gathering, the service, the cremation,
Preparing to resume what we'd deferred,
Putting out of our mind the sad occasion,

We saw the dark clouds being driven
In from the west, and a wind dragging them
Like a tarpaulin hastily hauled to cover
The darkening plain;

And the skies opened and from overhead
Poured down more tears than we had found to shed.

Matley Moore's memorial service
3 February 1982
In spite of the large congregation the gaunt Victorian church was cold—I do not think there were any heaters except one or two feeble electric fires in the chancel. The service was High Church (sung Eucharist), and James Shutt was wearing a very fine elaborate scarlet cope. But there was clearly something amiss, and there were many puzzling consultations among the officiants before the service got under way; and we had not proceeded far when James announced that an address, that was to have been given by Canon Leatherbarrow at that point, would be deferred till the end. Canon Leatherbarrow had already come and was sitting at the back of the church; but he was clearly not prepared to take part in the service because he was in mufti, and had equally clearly brought no gown or surplice with him. It was a confused and confusing service, and it was fortunate that the dead man was not there to have to endure it, because he hated muddle and inefficiency. Even when it ended we hardly knew what to do; but in the end Mr Blake stepped forward and delivered, very competently, an extempore tribute to the deceased, and we finally dispersed.

What a muddled affair! The service was such a rigmarole that it was impossible to follow it from the service book we were given. The kneelers were so thin and threadbare that it was a difficult job to get down to them, and an even more difficult job to get up. The no-doubt carefully thought-out ritual, the vestments, the sanctus bell, the comings and goings, the intonings—all seemed not to excite feeling so much as to douse it. It was a most unfitting tribute to a man who deserved something better—and a great embarrassment to Canon Leatherbarrow, who was in no way to blame for the contretemps. The fault was Elsie's. She had presumed that the Canon had been asked to preach the *oraison funèbre*, but had forgotten to make sure he was informed!

Plate 9: Fred in his study in Worcester, holding his 1982 book on Kilvert.

The Winter Thrush

The lights are on in the church, but as the priest
Moves through the collect, epistle, gospel, begins
To bid us all confess and then absolves
Us of our sins,

The morning light brightens beyond the window,
And suddenly that bird
Whose call comes sometimes through the advent air
And must be heard,

Calls out again. The vicar holds up the cup.
I do not hear a word
Of what he says. Nothing speaks to me now
Except my winter bird.

No word I know can interpret its thrilling summons.
What it is saying is a mystery.
It simply bids me listen, and I listen.
Nothing exists now but the call and me *(Plate 9)*.

Notes

1 Edmund Spenser (1552-99), Elizabethan poet. The single-line quotation comes from Spenser's Sonnet No 75, line 1.
2 Charles Greville (1794-1865), diarist.
3 The Deerhurst Angel is an Anglo-Saxon carving placed high up on a wall of the church.
4 R.L. Purdy and M. Millgate, *The Collected Letters of Thomas Hardy (1840-1892)*, Vol.1, 1980.
5 W. H. Hudson (1841-1922) was an Argentinian-British author, naturalist and ornithologist. In later life he wrote several books about the English countryside, including *A Shepherd's Life*, 1910.
6 The hoped-for breakthrough did not occur, and there is no evidence in Fred's writings that his enquiries were fruitful. We are left with Peter Alexander, Plomer's biographer, describing Plomer as editing the entire Kilvert typescript of the 22 notebooks by 'the apparently simple process of pencilling a line in the margin to mark passages he wanted the typist at Cape to copy for him', *William Plomer: A Biography*, 1989, p. 217; and Frederick Grice's observation that 'when the Kilvert typescript was destroyed or vanished, he [Plomer] did not trouble because he knew the original notebooks were still in existence...' But Mrs Essex Smith, who had inherited the notebooks at some date before 1955, 'without consulting Plomer set about the destruction of the precious notebooks she had inherited,' *Francis Kilvert and his World*, 1982 (p. 172). Neither facsimiles nor the missing transcripts referred to by Mrs Clarke-Irons have been located, and the record stands as it was left in the 1980s, with the exception of the publication of three out of the original Kilvert notebooks covering April to August 1870.
7 Queen Adelaide was German-speaking and the widow of King William IV.

Appendix 1

Frederick Grice's Poems: Titles and First Lines

Chapter 1
Song of the Pedestrians in the Shambles, 10 March 1956
Now, like that single heifer that will not sleep

Chapter 2
The Wind and the Book
Sunset from the Northbound Train, December 1957
The Gardener at Great Tew, 20 September 1959
Provençal Scene

Chapter 3
The Ruined Church at Edvin Loach, 7 February 1961
Wide Load, June 1961
The Middle-aged Poet, 3 March 1962
Motorbike Boys near Ludlow, 24 April 1962
Winter Plate
Border Landscape
Landscape of the Civil War, 17 August, 1963
Growing Old
Autumn Poem, October 1963
Whitsuntide, Whit Tuesday 1964
Aidan (at one and a half) 24 March 1967

Chapter 4
Cricket at Worcester
Night Poem, 30 October 1970
Lucky Man, 16 November 1970
This is Your Life, 2 January 1971
Students
Old Teacher, 19 June 1971
A Wet Night, 20 June 1971
Conker Time, 21 September 1971
Knightwick Station, 24 September 1971
Upland Country
Two for the Price of One (for Gwen), 5 May 1972
Seagulls on Ploughland, 17 November 1972
Widow, 5 September 1973
Tramp 5 September 1973
The Blackberry Year, 10 October 1973

Chapter 5
Sudden Shower, 3 October 1974
Storm, 11 November 1974
Whitley Court
Midwinter Day
Snake, 4 December 1975
Disserth Church, 2 February 1975
Home Thoughts (written after returning from Austria), 27 May 1975
For a Friend Preaching the Kilvert Sermon at Newchurch, October 1975

Chapter 6
The Gale, 19 January 1976
Men on the Road, 25 March 1976
Out of Touch – Newland
Islam, 25 April 1976
Vandalism, 26 May 1976
1917, 31 May 1976
Last Possessions, 15 September 1976 (suggested by a letter from Florence Hardy to Lady Hoare)
Damp Autumn
A Winter Child [Editors: written when Laura was a few weeks old]

Chapter 7
The Crane (after watching the Worcester Electricity Station being pulled down), 23 January 1977
Hard Times, February-March 1977
Dead Elms, May 1978

Misgivings, July 1978
Because he broke the law we sentenced him,
  4 November 1978

Chapter 9
Winter Scene, 4 January 1980
Birds in Winter
A still autumn day in a cemetery
Early Morning, Worcester,
  29 November 1980

Chapter 10
Late Poems
A Still Day, 22 February, 1981
Collection, 24 February 1981
Yobbos, 24 February 1981
Winter Scene, 24 February 1981
In the Station Buffet, 4 March 1981
A Lull, 23 March 1981
The fall of my feet on the rutted car track,
  23 April 1981
The Succubus, 10 May 1981
Emma's Room at Max Gate
The Abandoned House
For Kilvert at Hawkchurch
Rhulen Church, 1 November 1981
Queen Adelaide's window in
  Worcester Cathedral
As we drove north, we found to my surprise
The Winter Thrush

Appendix 2

Frederick Grice's Major Publications

Folk Tales of the North Country, London: Nelson, 1944.

Folk Tales of the West Midlands, London: Nelson, 1952.

Folk Tales of Lancashire, London: Nelson, 1953.

Aidan and the Strollers, London: Jonathan Cape, 1960.

The Bonny Pit Laddie, London: OUP, 1960.

The Moving Finger, London: OUP, 1962.

Rebels and Fugitives, London: Batsford, 1963.

A Severnside Story, London: OUP, 1964.

The Luckless Apple, London: OUP, 1966.

Dildrum King of the Cats, London: OUP, 1967.

The Oak and the Ash, London: OUP, 1968.

The Courage of Andy Robson, London: OUP, 1969

The Black Hand Gang, London: OUP, 1971.

Young Tom Sawbones, London: OUP, 1972.

Nine Days' Wonder, London: OUP, 1976.

Johnny Head-in-Air, Oxford: OUP, 1978.

Francis Kilvert and his World, Horsham: Caliban Books, 1982.

Water Break its Neck, Oxford: OUP, 1986.

War's Nomads: A Mobile Radar Unit in Pursuit of Rommel During the Western Desert Campaign, 1942-3. Oxford: Casemate, 2015.

Bibliography

Alexander, Peter F. (1989) *William Plomer: A Biography.* Oxford: Oxford University Press.

Bostridge, Mark (2019) 'Introduction' to *Kilvert's Diary, 1870-79,* pp *vii-xxv.* Selections from the diary of Francis Kilvert, chosen, edited and prefaced by William Plomer (based on the three-volume first edition published in 1944). London: Vintage.

Bostridge, Mark (2020) 'Dear diaries: archiving personal records,' *Times Literary Supplement,* 24 January, 2020, p 17.

Cheesewright, Paul (2008) *The University of Worcester: An Illustrated History.* London: James and James.

Commire, Anne (ed.) (1974) *Something About the Author: Facts and Pictures about Contemporary Authors and Illustrators of Books for Young People.* Detroit, Michigan: Gale Research, Vol. 6, pp 96-97.

Eliot, T. S. (1975) *Collected Poems, 1909-1962.* London: Faber and Faber. 'Little Gidding', one of the *Four Quartets,* appears on pp 214-23.

Gibson, Wilfrid (1928) *The Golden Room and Other Poems.* Macmillan: London, 'The Golden Room' cited p 172-3.

Grice, Frederick (1976) 'The Park Ornaments of Croome D'Abitôt,' *Transactions of the Worcestershire Archaeological Society,* Third series, Vol. 5, pp 41-9.

Grice, Frederick (1982) *Francis Kilvert and his World.* Horsham, Sussex: Caliban Books.

Grice, Frederick, edited by Gillian and Colin Clarke (2015) *War's Nomads: A Mobile Radar Unit in Pursuit of Rommel During the Western Desert Campaign,* 1942-3. Oxford: Casemate Publishers.

Hughes, Kathleen and Dafydd Ifans (editors) (1982) *The Diary of Francis Kilvert, April-June 1870.* Aberystwyth: The National Library of Wales.

Ifans, Dafydd (editor) (1989) *The Diary of Francis Kilvert,* June – July 1870. Aberystwyth: The National Library of Wales.

D. N. Lockwood and F. Grice, (Editors) (1980), *Blue Remembered Hills: An Anthology of Worcestershire Verse in Celebration of the Thirteenth Centenary of Worcester Diocese.* Worcester and London: Ebenezer Baylis.

Maber, Richard and Angela Tregoning (1989) *Kilvert's Cornish Diary,* 19 July to 6 August 1870. Alison Hodge Bosulval: Penzance, Cornwall.

Plomer, William (Editor) (1973) *Kilvert's Diary.* London: Jonathan Cape, Vol. 1, Vol. 2 and Vol. 3. William Plomer's first edition of the diary appeared in 3 volumes in 1938, 1939, and 1940.

Index

C

D

T

Y